0413

ry.o

iPhone and iPad Apps for Absolute Beginners, 3rd Edition

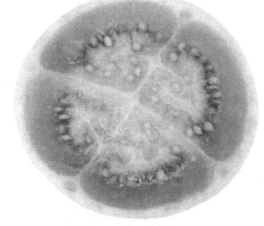

Dr. Rory Lewis and Chad Mello

Apress

iPhone and iPad Apps for Absolute Beginners, 3rd Edition

Copyright © 2013 by Dr. Rory Lewis and Chad Mello

All rights reserved. No part of this work may be reproduced or transmitted in any form or by any means, electronic or mechanical, including photocopying, recording, or by any information storage or retrieval system, without the prior written permission of the copyright owner and the publisher.

ISBN-13 (pbk): 978-1-4302-4617-6

ISBN-13 (electronic): 978-1-4302-4618-3

Trademarked names, logos, and images may appear in this book. Rather than use a trademark symbol with every occurrence of a trademarked name, logo, or image, we use the names, logos, and images only in an editorial fashion and to the benefit of the trademark owner, with no intention of infringement of the trademark.

The use in this publication of trade names, trademarks, service marks, and similar terms, even if they are not identified as such, is not to be taken as an expression of opinion as to whether or not they are subject to proprietary rights.

President and Publisher: Paul Manning
Lead Editor: Steve Anglin
Development Editor: Matthew Moodie
Technical Reviewer: Matthew Knott
Editorial Board: Steve Anglin, Mark Beckner, Ewan Buckingham, Gary Cornell, Morgan Engel,
    Jonathan Gennick, Jonathan Hassell, Robert Hutchinson, Michelle Lowman, James Markham,
    Matthew Moodie, Jeff Olson, Jeffrey Pepper, Douglas Pundick, Ben Renow-Clarke,
    Dominic Shakeshaft, Gwenan Spearing, Matt Wade, Tom Welsh
Coordinating Editor: Christine Ricketts
Copy Editor: Corbin Collins
Compositor: SPi Global
Indexer: SPi Global
Cover Designer: Anna Ishchenko

Distributed to the book trade worldwide by Springer Science+Business Media, LLC., 233 Spring Street, 6th Floor, New York, NY 10013. Phone 1-800-SPRINGER, fax (201) 348-4505, e-mail orders-ny@springer-sbm.com, or visit www.springeronline.com.

For information on translations, please e-mail rights@apress.com, or visit www.apress.com.

Apress and friends of ED books may be purchased in bulk for academic, corporate, or promotional use. eBook versions and licenses are also available for most titles. For more information, reference our Special Bulk Sales–eBook Licensing web page at www.apress.com/bulk-sales.

The information in this book is distributed on an "as is" basis, without warranty. Although every precaution has been taken in the preparation of this work, neither the author(s) nor Apress shall have any liability to any person or entity with respect to any loss or damage caused or alleged to be caused directly or indirectly by the information contained in this work.

To my best friend, my wife, my life, my light, my Kera.

—Dr. Rory Lewis

To my wife, Imelda. I can see nothing but beauty, eclipsed only by your grace. You have all of my love, admiration, and respect; Ab imo pectore.

—Chad Mello

Contents at a Glance

Contents

Foreword: About the Author

"Rory and I met in L.A. in 1983. He reminds me of one of my favorite film characters, Buckaroo Banzai—always going in six directions at once. If you stop him and ask what he's doing, he'll answer comprehensively and with amazing detail. Disciplined, colorful, and friendly, he has the uncanny ability to explain the highly abstract in simple, organic terms. He always accomplishes what he sets out to do, and he'll help you do the same."

Why You'll Relate to Dr. Lewis

While attending Syracuse University as a computer engineering student, Rory scrambled to pass his classes and make enough money to support his wife and two young daughters. In 1990, he landed a choice on-campus job as a proctor in the computer lab in the LC Smith College of Engineering. Even though he was struggling with subjects in the electrical engineering program, he was always there at the help desk. It was a daunting experience for Rory because his job was only to help his fellow students with computer lab *equipment* questions, but he invariably found his classmates asking deeper and harder questions: *"Dude, did you understand the calculus assignment? Can you help me?!"*

These students assumed that, because Rory was the proctor, he knew the answers. Afraid and full of self-doubt, he sought a way to help them without revealing his inadequacies. Rory learned to start with: *"Let's go back to the basics. Remember that last week the professor presented us with an equation. . .?"* By going back to the fundamentals, restating them, and rebranding them, Rory began to develop a technique that would, more often than not, lead to working solutions. By the time his senior year rolled around, there was often a line of students waiting at the help desk on the nights Rory worked.

Fast-Forward 17 Years

Picture a long-haired, wacky professor walking through the campus of the University of Colorado at Colorado Springs, dressed in a stunning contrast of old-school and drop-out. As he walks into the Engineering Building, he is greeted by students and faculty who smile and say hearty hellos, all the while probably shaking their heads at his tweed jacket, Grateful Dead t-shirt, khaki pants, and flip flops. As he walks down the hall of the Computer Science Department, there's a line of students standing outside his office. Reminiscent of the line of students that waited for him at the help desk in those early years as a proctor in the computer lab, they turn and greet him, *"Good morning, Dr. Lewis!"* Many of these students at UC Colorado Springs are not even in his class, but they know that Dr. Lewis will see them and help them anyway.

Past—Present—Future

Dr. Lewis holds three academic degrees. He earned a Bachelor of Science in Computer Engineering from Syracuse University. Syracuse's LC Smith College of Engineering is one of the country's top schools. It is there that Intel, AMD, and Microsoft send their top employees to study for their PhDs.

Upon completing his BS (with emphasis on the mathematics of electronic circuitry in microprocessors), he went across the quad to the Syracuse University School of Law. During his first summer at law school, Fulbright & Jaworski, the nation's most prolific law firm, recruited Rory to work in its Austin office, where some of the attorneys specialize in high-tech intellectual-property patent litigation. As part of his clerking experience, Lewis worked on the infamous *AMD v. Intel* case; he helped assess the algorithms of the mathematics of microprocessor electrical circuitry for the senior partners.

During his second summer in law school, Skjerven, Morrill, MacPherson, Franklin & Friel—the other firm sharing the work on the *AMD v. Intel* case—recruited Rory to work with them at their Silicon Valley branches (San Jose and San Francisco). After immersing himself in law for several years and receiving his JD at Syracuse, Lewis realized his passion was for the *mathematics* of computers, not the legal ramifications of hardware and software. He preferred a learning and creative environment rather than the fighting and arguing intrinsic in law.

After three years away from academia, Rory moved south to pursue his PhD in Computer Science at the University of North Carolina at Charlotte. There, he studied under Dr. Zbigniew W. Ras, known worldwide for his innovations in data-mining algorithms and methods, distributed data mining, ontologies, and multimedia databases. While studying for his PhD, Lewis taught computer science courses to computer engineering undergraduates, as well as e-commerce and programming courses to MBA students.

Upon receiving his PhD in Computer Science, Rory accepted a tenure-track position in Computer Science at the University of Colorado at Colorado Springs, where his research is in the computational mathematics of neurosciences. Most recently, he co-wrote a grant proposal on the mathematical analysis of the genesis of epilepsy with respect to the hypothalamus. However, with the advent of Apple's revolutionary iPhone and its uniquely flexible platform—*and market*—for mini-applications, games, and personal-computing tools, he grew excited and began experimenting and programming for his own pleasure. Once his own fluency was established, Lewis figured he could teach a class on iPhone apps that would include *non*-engineers. With his insider knowledge as an iPhone beta tester, he began to integrate the parameters of the proposed iPad platform into his lesson plans—even before the official release in April 2010.

The class was a resounding success, and the feedback was overwhelmingly positive, from students and colleagues alike. When approached about the prospect of converting his course into a book to be published by Apress, Dr. Lewis jumped at the opportunity. He happily accepted an offer to convert his course outlines, class notes, and videos into the book you are now holding in your hands.

Why Write This Book?

The reasons Dr. Lewis wrote this book are the same reasons he originally decided to create a class for both engineering and non-engineering majors: the challenge and the fun! According to Lewis, the iPhone and iPad are "...*some of the coolest, most powerful, and most technologically advanced tools ever made—period!*"

He is fascinated by the fact that, just under the appealing touchscreen of high-resolution images and fun little icons, the iPhone and iPad are programmed in Objective-C, an incredibly difficult and advanced language. More and more, Lewis was approached by students and colleagues who wanted to program apps for the iPhone and would ask his opinion on their ideas. It seemed that, with every new update of the iPhone, not to mention the advent of the expanded interface of the iPad, the floodgates of interest in programming apps were thrown open wider and wider. Wonderful and innovative ideas just needed the proper channel to flow into the appropriate format and then out to the world.

Generally speaking, however, the people who write books about Objective-C write for people who know Java, C#, or C++ at an advanced level. So, because there seemed to be no help for the average person who, nevertheless, has a great idea for an iPhone/iPad app, Dr. Lewis decided to launch such a class. He realized it would be wise to use his own notes for the first half of the course and then explore the best existing resources he could find.

As he forged ahead with this plan, Dr. Lewis was most impressed with *Beginning iPhone 3 Development: Exploring the iPhone SDK*, the best-selling instructional book from Apress written by Dave Mark and Jeff Lamarche. Lewis concluded that their book would provide an excellent, high-level target for his lessons—a stepping-stones approach to comprehensive and fluent programming for all Apple's multitouch devices.

After Dr. Lewis's course had been successfully presented, and during a subsequent conversation with a representative from Apress, Lewis happened to mention that he'd only started using that book about halfway through the semester, as he had to bring his non-engineering students up to speed first. The editor suggested converting his notes and outlines into a primer—an introductory book tuned to the less-technical programming crowd. At that point, it was only a matter of time and details, like organizing and revising Dr. Lewis's popular instructional videos to make them available to non-engineers excited to program their own iPhone and/or iPad apps.

So, that's the story of how a wacky professor came to write this book. We hope you are inspired to take this home and begin. Arm yourself with this knowledge and begin now to change your life!

—Ben Easton
Author, teacher, editor

About the Contributing Authors

Chad Mello is currently working on his PhD in Computer Science at the University of Colorado at Colorado Springs, with Dr. Rory Lewis as his mentor. Several research projects in machine learning keep him busy, such as research into epilepsy identification and predication models. Possessing Top Secret clearance, he is currently a freelance software consultant and architect for the U.S. Air Force, Army, and a number of private companies. His specialties are software architectures and framework design as well as geospatial applications. Chad currently lives with his wife and three children in the Rocky Mountains and loves every minute of it.

Ben Easton is a graduate of Washington & Lee University and has a BA in Philosophy. His eclectic background includes music, banking, sailing, hang gliding, and retail. Most of his work has involved education in one form or another. Ben taught school for 17 years, mostly middle school mathematics. More recently, his experience as a software trainer and implementer reawakened his long-time affinity for technical subjects. As a freelance writer, he has written several science fiction stories and screenplays, as well as feature articles for magazines and newsletters. Ben resides in Austin, Texas and is currently working on his first novel.

Acknowledgments

When I arrived in America in 1981 at the age of 20, I had no experience or money and didn't even know how to use an American payphone. Since then it's been a wonderful road leading to this book and my life as an assistant professor at two University of Colorado campuses. I am such a lucky man to have met so many wonderful people.

First, to my wife, Kera, who moved mountains to help with graphics, meals, dictations, keeping me working, and sustaining a nominal level of sanity in our house. Thank you, Kera.

To my mother, Adeline, who was always there to encourage me, even in the darkest of times when I almost dropped out of electrical engineering. To my sister, Vivi, who keeps me grounded, and my late brother Murray, a constant reminder of how precious life is. To Keith and Nettie Lewis, who helped me figure out those American payphones. To Ben Easton, Brian Bucci, and Dennis Donahue, all of whom invited me into their families when I had nobody.

A special thanks to Dr. Zbigniew Ras, my PhD advisor, who became like a father to me, and to Dr. Terry Boult, my mentor and partner in the Bachelor of Innovation program at UCCS.

Last, but not least, to Clay Andres at Apress—he walked me through this process and risked his reputation by suggesting to a bunch of really intelligent people that I could author such a book as this.

Many thanks to you all.

Preface

What This Book Will Do For You

Let me get this straight: you want to learn how to program for the iPhone or the iPad and you consider yourself to be pretty intelligent—but whenever you read computer code or highly technical instructions, your brain seems to shut down. Do your eyes glaze over when reading gnarly instructions? Does a little voice in your head chide, *"How about that! Your brain shut down six lines ago, but you're still scanning the page—pretending you're not as dense as you feel. Great!"*

See if you can relate to this: you're having an issue with something pretty technical, so you decide to Google it and troubleshoot the problem. You open the top hit, and somebody else has asked the exact same question! You become excited as the page loads, but, alas, it's only a bulletin board (a chat site for all those geeks who yap at one another in unintelligible code). You see your question followed by . . . but it's too late! Your brain has already shut down, and you feel the tension and frustration as knots form in your belly.

Sound Familiar?

Yes? Then this book's for you! My guess is that you're probably standing in a bookstore or in the airport, checking out a magazine stand for something that might excite you. Because you're reading this in some such upscale place, you can probably afford an iPhone, a Mac, a car, and plane tickets. You're probably intrigued by the burgeoning industry of handhelds and the geometric rate at which memory and microprocessors are evolving . . . and how quickly ideas can be turned into startlingly new computing platforms, powerful software applications, helpful tools, and clever games—perhaps even into greenbacks! And now you're wondering if you can get in on the action, using your intellect and technical savvy to serve the masses.

How Do I Know This About You?

Easy! Through years of teaching students to program, I know that if you're still reading this, you're both intelligent enough and sufficiently driven to step onto the playing field of programming, especially for a device as sweet as the iPhone or as sexy as the iPad. If you identify with and feel connected to the person I've just described, then I know you. We were introduced long ago.

You're an intelligent person who may have mental spasms when reading complex code—even if you have some background in programming. And, even if you do have a pretty strong background in various programming languages, you are a person who simply wants an easy, on-point, no-frills strategy to learn how to program the iPhone and iPad. No problem! I can guide you through whatever psychological traffic jams you typically experience and help you navigate any technical obstacles, real or imagined. I've done this a thousand times with my students, and my methodology will work for you too.

The Approach I Take

I don't try and explain everything in minute detail. Nor do I expect you to know every line of code in your iPhone/iPad application at this stage. What I will do is show you, step by step, how to accomplish key actions. My approach is simultaneously comprehensive and easygoing, and I take pride in my ability to instruct students and interested learners along a wide spectrum of knowledge and skill sets.

Essentially, I will lead you, at your own pace, to a point where you can code, upload, and perhaps sell your first iPhone/iPad app, whether it is simple or complex. Good news: the most downloaded apps are *not* complex. The most popular ones are simple, common-sense tools for life . . . finding your car in a parking lot, making better grocery lists, or tracking your fitness progress. However, when you complete this book, you may want to graduate to other books in the Apress and friends of ED series. You have quite a few options here, and down the road I'll advise you regarding the best ways to move forward.

May you experience great joy and prosperity as you enter this amazing and magical world.

Peace!

—Rory A. Lewis, PhD, JD

Preliminaries

This introductory chapter aims to make sure you have all the required tools and accessories to proceed with full confidence.

Three types of readers are likely to read this book. One group can skip to Chapter 2 immediately without reading Chapter 1. Another group may only need to read one small section in Chapter 1 before moving on to Chapter 2. The third group should read Chapter 1 very carefully before moving on.

- *Group 1*: You own a Mac. You have experience coding with Xcode on your Mac. You have an up-to-date iOS SDK and an up-to-date version of Xcode. You also have experience with DemoMonkey, and it's installed on your machine. If all this is true, meet me in Chapter 2.

- *Group 2*: You own a Mac. You have experience coding with Xcode on your Mac. You have an up-to-date iOS SDK and an up-to-date version of Xcode. But you have no experience with DemoMonkey or it's not installed on your machine. Please check out the section "Installing DemoMonkey" in this chapter and then meet me in Chapter 2.

- *Group 3*: You are a seeker of knowledge and have begun travelling down a wonderful road. We need to check your backpack and make sure you have all the tools you'll need for your journey. So let's start right here.

Necessities and Accessories

In order to program for the iPhone and/or iPad, and to follow along with the exercises, tutorials, and examples presented in this book, you'll need to meet six minimal requirements. You may not completely understand these requirements right now, but that's okay—just roll with me for a second, and I'll explain everything as we go through these steps.

> **Note**   Whenever I say *iPhone* or *iPad*, I'm referring to any iPhone or iPad OS device, including the iPod touch. And when I say *Macintosh HD*, yours may be named something different.

Briefly, you'll need six things:

- An Intel-based Macintosh
- The correct operating system for your Mac (OS X 10.8.1 Mountain Lion or later)
- To be a registered developer or be simulator-based (discussed in detail later in this chapter)
- To have the correct operating system for your iPhone (iOS 6 or later)
- To have the correct Software Development Kit (SDK) for your iPhone that runs a program called Xcode (version 4.4 and later)
- To have installed DemoMonkey

Let's go into each of these in a bit more detail.

Getting a Mac

As far as your Mac is concerned, I'll explain what you need in two ways—first a geeky way and then a newbie way.

- *In geek terms*: You need a Mac that has a 64-bit Intel-Core 2 duo processor or better.
- *In newbie terms*: You need a MacBook Pro that was manufactured from mid-2009 or later, or an iMac that was manufactured from mid-2007.

All the videos on the net that accompany this book are screencast from my MacBook Pro, bought in 2011; if I broadcast from my 2010 iMac, I first run the app on my MacBook Pro, bought in 2011.

You don't need the latest revved-up Mac. If you haven't bought one yet, get a basic, no-frills MacBook Air. See Figure 1-1.

Figure 1-1. *The author uses the cheapest 2011 MacBook Pro on the market to perform all the coding and compiling in this book. Many of the authors' students purchase the MacBook Air for $999, as illustrated here*

Or buy a secondhand MacBook Pro on eBay or another such site. If you do that, or own an older Mac, you may be able to add some RAM. I suggest you make a free appointment at the nearest Apple Store's Genius Bar and ask whether they can increase the RAM on your older model Mac. If so, ask about the maximum the RAM can be increased. Then ask explicitly: "Can this old computer run Mountain Lion, *at least* 10.8.1, and Xcode 4.4.1 or later?"

If you don't have a Mac, you'll need to buy one if you want to follow along with this book or program Objective-C to create iPhone apps. Keep in mind that, as mentioned, I've made a point to code and run every program in this book on Apple's smallest and cheapest model, the MacBook Air—many of my newbie students buy the MacBook Air for $999.

Getting OS X

You'll need the correct version of OS X. At the time of this writing, that version is OS X 10.8.1. You need to have the latest greatest operating system inside your Mac. I see a lot of emails and forum questions revealing that many people think: *"Ah, my code probably didn't compile correctly because Dr. Lewis has a different version of OS X or/and iOS on his machine…"*

Note   Even if you think your system is up-to-date, I suggest you follow along in this section to make sure your system has the latest OS X and the latest iOS inside it. I say this because as you follow along in this book and tackle all the programs, there will be times when your code doesn't work the first time you run it.

To make sure your system is recent enough to follow along with the book, please do the following:

1.   Close every program running on your Mac so that only the Finder is running.

2.   Click the little apple in the upper left-hand corner of your screen and select About This Mac. You'll see the window shown in Figure 1-2. Make sure it says OS X 10.8.1 (or later).

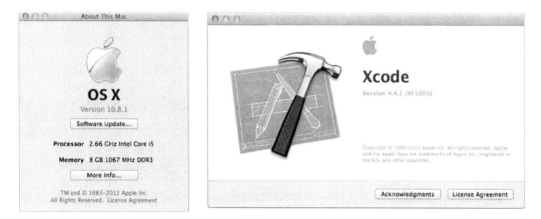

Figure 1-2. Here you can see that Dr. Lewis's iMac is using OS X 10.8.1. and Xcode 4.4.1

Now make sure your Mac has the latest software:

1.   With all your programs closed except for the Finder, click the apple in the upper left-hand corner again and select Software Update, as illustrated in top image in Figure 1-3.

Figure 1-3. *Top: Checking for new software.* *Middle: Download any new software and wait for software to download.* *Bottom: All software updated*

2. If updates are available, click Continue and follow the instructions and screen prompts, as shown in two bottom figures of the three Figures 1-3.

If your version of OS X or iOS makes my pictures seemed dated, don't freak out. Along with volunteers, I maintain a forum that has news about recent updates of OS X and iOS. You can visit the forum at www.rorylewis.com/ipad_forum/.

Becoming a Developer

If you're not already one, you need to become a registered developer via the iPhone/iPad DK for $99. Or you can get an introductory set of bells and whistles for free.

Making Your Choice

If you're a student, your professor has probably already taken care of this, and you may already be registered under your professor's name. If you're not a student, you need to decide which type of developer you'd like to be. Here are your options:

- *$0 option*: You can go to the App Store and download Xcode for free. That's fine, but bear in mind that unless you become a developer ($99), you'll only be able to see the apps you code and program in this book running on the iPhone or iPad *Simulator*. You won't be able to run them on a real physical iPad or iPhone. And you won't be able to sell your apps on the iTunes store. Nor will you be able to log in to the developer site to view code snippets and updates, beta-test new products, or be a part of the Apple online community. Still, the free route may be a very good choice for people who aren't sure whether they want to continue with Xcode and programming. If that's the case, then download the latest version of Xcode from https://developer.apple.com/xcode/ and meet me at Figure 1-10.

- *$99 option*: If you do want to run your apps on a real iPad or iPhone, sell apps on the iTunes store, and be a part of the developer group at Apple, simply continue reading.

Installing Xcode

Let's get started installing Xcode.

1. Go to `http://developer.apple.com/programs/ios/`. You'll see a page similar to the one shown in Figure 1-4. Click the Enroll Now button.

Figure 1-4. Click the Enroll Now button

2. Click Continue, as illustrated in Figure 1-5.

 Developer   Apple Developer Program Enrollment

Enrolling in Apple Developer Programs

Get everything you need to develop and distribute apps for iOS and OS X.

It's easy to get started.

✓ **Choose an enrollment type.**

Individual: choose this option if you are an individual or sole proprietor/single person company.

Company/Organization: choose this option if you are a company, non-profit organization, joint venture, partnership, or government organization.

✓ **Submit your information.**

Provide basic personal information, including your legal name and address. If you're enrolling as a company/organization, we'll need a few more things, like your legal entity name and D-U-N-S® Number.

Before enrolling as a company, check to see if D&B has assigned you a D-U-N-S Number. If not, please request one. Check now ›

✓ **Purchase and activate your program.**

Once we verify your information, you can purchase your program on the Apple Online Store. After you have completed your purchase, we'll send you an email within 24 hours on how to activate your membership.

Continue

Technical Requirements
You must have an Intel-based Mac running Mac OS X Snow Leopard or later to develop and distribute iOS and Mac apps.

FAQs
To learn more about the enrollment process, D-U-N-S Numbers, and how to check on your enrollment status, see our Frequently Asked Questions.

Figure 1-5. *Click the Continue button*

3. Most people reading this book will select the "Create an Apple ID" option (arrow 1 in Figure 1-6) and then click Continue (arrow 2). If you already have an account, then you've been through this process before; go ahead with the process beginning with the "Sign in with your Apple ID" option, and I'll meet you at step 6, where you'll log in to the iPhone/iPad development page and download the SDK.

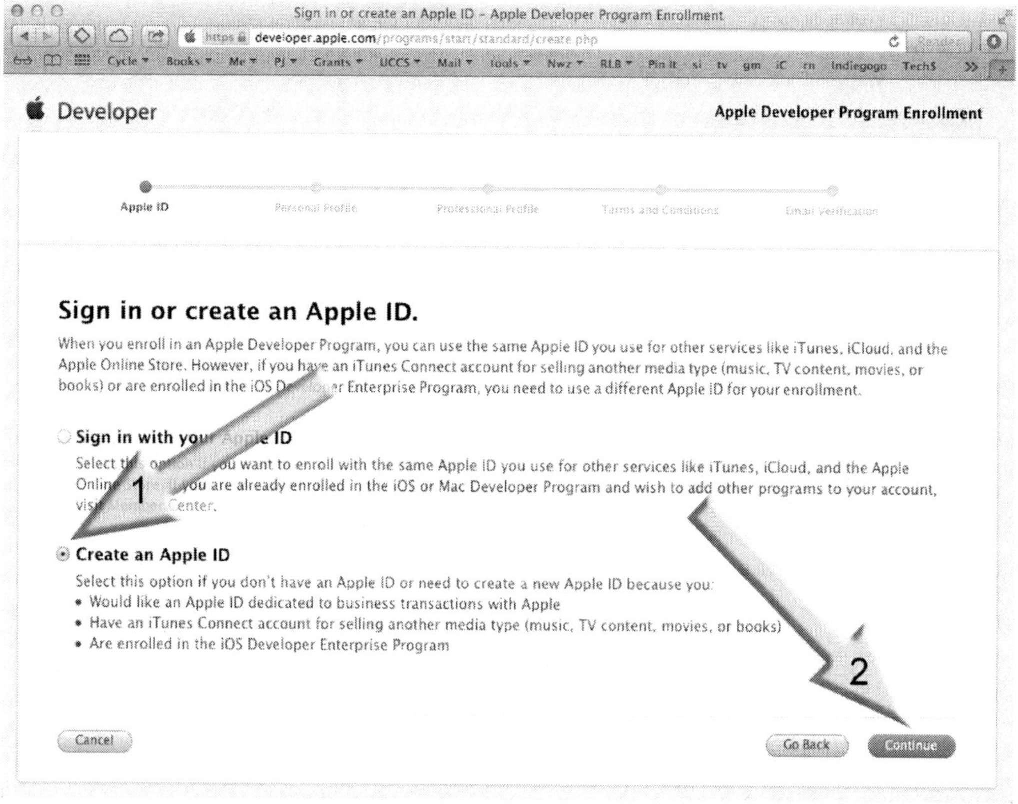

Figure 1-6. *Click the "Create an Apple ID" option to proceed*

4. You're probably going to be enrolling as an individual, so click the Individual button shown in Figure 1-7. If you're enrolling as a company, click the Company button to the right, follow the appropriate steps, and then skip to step 6.

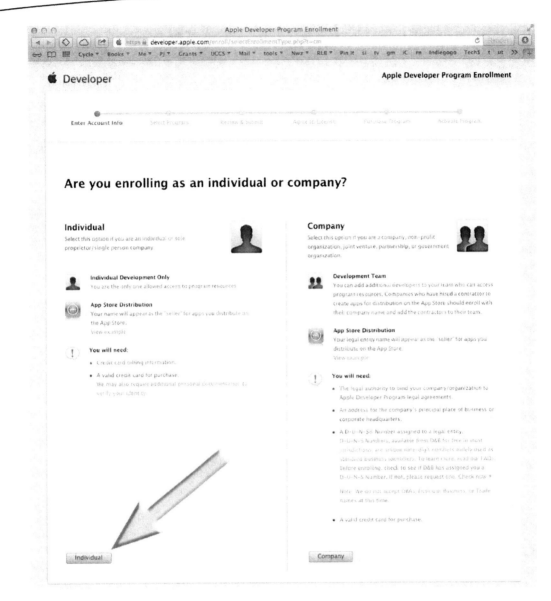

Figure 1-7. *Click the Individual option*

5. Enter all your information as shown in Figure 1-8 and pay the Standard program's $99 fee. The fee provides all the tools, resources, and technical support you'll need. (If you're reading this book, you don't buy the Enterprise program at $299—it's for commercial in-house applications.) After paying, save your Apple ID and username; you'll get a confirmation email.

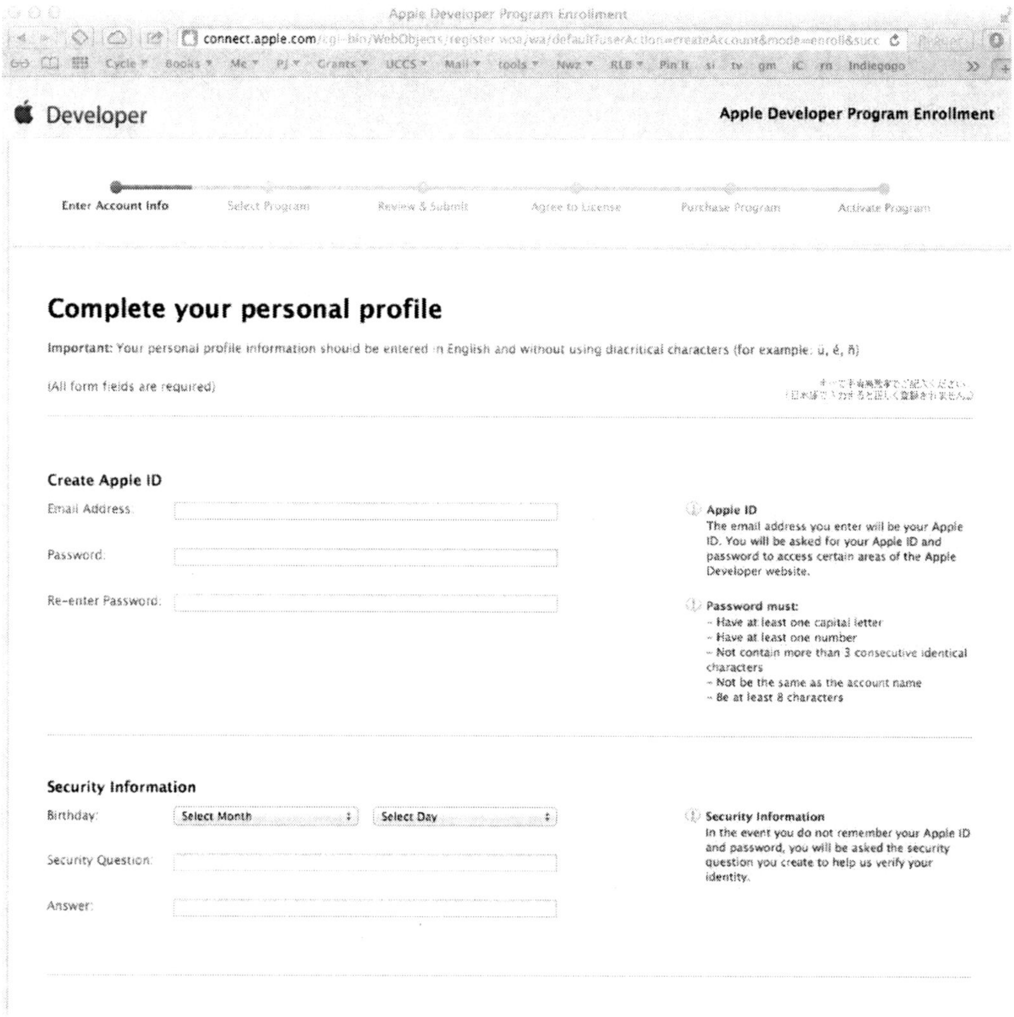

Figure 1-8. Enter all your information accordingly

Note   Before you move on to step 6, make sure you have received your confirmation email and chosen a password to complete the last step of getting set up as a bona fide registered Apple developer. Congratulations!

6. Use your Apple ID to log in to the main iOS development page at
    `http://developer.apple.com`. This page has three icons for the three types of
    Apple programmers. As shown on Figure 1-9, click the iOS Dev Center icon,
    which leads to the download page for iOS development software.

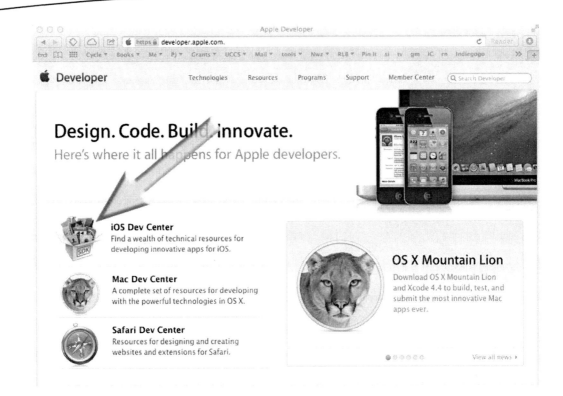

Figure 1-9. *For now click the iOS Dev Center icon as indicated by the arrow. Later you may want to program applications for Mac computers or the Safari web browser*

7. After logging in with your username and password as described in step 6, you'll see a screen similar to Figure 1-10. The iOS Dev Center contains all the tools necessary to build iOS apps. You'll spend more time here later, but for now just go to the Developer Page of the latest build of the iOS SDK by clicking the icon indicated by the arrow.

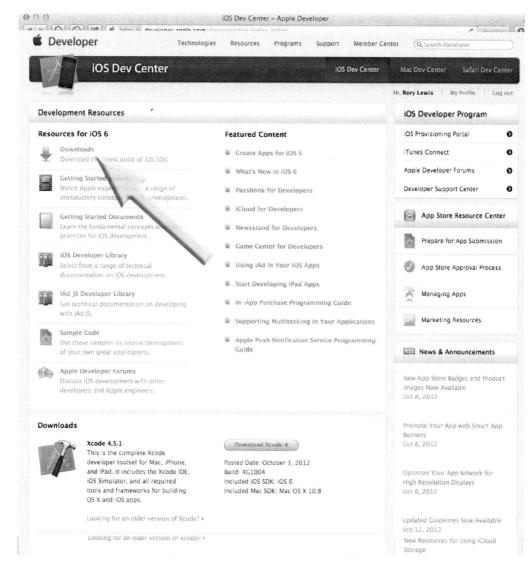

Figure 1-10. The Downloads link takes you to the bottom of the page

Note   At the time of writing, Xcode 4.4 and iOS SDK 6 are the latest environments. By the time you read this book these may well have larger numbers. That's not a problem—just go on to step 8. If by chance something has really thrown us a curve ball, it will be discussed and solved for you in our forum located at www.rorylewis.com/ipad_forum/ or http://bit.ly/oLVwpY.

8. Click the latest version. The figures in this section show the latest version at the time of print. These *will* be different by the time you read this. Right now the latest complete version is Xcode 4.5.1 for Lion, so click the Download Xcode 4 button indicated by the arrow in Figure 1-11.

Figure 1-11. Clicking the Download Xcode 4 button takes you to the Xcode 4 Developer page

9. Click the View in Mac App Store button. Remember that if it's a later version than shown in Figure 1-12, things may look slightly different, but I have confidence in you.

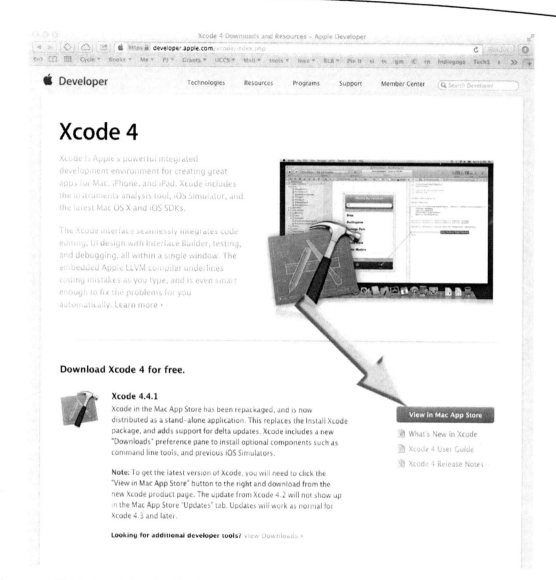

Figure 1-12. Click the View in Mac App Store button

10. Click the Install button, as shown in Figure 1-13. As the download continues, the Install button changes to say "Installing." When the download has finished, it changes to "Installed." Included with Xcode's iOS SDK is Apple's Integrated Development Environment (IDE). This is the programming platform that contains a suite of tools, sub-applications, and boilerplate code that enable programmers to do their jobs more easily.

Figure 1-13.   Click Install and wait for the download to complete

With your Xcode and iPhone/iPad Simulator tools installed and ready to access easily, you're almost ready to roll.

ABOUT DEMOMONKEY

Before you load the final tool—called DemoMonkey—let's step back and have a look at where you're going.

Through the years I've found that the most efficient way to teach students code is to take what I call the *subsystem* approach, teaching which pieces or sections of code will serve you in which situations. In this book I use a cool program you may have seen if you watched the latest WWDC: DemoMonkey. Essentially, in DemoMonkey you drag a heading explaining what needs to be done from the DemoMonkey palette. As you drop it into your code at the appropriate section of your Xcode file, it magically transforms into code that the author of the DemoMonkey file wrote. Before you can download and compile the Xcode project that creates DemoMonkey, you need to make sure Xcode works. So in the next section you first run a simple app to make sure all is in order in Xcode land.

Getting Ready for Your First iPhone/iPad Project

Before starting on your first app, you need to make sure that everything runs. Assuming you've already downloaded and installed Xcode, open it up:

1. Press Command + Shift + N (⌘⇧N) simultaneously to open a new window that showcases the different types of project templates in the land of Xcode.

2. Figure 1-14 displays the project templates: Master-Detail Application, OpenGL Game, Page-Based Application, Single View Application, Tabbed Application, Utility Application, and Empty Application. Click Single View Application, as shown in Figure 1-14, and then click Next.

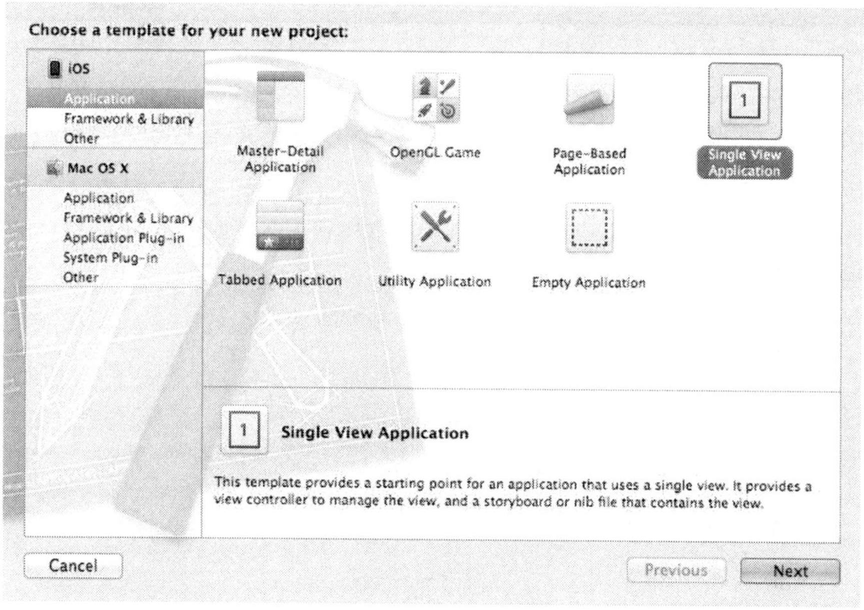

Figure 1-14. Select the Single View Application and then click Next

3. On your screen you should see something very similar to Figure 1-15. First call your project test as indicated by arrow 1. Choose iPhone (arrow 2) and then click Next (arrow 3).

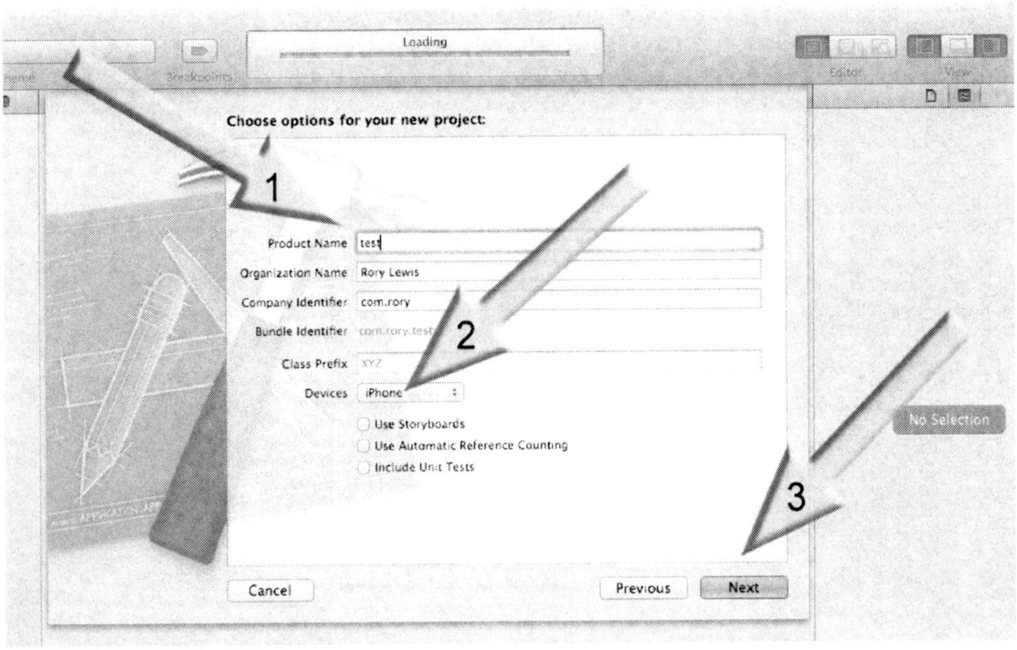

Figure 1-15. *Let's go for a test drive*

Note   This test doesn't use Storyboards. I just want you to see that Xcode builds a simple app. So keep everything unchecked—yes, including "Use Storyboard"—for now (as shown in Figure 1-15).

4. Figure 1-16 shows that you want to run your blank app. Click the "go" button, as indicated by the arrow.

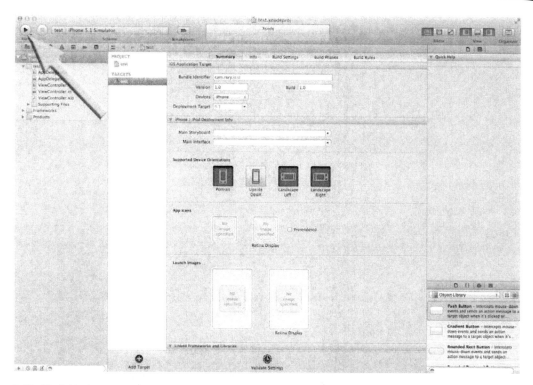

Figure 1-16. *The initial Integrated Development Environment (IDE)*

5.   The iPhone Simulator pops up, as shown in Figure 1-17.

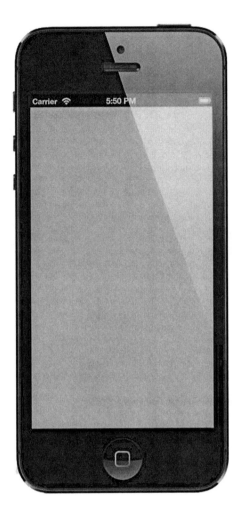

Figure 1-17. *Your first test drive*

Congratulations! You've loaded Xcode and have taken it for a test drive. Now let's get DemoMonkey running and start your first app.

Installing DemoMonkey

DemoMonkey is an optional tool intended to help you follow along with the book's projects. You only need it if you choose to use our .demoMonkey files for each chapter, which will allow you to drag and drop ready-to-use code snippets into the Xcode for most of the steps. If you don't want to do that, you can still type the code yourself, and if you choose not to use DemoMonkey for this book, you can skip the rest of this chapter.

DemoMonkey will make life easier for you by letting you focus more on the code you're using—but you'll still be challenged in this book. That's simply part of my pedagogy. The issue is really how to handle things when you get challenged.

Note When you find yourself in a tough spot, you can always reread the section, rewind the video examples, or—most importantly—visit the forum where you'll often find many people, including me, online and ready to help you immediately. We may refer you to somebody else's solution or we may help you directly. So go to the forum, say hello to the crowd, and become immersed by first seeking help from others and then going back to help others. The forum is at www.rorylewis.com/ipad_forum/ or http://bit.ly/oLVwpY.

With your Xcode running and building apps, you can now install DemoMonkey:

1. Apple provides DemoMonkey as an OS X sample code project that's available for download to anyone. Go to http://developer.apple.com/ library/mac/#samplecode/DemoMonkey/Introduction/Intro.html or http://bit.ly/v3BuKI, as shown in Figure 1-18. Click Download Sample Code, as indicated by the arrow, and save the zip file into a desired location on your machine.

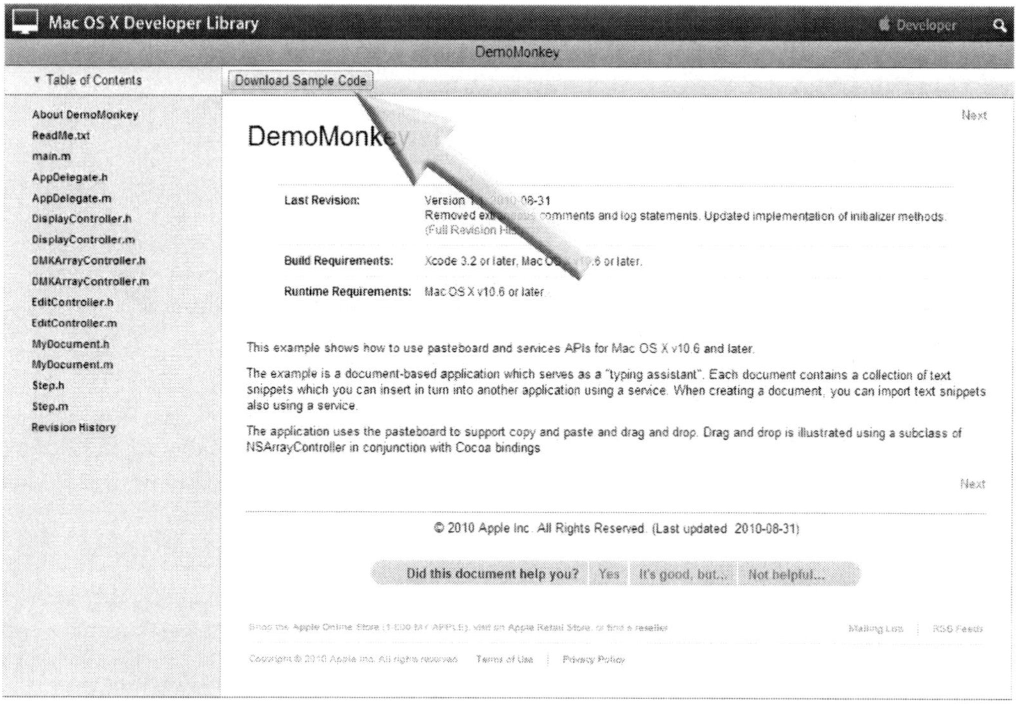

Figure 1-18. Download Sample Code

2. Unzip the zip file by double-clicking it, open the folder, and then double-click the DemoMonkey.xcodeproj file, as indicated by the arrow in Figure 1-19. Once the Xcode project is open, press Command + B (⌘B) simultaneously to compile the project.

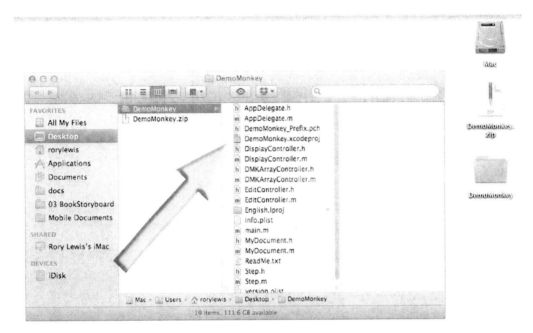

Figure 1-19. *Open the DemoMonkey Xcode project inside your DemoMonkey folder*

3. After the "Build Succeeded" message shows up, expand the Project Navigator, right-click the DemoMonkey.app icon, and then choose Show in Finder from the context menu, as shown in Figure 1-20.

Figure 1-20. Expand the Project Navigator and choose Show in Finder from the context menu

4. Lastly, once the Finder opens the folder containing the application you just built, drag the DemoMonkey.app to your Applications folder, as shown in Figure 1-21.

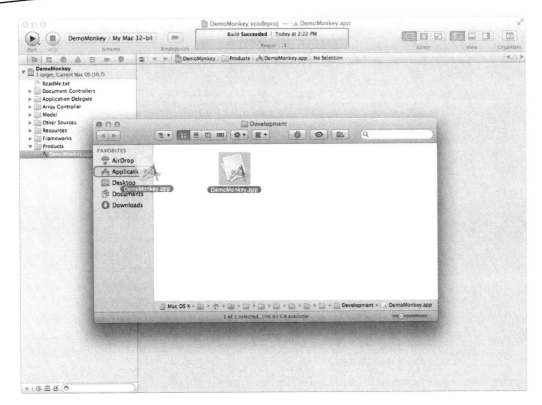

Figure 1-21. Drag the DemoMonkey.app to your Applications folder

> **Note**   If for some reason you were unable to reproduce the steps in this section, you can download a compiled DemoMonkey.app from my site using this link: `http://bit.ly/RpCtFj`. Then simply drag it to your Applications folder.

You're ready to roll now!

Chapter 2

Blast-Off!

The first program you'll attempt is a basic, generic Hello World app. This chapter follows precisely the method I have found, through experience, to work very well when teaching this subject. I use this simple Hello World app to introduce students to critical skill sets they'll use over and over again. As is the case with my own students, by the time you finish this chapter, you'll know how to run your first app in the three different ways described in this chapter:

- iPhone app on iPhone Simulator
- iPhone app on iPad Simulator
- iPad app on iPad Simulator

These three ways of running apps are critical because these are the most common ways that programmers in the real world code Xcode. Your first adventure with this new set of tools will be saying "Hello" to the world from the Single View Application template in Xcode.

> **Note** Besides the information I present here in this book, including screenshots, I also offer screencasts of me going through each of the examples in this book. Downloading those will help you get through this book, as will lecture notes, third-party resources, and pertinent YouTube videos—all of which can be accessed by clicking the blue iOS 6 icon on the top bar at `www.rorylewis.com`.

Running your App on the iPhone Simulator

In this first example, you're going to click a button, and text will appear above it that says "Hello World!"

1. Before opening Xcode, first close all open programs so you'll be able to optimize your processing capabilities and focus your undivided attention on this new material. Press ⌘+Tab and then ⌘+Q to close everything. Only the Finder should remain on your screen. Find and click the Xcode icon in your Dock to open it. The "Welcome to Xcode" screen appears, as mentioned in Chapter 1. See Figure 2-1.

Figure 2-1. Click the Xcode icon in your Dock to open it. You'll see the "Welcome to Xcode" screen

2. Open a new project in Xcode using either keyboard shortcuts or a mouse.
    I *strongly* suggest using keyboard shortcuts to save time and because the
    best way to *not* get work as an app developer is to use your mouse for
    functions that can be done with shortcuts. Press ⌘+⇧+N to open a new
    project. (If you were using your mouse to open a new project, you would
    choose "Create a new Xcode project.") Select Single View Application (see
    arrow 1 in Figure 2-2). Name it helloWorld_01 in the Product Name field,
    enter your name in the Organization Name field, and for the Company
    Identifier enter com.[your first name here]. Leave the Class Prefix field
    alone, select iPhone as your Device if it has not been selected by default,
    and uncheck the Use Storyboards, Use Automatic References, and Include
    Unit Tests selection buttons. Press Return or click Next as depicted by
    arrow 2 in Figure 2-2.

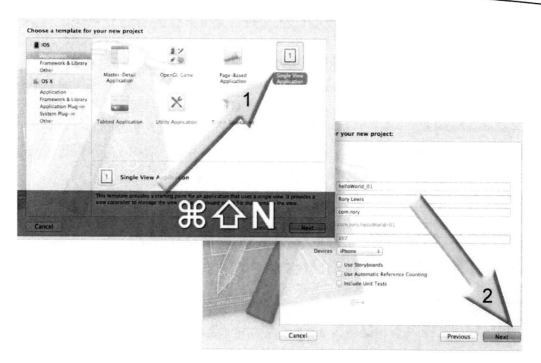

Figure 2-2. Name the project helloWorld_01 and use your name or company name for the Company Identifier. For Device, select iPhone

Note My Single View Application template icon was highlighted by default; yours may not be. Regardless, click it and save the new project to your desktop as helloWorld_01.

3. As soon as you save this project to your desktop, Xcode instantiates the helloWorld_01 project environment, as indicated by the name on the top of the window (see Figure 2-3). If this looks a bit scary, stay cool… don't freak out! This is Apple's way of arranging all the goodies that you'll eventually use to write complex apps. For now, just follow along and try to set aside all the questions you may be asking. Xcode has created six files:

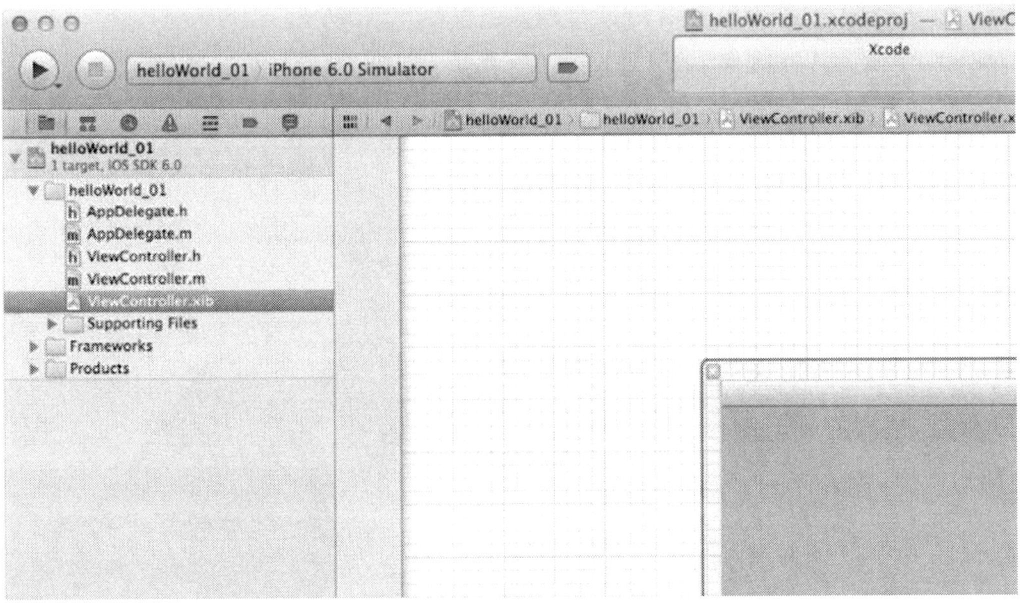

Figure 2-3. Click helloWorld_01ViewController.xib to open the Interface Builder

- *Two classes containing two files each*: A *header* file (.h) and an *implementation* file (.m). Two of them end in Appdelegate, and two of them start with ViewController. I'll get back to this later. Right now just know this: Each class is comprised of two files—a header file and an implementation file.

- *Two nib files* (.xib): *nib* stands for NeXT Interface Builder, used for interface files on Steve Job's NeXT computer before he came back to Apple. *xib* stands for Mac OS X Interface Builder, but both are pronounced "nib" for the most part and are used interchangeably.

As shown in Figure 2-3, double-click ViewController.xib to open the file, located in the manila-colored helloWorld_01 folder inside the blue Xcode folder at the top of the Navigator area of the Xcode environment.

Note   There is a slight possibility that your Navigation pane, which bears the folders seen in Figure 2-3, is closed. This is not a problem. To open your Utility area, go to the upper left of the workspace window, which includes inspectors and libraries. Use the View Selector in the toolbar to open and close the Navigator, Debug, and Utility areas. You may also need to again select the black folder Project Navigator icon, located directly under the Run button—the Run button looks like the Play button in iTunes.

4.   When you open your xib file, your workspace will appear, as shown in
     Figure 2-4. Note that if the shaded area on the right isn't showing the Utility
     area, which includes inspectors and libraries, navigate to your View Selector
     (which contains three icons). Click the far right icon, called the Utilities icon
     (see arrow 1 in Figure 2-4) and then click the Object Library icon. You may
     also want to select the icon's viewing option in your Library to view your
     objects (see arrow 2 in Figure 2-4)—doing so will make following along with
     me easier.

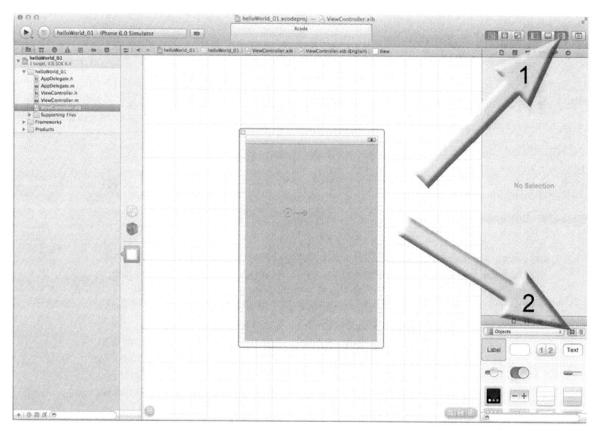

Figure 2-4. Your workspace

5.   You now need to drag some goodies from the Library onto your canvas,
     which includes everything on the graph paper area. First, though, think about
     what you're going to do. You're going to click a button, and text will appear
     above it saying "Hello World!" Therefore, you need the button to click and
     a label that will contain the "Hello World!" text. Easy! First drag a label onto
     your canvas, as shown in Figure 2-5.

Figure 2-5. Drag a label onto your canvas

6. Move the label to a height that suits you and then move it horizontally until the blue center line appears. At this point, let it go, nicely centered in the middle of your canvas. This label will eventually contain the text "Hello World!" so drag the label's side handle bars out to the right and left to make it a little larger, to about the size shown in Figure 2-6. In the Text box, delete the text label so that it's blank as shown in Figure 2-7. Lastly, still looking at Figure 2-6, notice how the Alignment "centered text" icon is highlighted? Do the same and click it so that when your "Hello World!" text appears in the label, it's nicely centered in the centered label. Beautiful. Now let's move on to the button.

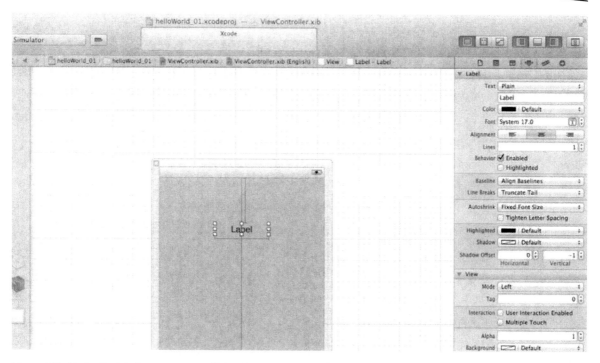

Figure 2-6. Center the label on your canvas. Delete its text and center its content

Note You'll also see the Vertical Line Constraint just slightly to the right of the center line. That tells you the how close or far apart the distance relationships to the top and bottom of the canvas amongst other things are.

7. Drag out a button and place it below your text, moving it left to right until the center lines tell you it's centered. Let it go, as shown in Figure 2-7. Double-click it and type *Press Me!* (see Figure 2-8).

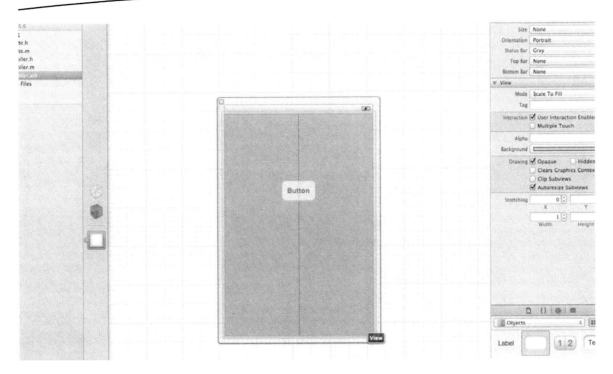

Figure 2-7. Drag a button onto the canvas

8. In View, select a color for the background, as shown in Figure 2-8. I selected light grey.

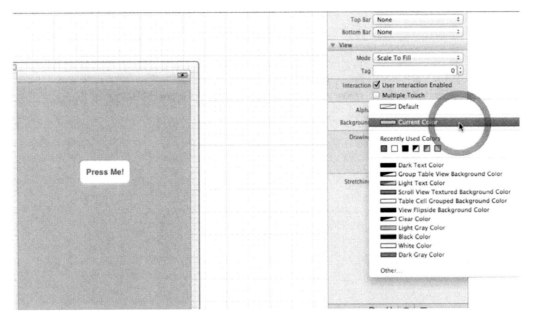

Figure 2-8. Choose a color for your background

9. You're now finished loading your two items onto the canvas. Close the Object Library icon again by clicking it, as shown by arrow 1 in Figure 2-9. Save the file with the shortcut ⌘ +S. (This is the preferred method of saving, rather than using your mouse.) Now you need to open the Assistant in the Editor Selector, located to the left of the View Selector and indicated by arrow 2 in Figure 2-9.

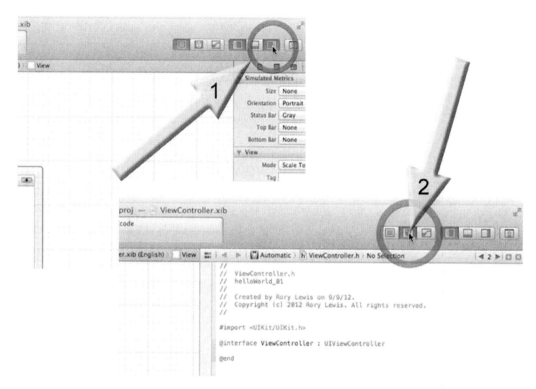

Figure 2-9. Close the Utilities folder, save your work, and open the Assistant

10. You're going to be using something here called the Open URL contextual menu. You want to tell the label to print out text that says "Hello World!" when the button is pushed. We call these background commands *"outlets"*. In the past outlets had to be coded from scratch, but now the source code is conveniently placed to the right of the graphical builder. You can simply Control-drag (holding the Control key while dragging your mouse) connections from the graphical builder to your code. First, check that the code on the right is your header file—the green print at the top ends with .h (see Figure 2-11) as explained at the beginning of this chapter. Click the label on your canvas (it's invisible because you took the text out, so you'll need to poke around where you placed it) and Control-drag over from your label to any place under your @interface method, as shown in Figure 2-10. Once the black label appears saying Insert Outlet, release the mouse button.

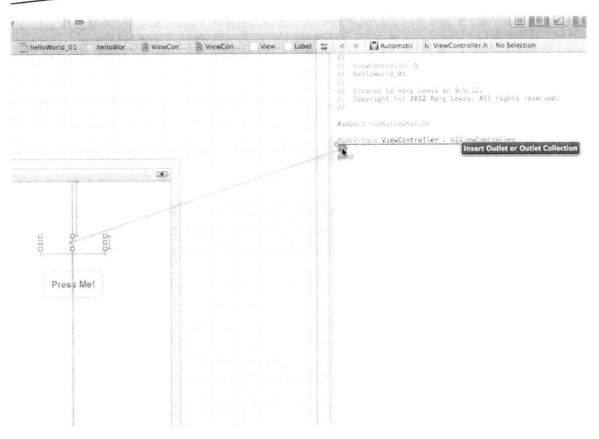

Figure 2-10. *Control-drag from your label to create an outlet*

Note   The Assistant uses a split-pane editor, but note that you can open the Assistant automatically by Option-clicking a file in the Project Navigator or Symbol Navigator pane.

11.   As mentioned in step 10, you want the Connection type to be Outlet (Apple figured this is what you probably need, so it appears by default). Don't worry about Object and File's Owner right now. You can name the label anything you like in the future, but for now name it *label* as in Figure 2-11, so your code will look the same as mine when you compare yours to my video, the images in this book, or the code you download from my web site. Don't worry about UILabel for Type now either. Press Return, and the code @property (retain, nonatomic) IBOutlet UILabel *label; magically appears. You can see it highlighted here:

```
#import <UIKit/UIKit.h>

@interface helloWorld_01ViewController : UIViewController
@property (retain, nonatomic) IBOutlet UILabel *label;
@end
```

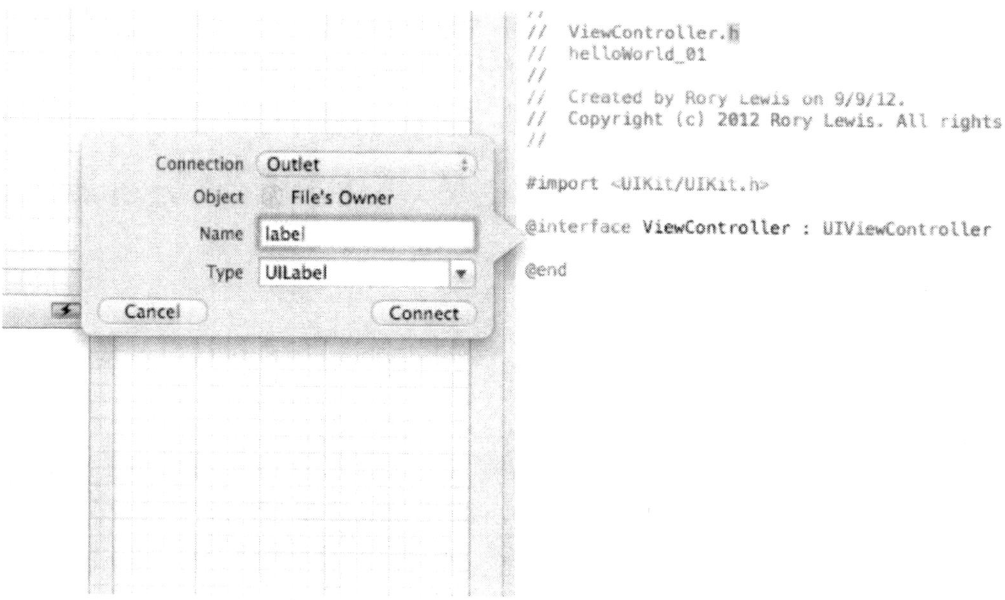

Figure 2-11. Make the IBOutlet a label – this automatically creates your Objective-C code

12. Now you need to place some code behind the button you dragged onto the canvas so it can do the action you want. In your case, you want the button to tell your label to do and say stuff. This is called *declaring an action*. For now, you just need to associate the button with action code; later you'll define exactly what these actions will be. So, just as you did before with the label, click the button in your canvas and Control-drag over from it as shown in Figure 2-12. Once the black label appears saying Insert Outlet, Action...release the mouse button.

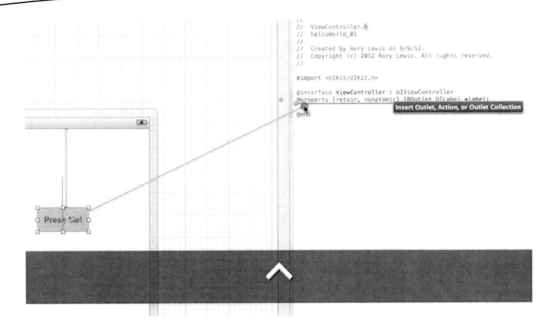

Figure 2-12. Control-drag from your button to create an action

13. Choose Action from the Connection drop-down menu. Again, don't worry
    about Object and File's Owner right now. Name it *button* and ignore
    everything else for now. This is illustrated in Figure 2-13.

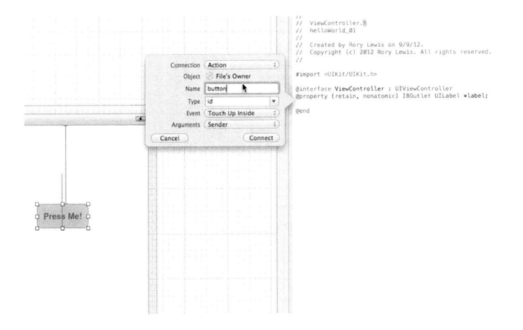

Figure 2-13. Create the action for your button

14. Press Return, and you'll see -(IBAction)button:(id)sender; which appears as shown below. I discuss this further in the section "Digging the Code" at the end of this chapter.

```
#import <UIKit/UIKit.h>

@interface ViewController : UIViewController
@property (retain, nonatomic) IBOutlet UILabel *label;
- (IBAction)button:(id)sender;

@end
```

Before moving on to step 15, let's look around and see where we're at. Back in step 3, I said you have two classes that contain two files: a header file (.h) and an implementation file (.m). Let me talk a little bit about the difference between these two files.

The ViewController class manages the interactions your code has with the display, and it manages the user's interactions with your code. It contains a view, but it's not a view itself. You only have a minimal understanding of the ViewController *class* so far. What I want you to get, though, is that every class consists of two parts: the header (.h) file and the implementation (.m) file.

I want you to read this next part aloud, okay? *We tell the computer in a header file what types of commands we will execute in the implementation file.* Now, say it again in the context of your code: *We tell the computer in the* ViewController.h *file what types of commands we will execute in the* ViewController.m *file.*

Well, admit it—that wasn't so bad! Let's get back to the example.

15. To move on to the implementation file at this point, get into the habit of first switching views and going from the Assistant Editor to the Standard Editor. To do this, simply click the button immediately to the left of the Assistant Editor (remember arrow 2 in Figure 2-9). This is the Standard Editor.

16. Once in the Standard Editor, select your ViewController's implementation file, as shown in Figure 2-14.

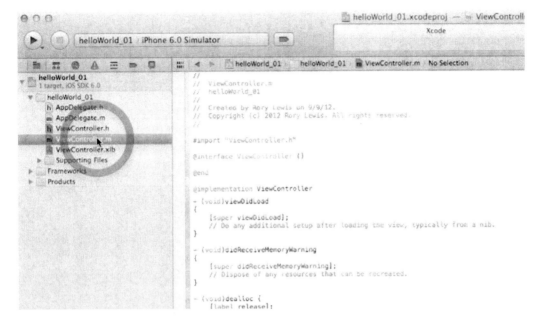

Figure 2-14. Open your helloWorld_01ViewController's implementation file

Recall how in step 13 (Figure 2-13) you *declared an action* when you Control-dragged the button into your header file's code? Remember that in the header file you *declare* actions, whereas in the implementation file you *implement* actions. Here in your `ViewController`'s implementation file, you're going to implement the actions that you want to happen when somebody presses the button. Specifically, you want the label to say "Hello World!" How do you do that? Well, you need to type your very first code to start your journey toward geekdom. Yup, you're going to code text. Take a deep breath and follow along.

Looking at the text of your `ViewController`'s implementation file, you can see that the clever people at Apple programmed Xcode to write a number of methods already that need to happen in the background just to get your app with label and buttons running on your iPhone. For now, I'll ignore these methods. Just scroll down to the end until you get to one named - `(IBAction)button:(id)` `sender`. Hmm ... wait a minute, that's the code that appeared in step 14, right? Well, almost. That code ended with `;` (semicolon) because in the header file, you declared this action. Xcode knows you now need to implement whatever actions you tell it to do inside the squiggly brackets. You need to remember this rule. You'll use it over and over again.

> **Note**   A declaration in the `.h` file becomes a method in the `.m` file by replacing the colon with squiggly brackets.

After reaching the implementation of the action you declared in the header, I want you to place your cursor in between the two squiggly brackets, as indicated in the following code. Click there and read below.

```
#import "helloWorld_01ViewController.h"
@implementation helloWorld_01ViewController
- (void)dealloc


- (IBAction)button:(id)sender {
}
@end
```

17. The code I want you to type is `label.text = @"Hello World!"`. But it's not
     that straightforward, because as you type, something really cool happens.
     Xcode figures out what you're probably going to want to code in its
     autocompletion window, as illustrated in Figure 2-15. If you agree with the
     selection, press Tab, and Xcode places the completed, correctly typed and
     spelled command into your code. If the one it suggests is not the correct
     one, but you see the correct one a few commands down, just arrow down
     (↓) until you reach the correct selection and then press Tab. Cool, huh? After
     you've written `label.text`, continue on to step 18.

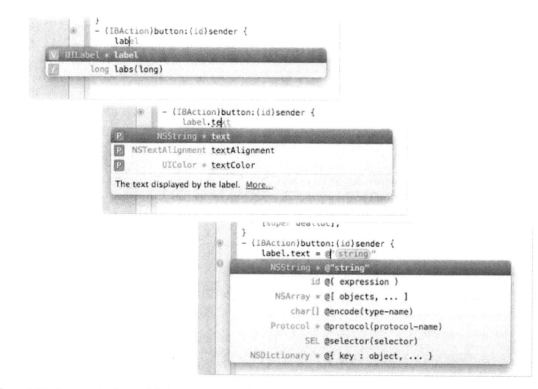

Figure 2-15. As you enter the text label.text, autocompletion suggests code. Type the text you want the label to say after the @ directive

18. Your code should look like that depicted in Figure 2-16. If you wanted to say *I can feel I'm becoming a geek!* instead, you'd type `label.text = @"I can feel I'm becoming a geek!";`. Save your work too (⌘+S as shown in Figure 2-16). Please try not to use your mouse; try to use Command + S (⌘+S) every time you save. You may also want to check that your header files and nib files are also saved because, during the course of reading these instructions, you may have had to go back and change files. Well, you need to go back and save them. So, go ahead and save everything now. If the file is highlighted in gray, it means you need to save it too.

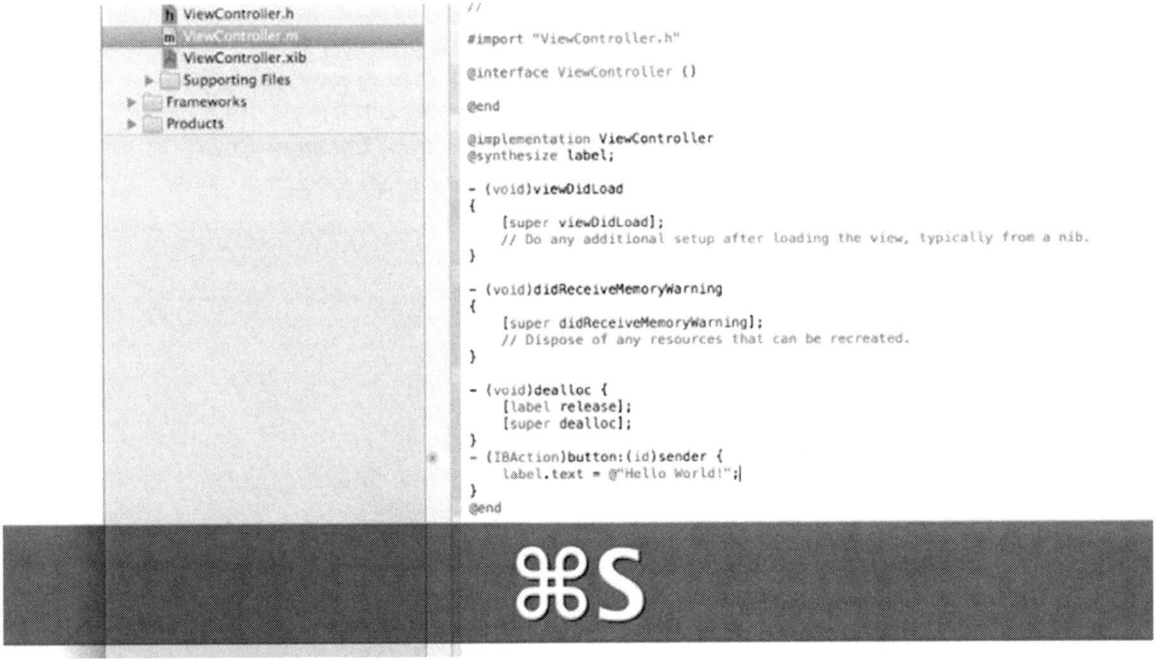

Figure 2-16. Save your work with ⌘+S

19. Ok! Let's run it. Click on the run button as shown in Figure 2-17.

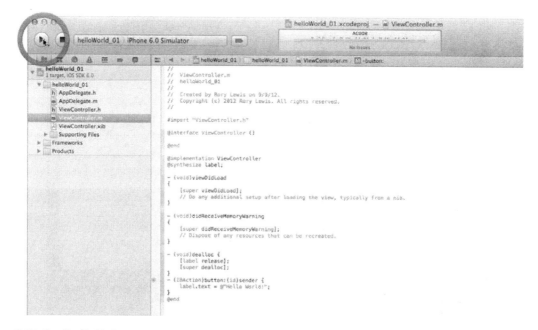

Figure 2-17. Run it with ⌘+R

As Figure 2-18 shows, the iPhone Simulator loads your very first app, waits for you to press (click) the button, and then says "Hello World!"

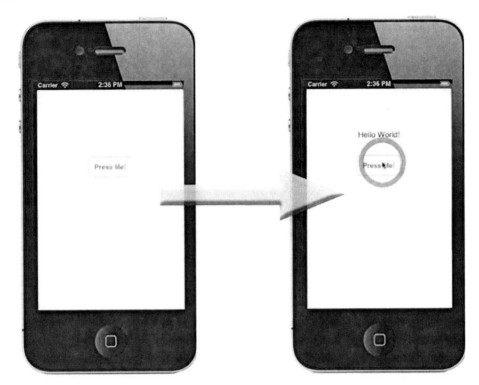

Figure 2-18. The iPhone Simulator is loaded and waiting for the user to press the button. Then it will say "Hello World!"

Congratulations, my friend! You've really done something very special today. You may have cursed me a couple of times or floundered here and there, but in getting here you've taken that very difficult leap from being a user of technology to being a coder of technology.

We still have a few things to do, so take a break. Walk the dog. Do something that doesn't involve technology, even if it's just taking a walk. Take a minute to realize that you're beginning a long journey, one that will be difficult at times, but one wherein you can hold your head high and say, "Yeah, I code iPhone and iPad apps!"

Running Your iPhone App on the iPad Simulator

As you will see, apart from specifying that the app will be on an iPad rather than an iPhone, the app will be the exact same thing. But let's go through it so you know that this is indeed the case.

1. First, change the environment from the iOS Simulator. While still in the iPhone Simulator, click Hardware ➤ Device ➤ iPad so you can see how your first app would run if it were being run on an iPad (see Figure 2-19).

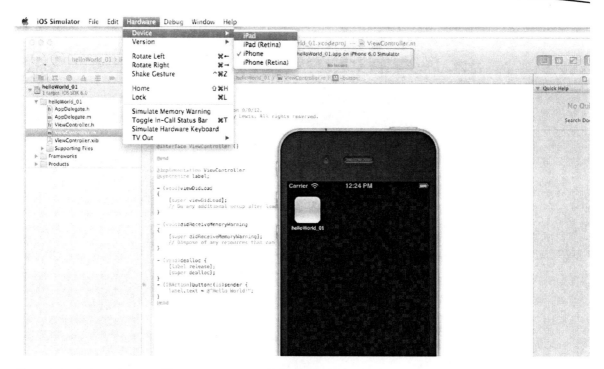

Figure 2-19. *Let's see how your iPhone app runs on the iPhone Simulator*

2.   The result is the display shown in Figure 2-20. The Simulator may initially appear
     with the default screen, so click to the right of the highlighted middle dot.

Figure 2-20. *The initial screen of the iPad Simulator. If it initially it appears in default screen, click to the right of the highlighted middle dot*

3. Once it shifts to the screen that has the button for your app, double-click it, as shown by arrow 1 in Figure 2-21. Your app appears as a small iPhone-sized image as shown on the right. It can work like this, but go ahead and enlarge it to iPad size by clicking the zoom button, indicated by arrow 2 in Figure 2-21.

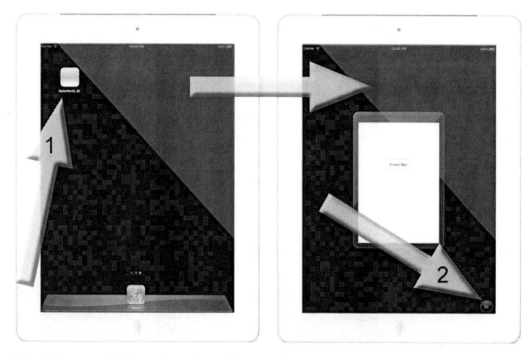

Figure 2-21. *Click your app's button and zoom it up with the zoom button*

4. Click on the Press Me! button you created, and you see it works (see Figure 2-22).

Figure 2-22. Click "Press Me!" It worked on the iPad

Running Your iPad App on the iPad Simulator

At the beginning of this chapter, I made a deal with you. I said you were going to make a very simple app and run it in three ways:

- iPhone app on iPhone Simulator

- iPhone app on iPad Simulator

- iPad app on iPad Simulator

You've already completed the first two. But it's still not really an iPad app. If you look closely, you'll see pixilation (jagged pixels)—what we often call *pseudo iPad* style. What you really want to do is program your app specifically for the iPad. A real iPad app is made specifically for the iPad and cannot be run on an iPhone. All the graphics and screen sizes are specifically designed for the iPad and are too large for the iPhone. So let's go ahead and make an app specifically for the iPad.

1. Close your helloWorld_01 app in Xcode by pressing ⌘+S to save it and then ⌘+Q to quit Xcode. You should now be looking at your empty desktop, except for the helloWorld_01 folder right under your Mac hard-drive icon. Good. You're now going to run helloWorld_02, which will be exactly like helloWorld_01 except for a couple of steps.

2. Open Xcode and press ⌘+⇧+N. Select View-Based App and then press Return. Now look at Figure 2-23: in Figure 2-2, you named it helloWorld_01. In Figure 2-23, you name it helloWorld_02. Most importantly, in Figure 2-23, you select iPad, *not* iPhone as you did in Figure 2-2 (that's why it is selected by default in Figure 2-23). Once you have changed it to iPad, I want you to try remember all the steps you performed in helloWorld_01 and implement them on the iPad.

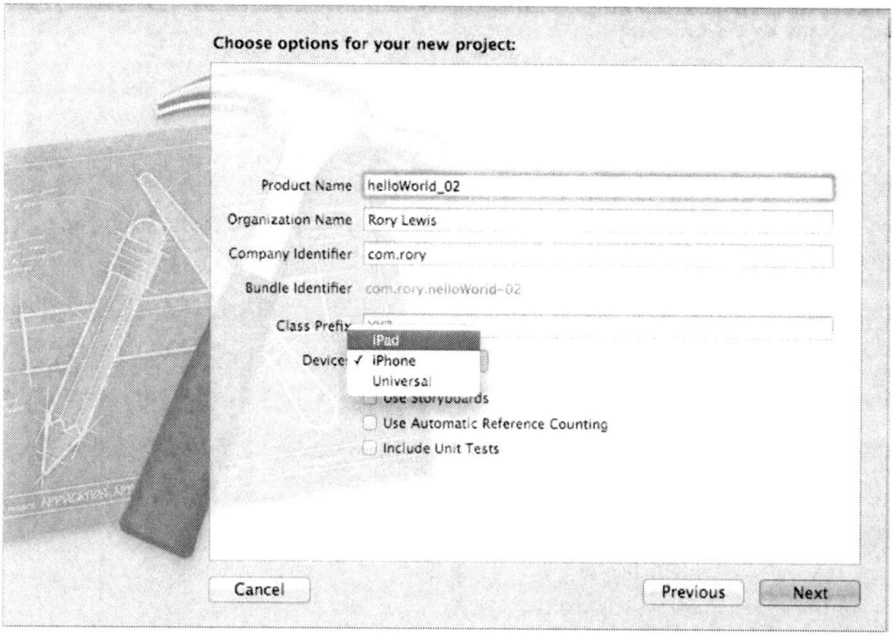

Figure 2-23. *Open Xcode, select the View-based Application template, and then save a new project file to your desktop*

Huh? Yes, that's what I said. I make my students in the lecture hall redo helloWorld all over again, but now as an iPad app, and I encourage them to try not to peek at their lecture notes. I want them to try doing it on their own. If you need to refer back to earlier steps in this chapter, that's okay—but then do it again and again until you can do it by memory. Students usually need to do it between three and six times before they can repeat it identically without referencing notes.

Note You may have noticed the Universal option in the drop-down menu in Figure 2-23. Universal allows you to code for the iPhone and the iPad at the same time. When run by your user, the app adapts the screen size to the current device. You'll use Universal later in the book, but you can experiment with it now.

Now that you've created your new apps, you need to do a few organizational chores. Right now, on your beautiful clean open desktop, you only have two folders containing your two helloWorld programs. You need to make a place to store all your programs that will make sense to you as you continue to read this book. Create a subfolder in your Documents folder called My Programs and then save the files helloWorld_01 and helloWorld_02 there by dragging them to that folder. Now, with a fresh, clean, empty desktop, close all programs. Press ⌘+Tab and then ⌘+Q to close everything until only the Finder is left on your screen.

Digging the Code

At the ends of chapters, I include this section called "Digging the Code," wherein I start feeding you insights into the meaning of much of the code that miraculously appeared or that I instructed you to type. What I've found, though, is that the human brain makes its own associations if it keeps on doing something over and over again, and certain outcomes occur each time we repeat that action. I've found that if I first allow students to fly through huge amounts of code in sheer ignorant bliss, it does a great deal of good because it allows their brains to make connections that only they can make. So here in "Digging the Code" I start feeding you little snippets, just the right ones that connect the dots as to why you put this code here or that code there. Later, as you approach the end of the book, you'll feel totally comfortable really digging the code and getting into it. For now, take a deep breath, relish the fact that you coded an app in the fundamental ways necessary for iPhone and iPad apps, and I'll see you in Chapter 3.

Good job!

Keep on Truckin'

Now that you've gotten your feet wet from programming your first two iPhone and iPad apps, I want you to tell yourself that you have to *keep on truckin'* with more apps and more practice. You need to create a more natural connection between the synapses in your brain.

Initially, many of my computer science colleagues had disdain for my approach of blindly hauling newbie programmers through code without explaining it all. Over the years, I've learned exactly when to tell you what's going on and when to just jostle you through the code. Most importantly, you need to keep on truckin' and keep your brain dialed into Xcode.

The third Hello World app introduces you to user interaction and `if-else` statements, which results in slightly more complex code. Remember, this is Objective-C—a pretty complex and difficult language—so I explain only what I deem necessary. That brings up one difference between Chapters 2 and 3. In Chapter 2 we did not repeat enough actions for you to make your own associations." Well, here in Chapter 3 you will make these associations and therefore it will be appropriate to start digging the code.

So let's get on with the next application. When it's done, take a break and then be ready to go back and review lines of your input, as you focus on certain portions of the code and see how it all works together.

> **Note** Besides the information I present here in this book, including various screenshots, I also offer screencasts on my website. Go to rorylewis.com, click the iOS 6 Tutorials icon, and then click either Video tutorials or Downloads for this book.

helloWorld_03: An Interactive Single View App

In the first two programs you did by yourself, helloWorld_01 and helloWorld_02, you said hello to the world using a Single View platform that housed a button. This third app will also be a Single View Application, but with a little more complexity. In your third app, the user is asked whether he's a geek. When he taps the Are you a Geek? button, teasing text will appear. First it says, "You Are!" When the user taps it again, it says, "Shut up you're not!"

Before you get started with the next method, save helloWorld_01 and helloWorld_02 in a folder of your choice that is *not* on the desktop. Create a folder in your Documents folder called My Programs and save the file named helloWorld_01 there by dragging the entire folder inside your My Programs folder. Now, with a fresh, clean, empty desktop, close all other programs you may have running by selecting programs. Press ⌘+Tab and then ⌘+Q to close everything until only the Finder is left on your screen.

1. As you did in the first example, launch Xcode and open a new project with your keyboard shortcut: ⌘+⇧+N. Your screen should show the New Project with Single View Application template, as shown in Figure 3-1. You may find that your Single View Application template was highlighted by default because of the last example. If not, click the Single View Application icon and then click Next button.

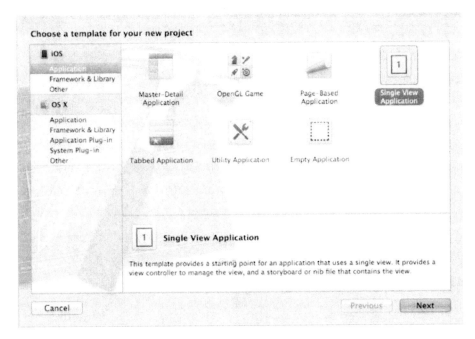

Figure 3-1. Open Xcode, select the Single View Application template, and click Next

2. You're going to call this third project helloWorld_03, so type that in the Product Name box, as shown in Figure 3-2. The Organization Name and Company Identifier should automatically be defaulted to your Xcode license name. Remember that helloWorld_02 was created for an iPad, so the Devices setting on your computer may still be set to iPad. Whatever the case, make sure that the helloWorld_03 Devices setting is set for the iPhone. If Use Storyboards, Use Automatic Referencing Counting, or Include Unit Tests are checked by default, uncheck them. Click Next.

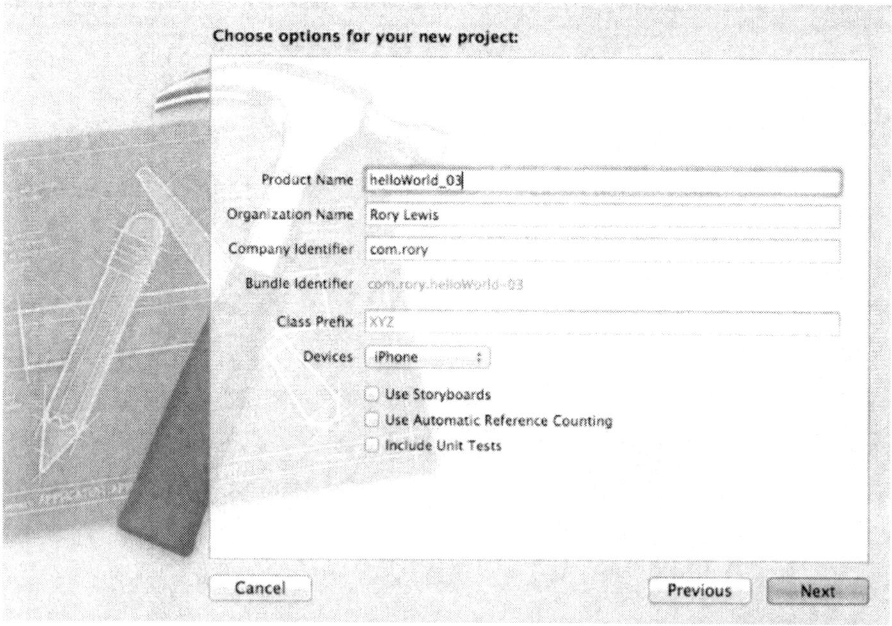

Figure 3-2. Name your project, make sure it's for an iPhone, and then click Next

3.   For this homework assignment, my students are required to take photos of themselves, crop them to 320 × 480 images, and save them as .png files. This way, I can more quickly associate names with the correct faces. If you're not my student, go ahead and get a picture of yourself, crop it to 320 × 480, and save it onto your desktop as a .png file. (If you don't have access to a graphics editor, feel free to use the picture I used for this project. You can download it at http://bit.ly/PFXJGe (scroll down to the third video tutorial from the top, helloWorld_03, and click the box icon). A compressed file will be downloaded to your computer with the picture I used in this example, named DrLewis.png.) Place the image on your desktop. Press ⌘+Tab until Xcode is highlighted. When you release the ⌘+Tab keys, Xcode will fill your screen again. Resize Xcode slightly so you can see the desktop with the image, as indicated by arrow 1 in Figure 3-3. Grab it, drag it over to your Supporting Files folder, and drop it there as indicated by arrow 2 in Figure 3-3.

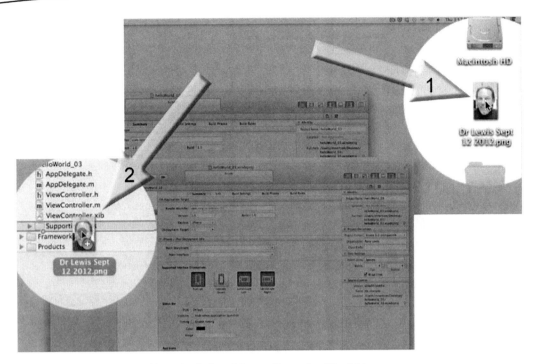

Figure 3-3. Drag a picture of yourself from the desktop into your Supporting Files folder

4. One of the most common mistakes students make happens at this simple
    stage of Xcode management: They forget to check the "Copy items into
    destination group's folder (if needed)" checkbox. When you import a file into
    the Supporting Files folder on your computer, if you don't check "Copy
    items into destination group's folder," everything will seem fine, giving you
    a false sense of security. In this case, even though Xcode is told that your
    supporting files, such as the image in this example, reside in your Supporting
    Files folder, what's really happening is that there's a little note saying: "Dude,
    I take no responsibility for this, but the file is not here, it's still on the owner's
    desktop!" So you, the writer of your code, go on doing your homework. Every
    time you run your code, and Xcode calls to access a supporting file, this
    irresponsible "pointer reference" guy just keeps saying, "It's not here—it's still
    on your desktop!" So you finish your homework and everything works great.
    You smile as you zip up your work and send it to me. I give you a zero and
    then you cry. Why? Well, the irresponsible pointer reference is telling me that
    your reference files are on *my* desktop. Nope! They're not on my desktop,
    they're on yours, and you get zero for being negligent and depending on a
    pointer reference dude rather than selecting the "Copy items" check box. So,
    after dragging your picture into the Supporting Files folder, check the "Copy
    items into destination group's folder (if needed)" check box, as shown in
    Figure 3-4, and then click Finish. Now you're in good standing, and won't be
    brought to tears by the pointer reference dude.

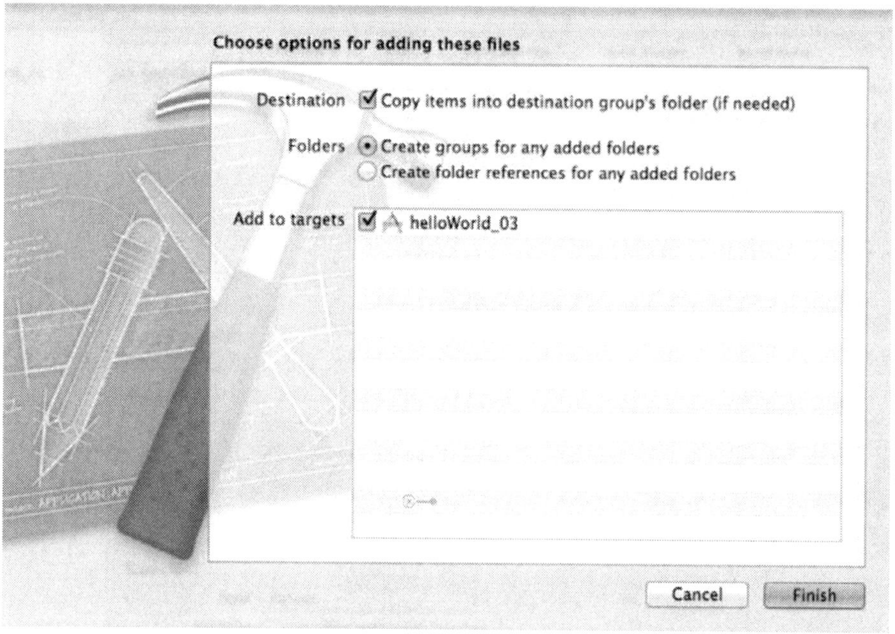

Figure 3-4. Complete importing your image by selecting the "Copy items into destination ..." option and clicking Finish

Note I can hear you asking, "Why even give us this option, then?" Here's a simple answer that covers most but not all bases: Let's say you were designing a game or program that has a database of millions and millions of files, and this database was too large to fit on an iPhone or iPad. Here, you would not check the "Copy items" box. You would allow the pointer reference dude to say, "Yo, I take no responsibility for any of this, it's not really here, it's at this URL located at www.wherever.com."

Creating the User Interface

Okay, now you're ready to start dragging and dropping items onto your View Design area, which is what the user sees when she looks at her iPhone.

5. Open your nib file, as you did in the two previous apps. Open your helloWorld_03 folder and select the ViewController.xib file, as illustrated in Figure 3-5.

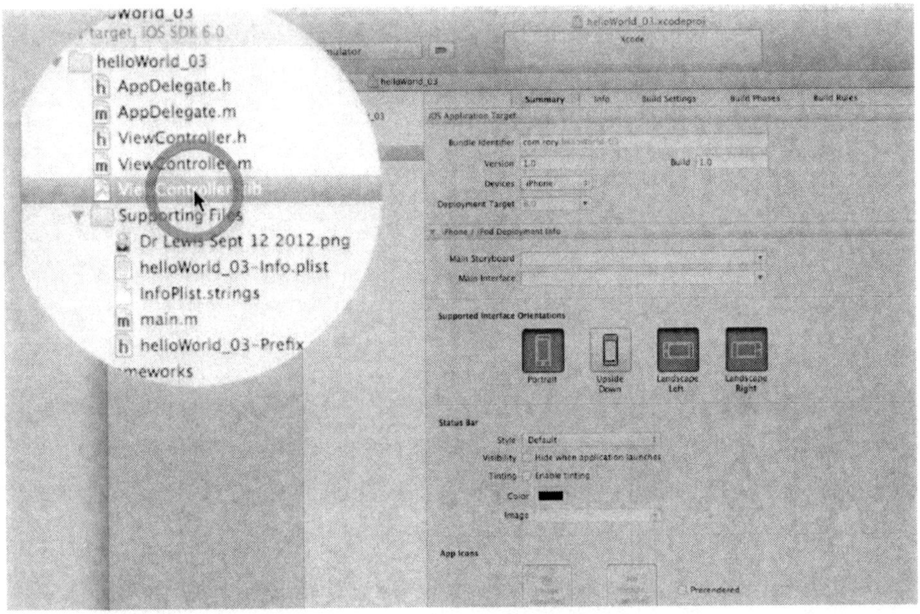

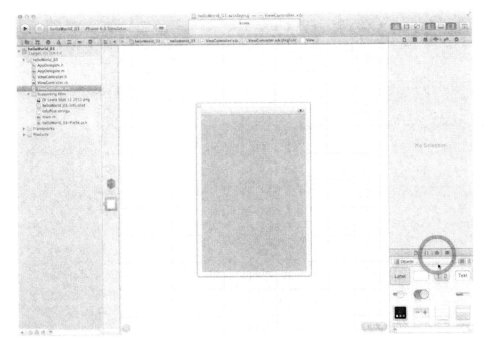

Figure 3-5. Open your nib file

6. Click the Object Library icon and make sure you're in Icon View (the icon with four little squares, above the Text icon in Figure 3-6, is highlighted). You'll be dragging screenviews, labels, and buttons onto the View Design area.

Figure 3-6. Open the Object Library

7. With your Utilities pane open, as shown in Figure 3-7, from the bottom
    section of the panel, drag an Image View (most often referred to by its full
    name, UIImageView, by coders and at Apple demonstrations) onto your View
    Design area. You need a UIImageView because you need to have an image
    of you underneath the buttons and text labels. That picture that you just
    dragged in needs to have a place to live, and a UIImageView is just the thing
    for this job. It's going to reside underneath all your buttons and embrace
    whatever picture you tell it to embrace.

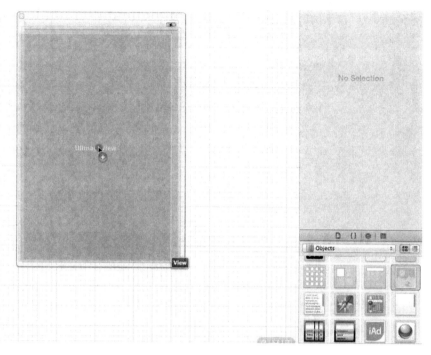

Figure 3-7. Drag a UIImageView onto your View Design area

8. Remember the image you dropped into the Resources folder back in
    Figure 3-3? That's the image you will want the UIImageView to be, so drag it
    onto your View Design area to encapsulate it. Make sure you've selected the
    Attributes Inspector in the Inspector Bar. With the Attributes Inspector open,
    click the Image drop-down menu, and guess what you'll see. You'll see the
    name of the file you dragged into the Resources folder. Select it, and *voila!*
    The image appears in your View Design area. Isn't that cool?

Figure 3-8. Associate your selected image with your UIImageView

9. Drag a label from your Library onto your View Design area and place it at the bottom, as shown in Figure 3-9. Make sure it's nicely centered as indicated by the blue line. Just to remind you: when you click a button you've yet to drag onto the View Design area, your code will invoke an action that will change the text in this label field object (depending on whether the code thinks the user elevated himself to the rank of geek or not).

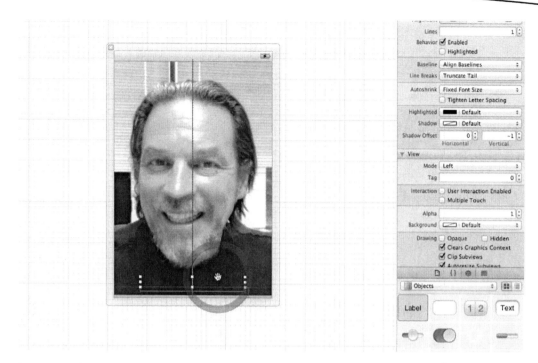

Figure 3-9. Drag a label onto your View Design area

10.   After releasing your label, with it still selected, in the Attributes Inspector and as illustrated in the three images in Figure 3-10, you'll do three things:

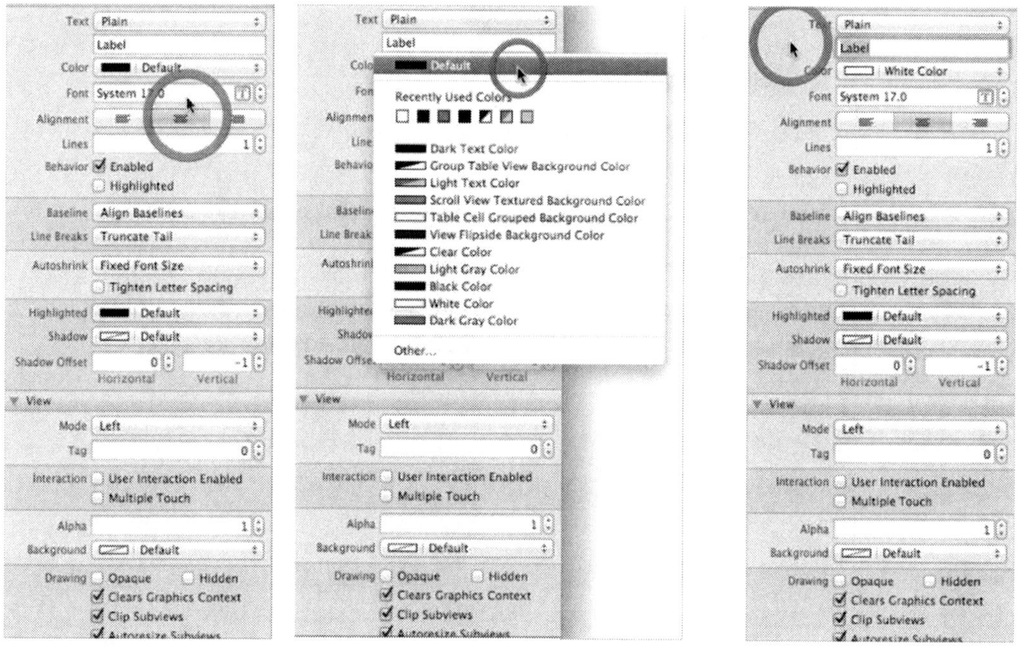

Figure 3-10. Center, change color, and delete the label text

    a.   Center the text (left image).

    b.   If the text is over a dark area, change the text color to white (center image).

    c.   As weird as this sounds, delete the text inside it because you'll be generating your own, changing text, through code with an `if-else` statement (right image).

11.   Drag in a button and place it, centered horizontally, toward the upper portion of your View Design area, as shown in Figure 3-11.

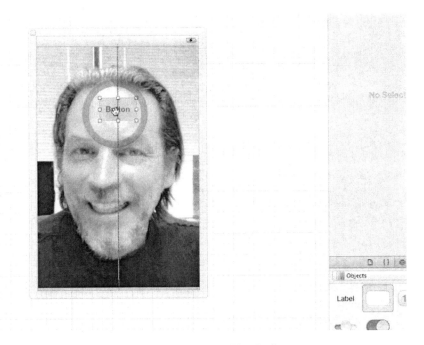

Figure 3-11. Drag in a button and center it toward the upper portion of your View Design area

12.   You need to ask the user: "Are you a Geek?" Double-click the button and enter the text, as shown in Figure 3-12. Don't worry about resizing the button to accommodate the text—Xcode automatically figured that out for you.

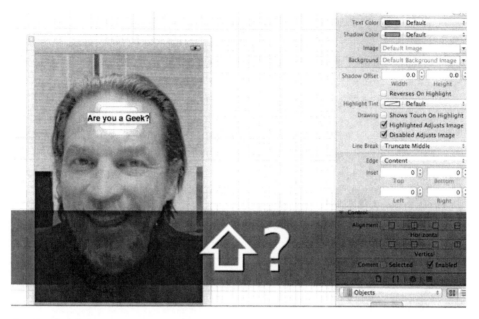

Figure 3-12. Double-click the button and enter your text

Connecting to the Code

You're done with dragging objects from the Library to the View Design area. It's time to connect these objects to your file's owner, so you can associate it with code.

13. You need to make more space and adopt the habits of seasoned coders.
Close the Utilities Inspector (arrow 1 in Figure 3-13) and select the Assistant
Editor (arrow 2), which looks like the chest of a person wearing a tuxedo.
See how the layout changes. Just for fun, you may want to temporarily click
the button immediately to the left of the Assistant Editor, called the Standard
Editor, and you'll see that now you have one screen. Make sure the Assistant
Editor selected before moving on.

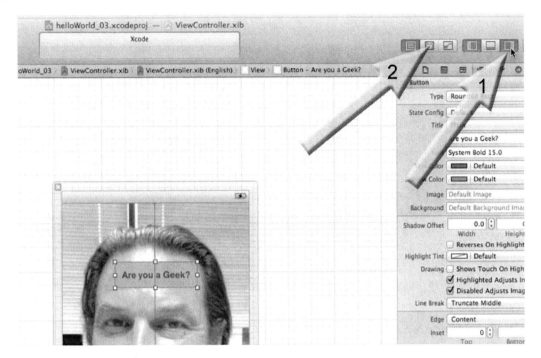

Figure 3-13. Hide the Utilities Inspector and open the Assistant Editor

Note   You can also use keyboard shortcuts to open the Assistant Editor (Option+⌘+Return) and the Standard Editor (⌘+Return). There are thousands of keyboard shortcuts; some achieve superstardom, and some never make it out of books and blogs.

14.   As you can see, you're back at a familiar screen that shows Interface Builder with your header file centered in the middle. Here you want to associate outlets and actions with the buttons and labels you dragged to the View Design area. The last two times you did this, you were told to drag from this to that. Now you're going to use a bit more of the correct nomenclature so you can sound geekier. Click once inside the button and then Control-drag from the button to your header file, placing it under the @interface directive. If you were to Control-drag to an invalid destination, Xcode wouldn't display the insertion indicator, shown in Figure 3-14. Note that as you drag over to this area, Xcode already knows that this could be one of three options, not two, as shown in the insertion indicator for label and text box outlets.

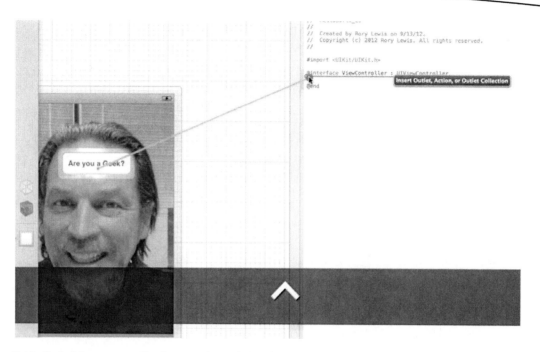

Figure 3-14. Control-Drag a connection from your button in Interface Builder directly into your header file

15. Change the Connection type in the top drop-down menu in the dialog box from Outlet to Action, as shown in Figure 3-15.

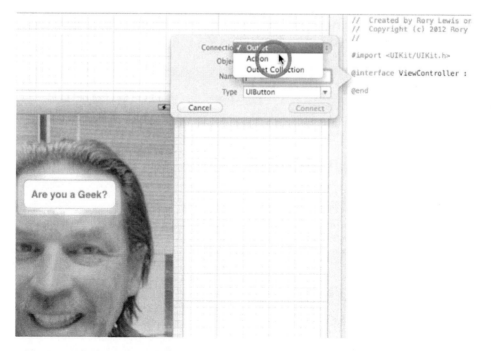

Figure 3-15. When the button's connection dialog appears, specify what type of connection you plan to use in your code

16. Click once inside the Name field and call your button button, as shown in Figure 3-16.

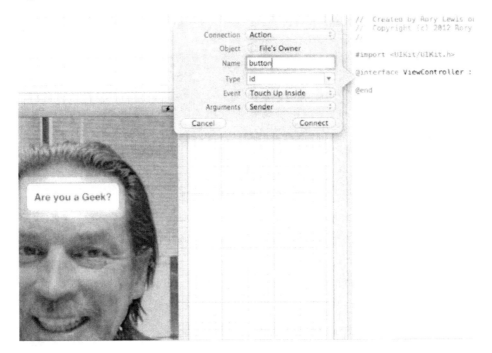

Figure 3-16. *Name your button button*

17. Control-drag from the label to your header file, placing it under the Button's IBAction line of code, as shown in Figure 3-17.

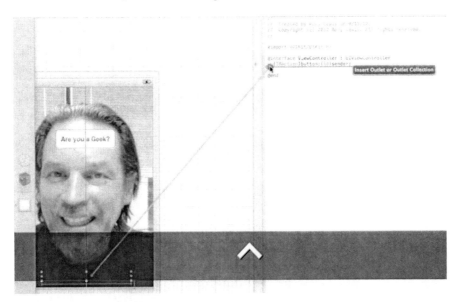

Figure 3-17. *Control-drag from the label into your header file*

18. You want to keep the label as an outlet, so leave the Connection type alone. You do want to give it a name, though. Name it label for now (see Figure 3-18).

Figure 3-18. When the label's connection dialog appears, specify what type of connection to use in your code and name it label

19. Figure 3-19 shows the header file coded without your typing a single letter. Before moving on, make sure your code looks like that shown in Figure 3-9 and as follows:

Figure 3-19. Header code is written without typing

```
-(IBAction)button: (id)sender; //This creates an action for a button (see details below)

IBOutlet UILabel *label; //This adds an outlet to a label, just as you did in
previous examples.
```

Digging the Code: -(IBAction)button: (id)sender;

After changing the button from outlet to action, as shown in Figure 3-15, you still need to name it. In Figure 3-16, it's named `button`. Let's talk about this code briefly. Don't worry if you space out.

When you made the button an action, you created something that is *critical* to know: you created a *method*, and you could have named it monkey if you wanted to. If you did, it would look like this:

```
- (IBAction)monkey:(id)sender;
```

I only want you to know two things about this method you called monkey. First, it has a *return type.* Second, it has an *argument*.

> monkey's return type: Your monkey method returns stuff, which is explained by saying: "Method monkey's return type is an `IBAction`." Read the bold code louder:

```
- (IBAction)monkey:(id)sender;
```

> monkey's argument: Your monkey's argument is of type `(id)`, which in your case, points through the `sender` to the button you dragged into the header file in Figure 3-14. Read the bold code louder:

```
- (IBAction)monkey:(id)sender;
```

Now, take a nice deep breath. You're done peeking under the hood for a while. You're also done with the header file, and now you can move on to the implementation file.

Setting up the Coding Environment

Before typing code, you need to do a little more housework. You need to set up your working environment.

20. Get your screen in a condition conducive for writing code by closing the Assistant Editor you opened (see arrow in 2 Figure 3-13) and then opening the Standard Editor, as shown in Figure 3-20.

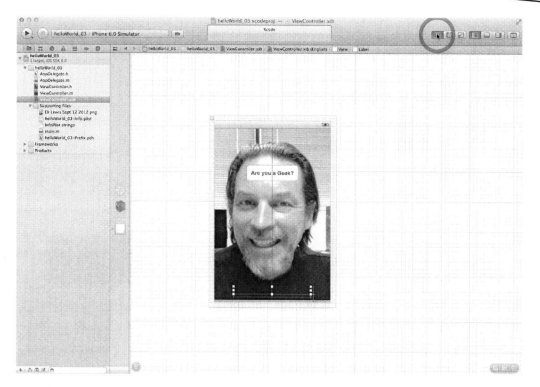

Figure 3-20. Close the Assistant Editor and open the Standard Editor

21. I hope you're already in the habit of saving things. Go over to your nib, header, and implementation files that are now colored dark grey, as shown in Figure 3-21. (Note that my ViewController.h is not greyed because I am in the process of saving it.) Click each one and save them by pressing ⌘+S. Or use ⌘+Option+S to save all. Please don't use your mouse to save, as I will magically appear, take your book away, and declare that you have failed in your endeavor to become a geek.

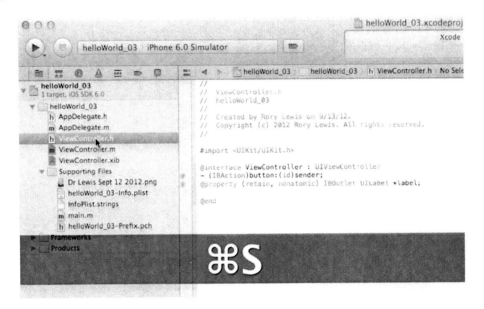

Figure 3-21. Save everything

22. You have one more thing to do before you can code. Open
     ViewController.h, as shown in Figure 3-22.

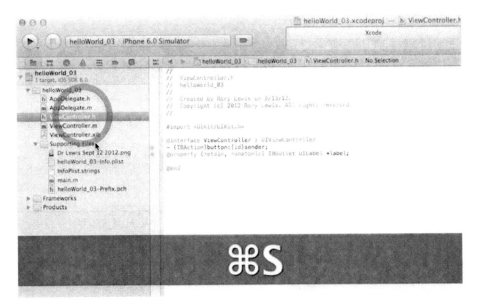

Figure 3-22. After saving, open your ViewController's header file

Creating a Programming Roadmap

You're now ready to get into some code that does something useful.

23.   Your app is going have a user tap the button asking whether they are a geek or not, and the label text will alternate between two messages. Regardless of what the content of these messages is, it needs to switch between one message and the other. In other words, you need to make one situation *false* and the other *positive*. That means you have to create something called a *variable* that can switch between states of *positiveness* and *falseness*, also known as Boolean. Let's name your variable ruaGeek. To program it, you have to first declare it in your header file as being *of type* Boolean. Make a space under the #import line and type bool ruaGeek, as shown in Figure 3-23 and the following code. Now, when you go to the implementation file and program what you want it to do, you can have it be in a false or positive state.

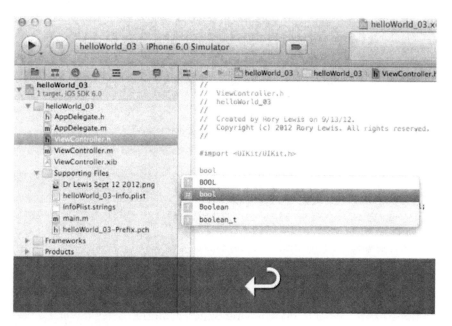

Figure 3-23. Create a Boolean variable

```
- #import <UIKit/UIKit.h>

bool ruaGeek;

@interface ViewController : UIViewController
- (IBAction)button:(id)sender;
@property (retain, nonatomic) IBOutlet UILabel *label;

@end
```

24. You need to tell the button's action what to do. You know you'll use a variable called ruaGeek to be in a state of positiveness or falseness, and you also know that the code you'll write will be for (IBAction), so let's do it. Open the implementation file and do what we love to do: code!

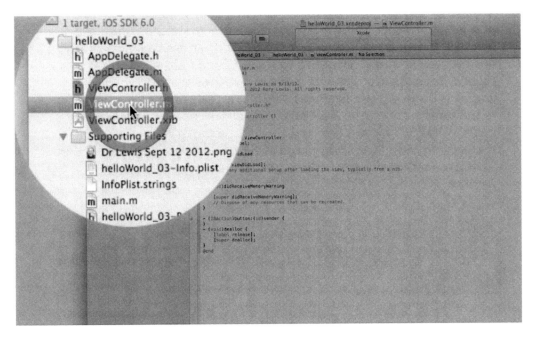

Figure 3-24. Open the implementation file

25. Scroll down to the button method you created when you dragged in and created the button in Figures 3-14 through to 3-16. For now, ignore the @directives at the top of the page and the ViewDidLoad and didReceiveMemoryWarning methods the clever people at Apple instantiated for you. Focus on the button method. Remember my saying that you could have named this method monkey—the one that tells the code what to do when the button is tapped? Inside the squiggly brackets, you're going to tell the iPhone exactly what to do when the button is tapped. If it's the *first* time the button is tapped, it will say one thing, and if it's the next time the button is tapped, it will say another thing. Then repeat. To decide whether it's the first time, you'll use an if-else statement, which is something used every day in coding. So let's drag a snippet of if-else code from the library.

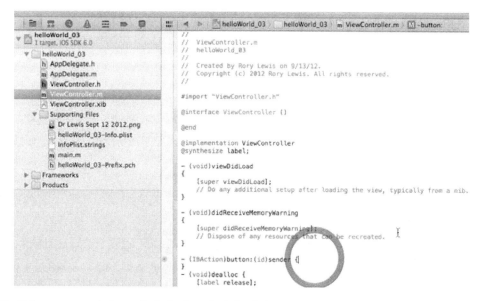

Figure 3-25. *Make some space between the button's squiggly brackets*

26. To find the `if-else` snippet of code you need, you'll have to open a section of the Library that you've not gone to before. As shown in Figure 3-26, open the Code Snippet Library by clicking its icon.

Figure 3-26. *Open the Code Snippet Library*

27. Scroll down until you reach the If-Else Statement snippet, shown in Figure 3-27.

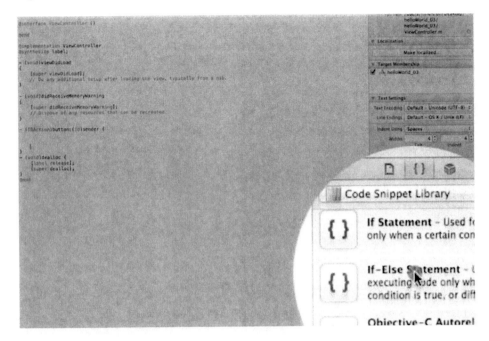

Figure 3-27. Select the If-Else Statement snippet

28. Drag the snippet of code onto the canvas and drop it between the two squiggly brackets of the button method, as shown in Figure 3-28.

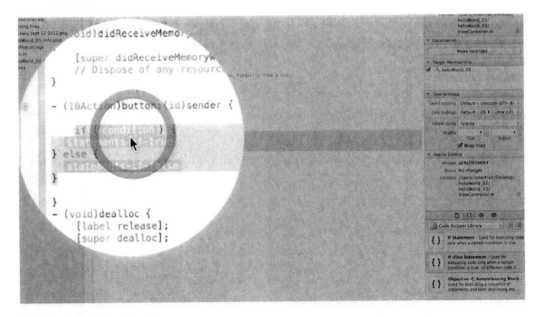

Figure 3-28. Drag the snippet into place

29.   Look at the `if-else` statement. What it's saying is that *if* something is true, do "this"—*else* do "that." Here's how to go from English to pseudo code:

Top level:

if (**First Condition**){Do **this**} else {Do **that**)

Next level down, a little deeper now:

if (<#**condition**#>) { <#statements-if-**true**#> }
else {
<#statements-if-**false**#>
}

You want to replace the <#condition#> with the Boolean variable you declared in the header file ruaGeek. You want to first set the state of ruaGeek to be `true` and then have your app say one thing. Then set the state of ruaGeek to `false` and have it say another thing. Easy! Let's set the variable to `true` and test for this condition; type ruaGeek==true, as shown in the following code and in Figure 3-29 and completed in Figure 3-30.

Figure 3-29. *Make some space between the button's squiggly brackets*

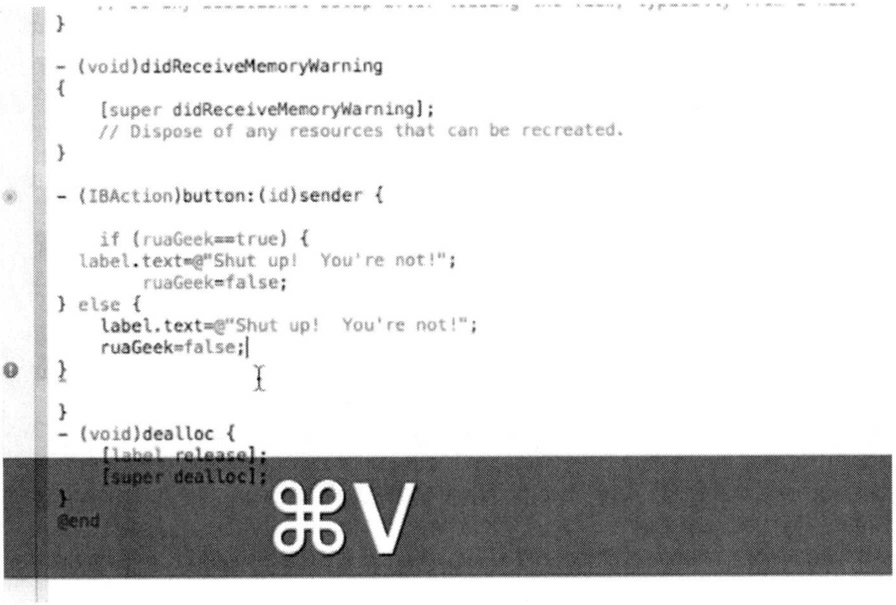

```
    }
    - (void)didReceiveMemoryWarning
    {
        [super didReceiveMemoryWarning];
        // Dispose of any resources that can be recreated.
    }
    - (IBAction)button:(id)sender {

        if (ruaGeek==true) {
    label.text=@"Shut up!  You're not!";
            ruaGeek=false;
    } else {
        label.text=@"Shut up!  You're not!";
        ruaGeek=false;|
    }

    }
    - (void)dealloc {
        [label release];
        [super dealloc];
    }
    @end
```

⌘V

Figure 3-30. Make some space between the button's squiggly brackets

Pseudo code: setting ruaGeek to be true for the initial condition:

```
if (ruaGeek==true) { <#statements-if-true#> }
else {
<#statements-if-false#>
}
}
```

30. The first message is "Shut up! You're not!" (For those not in a university
     or high school setting, this is not an insult—it's a joyous affirmation. For
     example, a student says to her friend, "I got an A for the exam." Her friend
     affirms the joy of receiving the A and says, "Shut up! You did not get an A!")
     So your first statement, when ruaGeek is true, has to say "Shut up! You're
     not!" to the user. Then you need to change the value to false so you can
     invoke statements-if-false later. Type the following code:

```
if (ruaGeek==true) {
    label.text=@"Shut up! You're not!";
    ruaGeek=false;
} else {
        <#statements-if-false#>
}
```

Now, rather than typing everything again for the else part, copy what you just coded and paste it
into the second condition, as shown in Figure 3-30.

31. Change label.text=@"Shut up! You're not!"; to label.text=@"You are";.
     Then you need to change the value from ruaGeek=false to ruaGeek=true so
     you can invoke the next statement, as shown in Figure 3-31.

```
    [super viewDidLoad];
    // Do any additional setup after loading the view, typically from a nib.
}

- (void)didReceiveMemoryWarning
{
    [super didReceiveMemoryWarning];
    // Dispose of any resources that can be recreated.
}

- (IBAction)button:(id)sender {

    if (ruaGeek==true) {
    label.text=@"Shut up!  You're not!";
        ruaGeek=false;
} else {
    label.text=@"You are";
    ruaGeek=true;
}
                ▦    TRUE
}               ▦    true
- (void)dealloc {
    [label release];
    [super dealloc];
}
@end
```

Figure 3-31. Set the initial condition to true

32.   Now run it, as shown in Figure 3-32. Uh-oh, there are two things you need to correct!

Figure 3-32. Let's run it!

In the real world, clients always want you to change everything around, so get used to this. Making changes also helps you learn what you just did. When I ran it, I saw two errors, seen in my video. Yours may not have had one of them, but let's go back and tweak the code a little.

33. Looking at the image on my screen (not your screen, you probably placed the image perfectly), there is a grey gap between the bottom of my image and the iPhone body. Let's fix that. Also, let's say your client first wants to see "Shut up! You're not" when the user clicks on the phone button! No problem. Just adjust the UIImageView down until it fits perfectly. Then leave the xib file and open your implementation again; it seems to be running the statements in the else section (that is, the value of ruaGeek is false) to begin, so you can either change all the values of ruaGeek to their opposite or simply swap out what you say. Figure 3-33 and the following code do the latter:

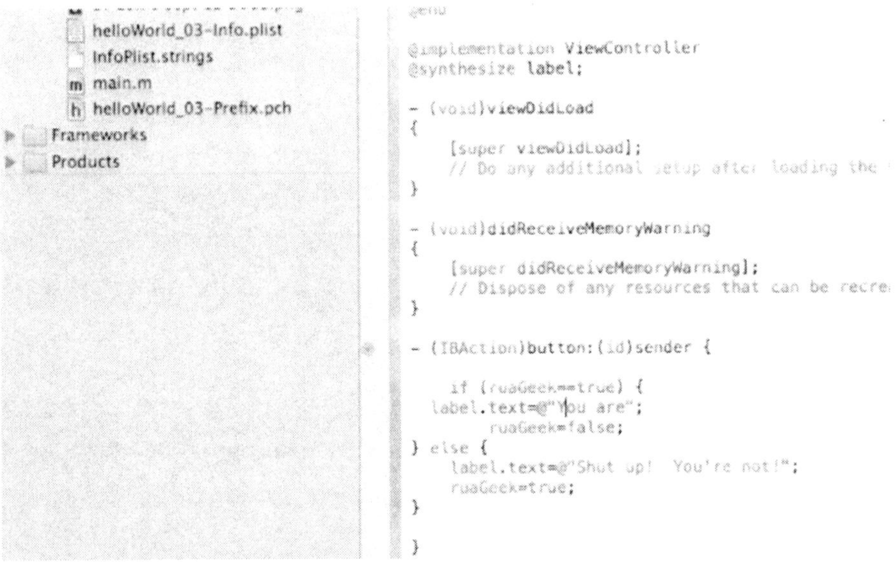

Figure 3-33. Swap out the if statements

```
if (ruaGeek==true) {
 label.text=@"You are";
    ruaGeek=false;
} else {
  label.text=@"Shut up! You're not!";
  ruaGeek=true;
}
```

34. Run it and click, as shown in Figure 3-34! Yeah!

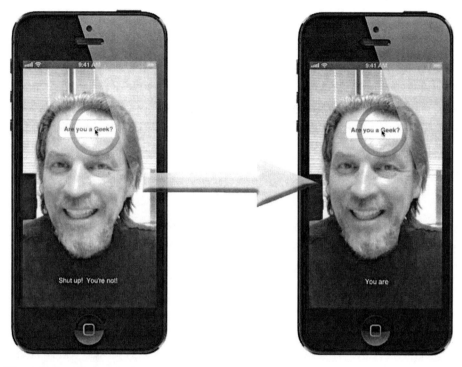

Figure 3-34. Wow, talk about Geek power!

Digging the Code

In the following reviews, I go over some of the code from this chapter, referencing familiar code and explaining the processes in more detail. I introduce you to more technical terms that you'll use in future chapters and in communicating with other programmers.

Consider this analogy: In helloWorld_01 and helloWorld_02 I taught you how to get into a car, turn the ignition, press the accelerator, and steer as you moved forward. In helloWorld_03, I guided you with similar directions, but as you drove toward your destination, I explained how the car is a hybrid engine and that it has some gasoline components and some electrical components. We talked about methods, outlets, and actions.

Now you've arrived at your destination; you've completed helloWorld_03. I'm about to open the hood and show you how, when you pressed the accelerator, it either pumped gasoline into the engine or used the electric motor. Under the hood, I'll show you where these components are located. And by the time you finish this book, looking under the hood and digging the code, I will have described the amount of gasoline being squirted onto the pistons by the carburetors, the exact torque and heat emission of the electric motor, and so on. And guess what—you'll be able to handle it!

One last comment about this section that is *really important*: "Digging the Code" is a section that I encourage you to read *without* definitive understanding. It's okay if you only partially "get it." Of course, if you happen to attain full comprehension of the subject in all its details, well, that's great. What I suggest, though, is that you read these sections at the end of each chapter loosely because:

- I have received hundreds of emails from readers from the first and second editions of this book saying that knowing it was okay to blank out and not feel pressured to understand the code really worked out for them.

- My students love it when, at the end of each class, I make them turn off their Macs, put down their pens, Zen and zone out, and just casually listen to me. I've had students knocking on my office telling me in many colorful ways how the Zenning and zoning really worked for them.

Note that my research is in neurological acute brain injuries, where I study the brain and neural interconnectivity. This methodology of first connecting neurons and then infusing the deeper connective associations when the brain is relaxed is one that I've developed over the years. So, I want you to consider my former readers' and students' opinions about this matter and absorb my theorem concerning neurological leaps.

> **Note**   Becoming an eloquent, knowledgeable, and financially thriving coder takes neurological leaps, during states wherein your brain is open to absorbing new data without the hypothalamus releasing anxiety hormones that pollute the ability of your neurons to create new connections, which allows linking logic and code to ontological reasoning.

So Zen out, zone out, and read in a meditative state with no fear. When that voice says, "You're not understanding it all," say, "That's okay, Dr. Lewis said so, now go away!" You will Zen and zone through the following:

- Nibs, zibs, and xibs: Instances and Instantiation
- Methods: Instance methods and class methods
- Header files
- The Inspector Bar
- Memory management

Nibs, Zibs, and Xibs

Back in Figure 3-5, I instructed you to open your nib file. You could see that it was written *xib*, and to make it more confusing, some coders call them "zib" files. Just ignore them. Refer to xib files by pronouncing them as "nib." At the recent 360iDev for iPhone Developers Conference in Denver, it was clear most of the presenters referred to xib files as "nibs," not "zibs." But no matter how you refer to them, it's important that you understand what's going on with these files. What are they? Do we need them? Do you need to know how they work?

Do you recall, from step 5, Figure 3-5, how you opened Interface Builder View when you clicked on that nib file? It was here that you saw, for the second or third time, your view and began dragging and dropping items onto your View Design area. What's going on here?

It turns out that when you examine nib files at the level of Objective-C, you see that they contain all the information necessary to activate the user interface (UI) files, transforming your code into a graphical iPhone or iPad work of art. It's also possible to join separate nib files together to create more complex interactions, as you'll see later in this book. But to follow along, you need to add two words to your vocabulary: *Instances* and *Instantiation*.

- *Instances*: All the information that resides in these files is put there so that it can *create an instance of* the buttons, the labels, the pictures, and so forth that you've entered. This collection of commands is plonked down and saved into your nib files to become the UI. The code and the commands taken together become real, and they're sensed by the user—seen or heard, or even felt.

- *Instantiation*: Remember in step 25 and Figure 3-25, I explained that you can see that you have the method - (IBAction)button:(id)sender{...}? Well, the term *instantiate* can be usefully explained if you consider what happens when you first save a new project. The computer *instantiates*—makes real and shows you the evidence for—a project entity created by assigning it a body of subfiles. In helloWorld_03, you saw how in Figure 3-21 I asked you to go over to your nib, header, and implementation files that were colored dark grey and save them? Well, excuse me, how did these files get here? Did you program them or make them? Nope, Xcode instantiated them when you created your project. Xcode gave your project "arms and legs": two AppDelegate files and two ViewController files. The same happens when your app instantiates buttons and other objects as part of its operation; the app does it for you.

> **Note**   You'll be manipulating these arms and legs to do cool stuff in apps and selling them on the iTunes store.

You've *created an instance* of something when you've told the computer how and when to grab some memory and set it aside for some particular process or collection of processes such that, when the parameters are all met, the user has an experience of this data (that is, whatever was assigned in memory). Sometimes we refer to these collections or files of descriptions and commands as *classes*, *methods*, or *objects*. In this code-digging session, these terms might seem to run together and appear as synonyms, but they're not. As you read on, you'll come to understand each term as a distinct coding tool or apparatus, to be employed in a particular situation, relating to other entities in a grammatically correct way.

When I say that you *created an instance* of the buttons and labels in your nib file, what I'm really saying is that, when you run your code, a specific portion of your computer's memory, known by its address, will take care of things in order to generate the user experience you've designed. Each time your application is launched on an iPhone or iPad, the interface is recreated by the orchestrated commands residing in your nib files. Consider the nib file associated with the action depicted in Figures 3-14 through 3-16. You dragged a button from the Library into the View window, thus *creating an instance* of this button. If somebody were to ask you what that means, you might look them in the eye, with a piercing and enigmatic look, and say: "By creating an instance of this button, I have instructed the computer to set aside memory in the appropriate xib file, which, upon the launching of my app, will appear and interact with the user, precisely as I have intended."

Wow!

Methods

The next concept I would like to explore a little more deeply is that of *methods*. As with nibs, I'm only going to give you a high-level look this time. You've already used methods pretty extensively, so I'm simply going to tell you what you did.

Looking at Figure 3-15, after you dragged the button into your header file, you changed it from an outlet to an action and clicked the Connect button. Then you saw some code appear:

```
- (IBAction)button:(id)sender
```

I suggested that to make things clearer, you could have named the method monkey, making it become the following:

```
- (IBAction)monkey:(id)sender;
```

Here, you're instructing the computer to associate an action with a button:

- The first symbol in this piece of code is a minus sign (-). It means that monkey is something we call an *instance method.*

- On the other hand, if you had entered a plus sign (+) there instead, as in + (IBAction), it would be called a *class method.*

What these two statements have in common, though, is the method monkey. Furthermore, just by the name of IBAction alone, you can see that this is an action that will be performed in Interface Builder. Yup, that's what that IB in front of Action means. See how Steve Jobs was really saying to himself, when he designed Objective-C on his NeXT computers, that he wanted Actions—and called them IBActions to remind himself and others who used his code that when we typed IBAction it was for Actions used in Interface Builder.

Consider this analogy: a programmer says, "Here comes an app that will help you draw a nice, pretty house." That's a header type of announcement. Then the programmer enters specific instructions for how the house will be constructed, how it will sit on/against the landscape, what kind of weather is in the background, and so on. "Draw a slightly curving horizon line one third from the bottom of the display, and midway on this, place a rectangle that's 4 × 7, on top of which is a trapezoid with a base length of…" and so on. These specific, how-to instructions belong in the implementation file, for they describe the actual actions—the *method*—of drawing the house. So, for example, if you wanted to connect a button to a method named hello, you'd add this code to the following:

```
- (IBAction)hello:(id)sender;
```

This creates a place in memory to execute the code inside your hello method.

Header Files

Look at the following code, not in terms of methods but in terms of it being a header file and how it relates to its implementation file. Go back to after you created the variable ruaGeek of type Boolean in your header file, as shown in Figure 3-19. Look at the following and calmly absorb the two lines under your ruaGeek of type Boolean—look and absorb as much as you can:

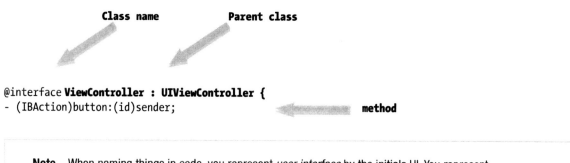

```
@interface ViewController : UIViewController {
- (IBAction)button:(id)sender;                                    method
```

> **Note** When naming things in code, you represent *user interface* by the initials UI. You represent *Interface Builder* by the initials IB.

There are two things to note here: first, the @ symbol talks to the innermost part of Xcode, which transforms your code into actions, and second, that the @ symbol has something essential and important to announce. In fact, we call any statement beginning with @ a *directive*. This @interface directive tells Xcode that you have interface stuff concerning helloWorld_03, and that the particulars will be enclosed within brackets {}. Now take a look at Figure 3-35. The ViewController and the UIViewController interact with the buttons and labels we created. Just gleem over this for now; it'll all make perfect sense by the time you complete this book.

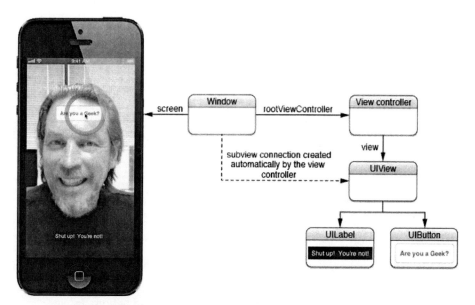

Figure 3-35. UILabel and UIButton in relation to the UIViewController and the ViewController

The Inspector Bar

You've been playing around with the Inspector Bar, so here's some insight into how the Inspector Bar is set up. Figure 3-36 shows how I illustrate the Inspector Bar on the marker board in class.

As you become familiar with the Xcode environment, you'll find yourself using the Inspector Bar to choose a workspace you will need at any phase of your coding. For now, let's zoom in on the most intense view: the Utilities View. Clicking Utilities View, as shown in the top right of Figure 3-36, you'll see how I've created a zoomed up version of the Inspector Bar, with its submenus located to the left of the panel. Starting at the top, the Inspector Bar contains the following:

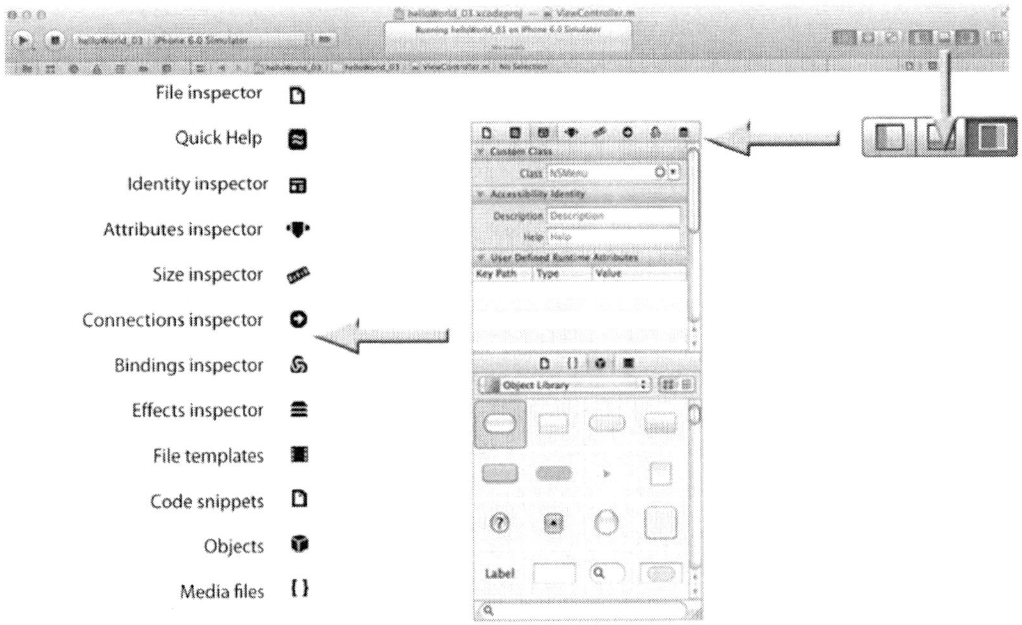

Figure 3-36. Focusing on the Inspector Bar

- *File inspector*: This is where you manage file attributes such as name, type, and path within your project.

- *Quick Help*: Just what it says.

- *Identity inspector*: Gives access to deep stuff such as class names, access, and labels.

- *Attributes inspector*: For adjusting attributes available to an object.

- *Size inspector*: Allows you to tinker with an interface object's initial size, position, and autosizing.

- *Connections inspector*: Allows you to view the outlets and actions for your interface objects.

- *Bindings inspector*: For configuring bindings for view objects.

- *Effects inspector*: To adjust animation protocol such as transitions, fades, and other visual characteristics of selected objects.

- *File templates*: Common templates that you can drag from the library to the project navigator.

- *Code snippets*: Like clip art but for coders—snippets of source code that you can use by dragging into your files.

- *Objects*: You use these interface objects by directly dragging onto your nib file in the Interface Builder editor window.

- *Media files*: Just as it says, they are graphics, icons, and sound files that can be dragged directly to your nib file in the Interface Builder editor window.

You're still here! Awesome! Take a break for at least six hours and don't sweat over not "getting" all the code you've been digging around in here. Hope you Zenned and zoned out beautifully. See you in Chapter 4.

Buttons and Labels with Multiple Graphics

In this chapter, you'll tackle your fourth program, and it's time to quicken the pace a bit. As in Chapter 3, you'll be able to simply view the screen shots and implement the code if you remember most of the details—steps that have been described repeatedly in the previous examples. You'll get fewer figures pertaining to each step, yet more procedures; I'll be using the short bursts of information introduced in Chapter 3.

In addition, as in Chapter 3, once you've completed the program, you'll get a code review in the "Digging the Code" section. Initially, I'll cover some of the same aspects and concepts discussed in that section in Chapter 3 and then I'll zoom in on some of the new code. Not only will I go a little deeper, but I'll consider other computing concepts that link up to this deeper level of analysis.

You will probably also notice a change of style in this chapter. I'll be moving away from the "elementary" language used in previous chapters. I'll also be doing less hand-holding for you with the images. I'll start weaning you off arrows—all the information is there, so if you can't immediately find what I'm referencing in the text, you'll need to think a little and look to find it. Think of it as an exercise to force your neurons to make some associations by taking baby steps. We're picking up the pace—a little faster, a little more advanced, and using more of the technical nomenclature.

Most importantly, at step 30 I open the hood, and you'll really get our hands dirty, delving into some critical code concepts that you'll need to wrap your head around in order to move on through the book. Don't worry; I make it easy.

Again, if you don't grasp every concept and technique fully, that's perfectly okay. Relax and enjoy this next example. But before we start our fourth app, let's take a brief glance at our roadmap.

Roadmap Recap

Thus far, we've gone through three Hello World examples. You've had an opportunity to familiarize yourself with the creative process in the context of programming apps: go in with an idea and come out with a tangible, working product. Several times I've asked you to ignore heavy-duty code that I judged would be distracting or daunting. You may have also noticed that when you did try to understand some of this thicker code, it made sense in a weird, wonderful, chaotic way. Well, as we progress, we're going to make the chaos of the unknown less unsettling.

Before dealing with this issue, let me also put you at ease by telling you that when it comes to Objective-C, I have yet to meet a single advanced programmer who knows every symbol and command. Just as in other industries, people tend to get very knowledgeable in their specific domains and specializations (for example, integrating Google Maps to a game or an app).

Car mechanics used to be able to strip an engine down completely and then build it back up—presumably better than it was. Nowadays, car mechanics are very specialized, with only a handful knowing how to completely strip down and rebuild any given new car. You get an expert in Ford hybrid engines, Toyota Prius electrical circuitry, the drum brakes that stop big rigs, and so on. There's nothing wrong with this.

It's similar to how you're proceeding. You've just gotten your hands greasy and dirty by *successfully* programming three apps. Now, if all goes according to plan, you're going to delve even deeper when you get to step 30. Soon you'll be brimming with confidence. I know from experience that the confidence of my students can be derailed if they're intimidated—they can be blown away by too much complexity or technicality. I've found that students can handle bumps in the road if they know where they're going, and if they know that the rough stretches won't get too scary or dangerous.

helloWorld_04: A View-Based Application

Right this second—feel good about yourself! You're already quite deep into the Objective-C forest. If you lose your way, remember that besides the book and its screenshots, I also offer you screencasts, available at my website. http://bit.ly/PFXJGe is the short URL, or go to rorylewis.com, click the iOS6 icon, and click either Video tutorials or Downloads.

1. As usual, let's begin with a clean desktop and only five icons: your Macintosh HD (if you've kept it visible like I do) and four image files shown as icons in Figure 4-1. As I'm sure you've gathered by now, I think having an uncluttered desktop is essential, and I want to encourage you to continually hone your organizational mindset. Using our familiar shortcuts, close all programs. You're welcome to download these images from http://tinyurl.com/9r7lnuw from the Downloads page or from the Videos page at http://tinyurl.com/8rvwzdk. Icons will become key building blocks of this project, but I really want to encourage you to find and prepare images of your own. That way, you'll have more passion about this assignment. If you create your own images, pay attention to the following guidelines.

Figure 4-1. Create or download three .png image files: a bottom layer, a top layer, and a desktop icon. Save them all to a beautiful, clean desktop

2.   The size of the first picture, STAIR.png, as shown in Figure 4-2, will be the iPhone standard of 640 pixels in width by 1096 pixels in height. This will be the bottom layer of two images, so we'll call it the *background* layer. Our background, then, is a photograph of the stairs leading out the back of the Engineering Building here at the University of Colorado at Colorado Springs. We will use this picture as a backdrop for a picture of Immanuel Kant—the greatest philosopher of all time—a man whose philosophy formed the basis of that of many of our founding forefathers who framed the Constitution. More importantly to us, he was the man who began mapping parallels between mathematical logic and words in speech. When the program is run, the background will display and, once a button is clicked, up will pop the photo of Immanuel Kant at the top of the stairs. Take a quick peek at Figure 4-3. How nice—Immanuel Kant has decided to return to university! This is our scenario then: Many times in programming, you'll find that you want your user to see a familiar background, and then when a button is tapped, somebody (or something) unusual or unexpected suddenly appears. This program helloWorld_04 will teach you how to do that.

Figure 4-2. STAIR.png is the background image—or bottom layer

Figure 4-3. This is the modified top-layer image, which will overlay the background

3. To create the second image, which we'll call the *top* layer, copy the
   background layer photo, which, in my case at least, was STAIR.png. Then
   crop this copy to create an image with these exact dimensions:
   640 × 698 pixels. Yes, I know the height is a strange number—but trust me,
   the new Apple overlay code transforms the pixilation schema in a way that
   makes this weird size perfect! Now you have a roughly square copy of the
   bottom two-thirds of your background photo. Next, paste onto this a partial
   image—probably a cut-out of some interesting or unusual object. This will
   yield something like the image in Figure 4-3: Immanuel Kant, in front of the
   background scene. This modified top layer will, of course, be saved as a
   .png file. Thus, you will end up with a prepared top layer that consists of
   the bottom section of the original background photo, with some interesting
   person or object pasted over it. You can probably guess that you're going
   to program the device to start with the background image, and then, with
   some user input, insert the top layer—with bottom edges matching up flush,
   of course. This will give the illusion that your interesting guest, or object,
   suddenly materialized out of nowhere. The top layer will not affect the space
   near the upper part of the background; you're reserving this region for the
   text that you'll also direct the device to insert.

4.   The third image file is an icon of your choice. As in the previous chapter, you may want to customize your icon. In my case, I took a portion of the photograph of Immanuel Kant's face and put it into my icon file, as shown in Figure 4-4. Once you have all three of these images—the bottom layer, top layer, and icon—save them onto your desktop, which will make it look similar to Figure 4-1.

Figure 4-4. This is the image for the screen icon

Note   Remember that icons for the iPhone 5 have a recommended size of 114 × 114 pixels, as illustrated in Figure 4-4. However, note that if your app is to run on previous models of the iPhone, include a 57 × 57 version of this icon and drag it in as specified the steps coming up. Be sure to stay mindful of these dimensions.

5.   Now, just as you did in the first example, launch Xcode and open a new project by using your keyboard shortcut (⌘+⇧+N). Your screen should show the New Project Wizard, as depicted in Figure 4-5. You may find that your Single View Application template was highlighted by default; if not, click the Single View Application icon and then click Next, as indicated in Figure 4-5.

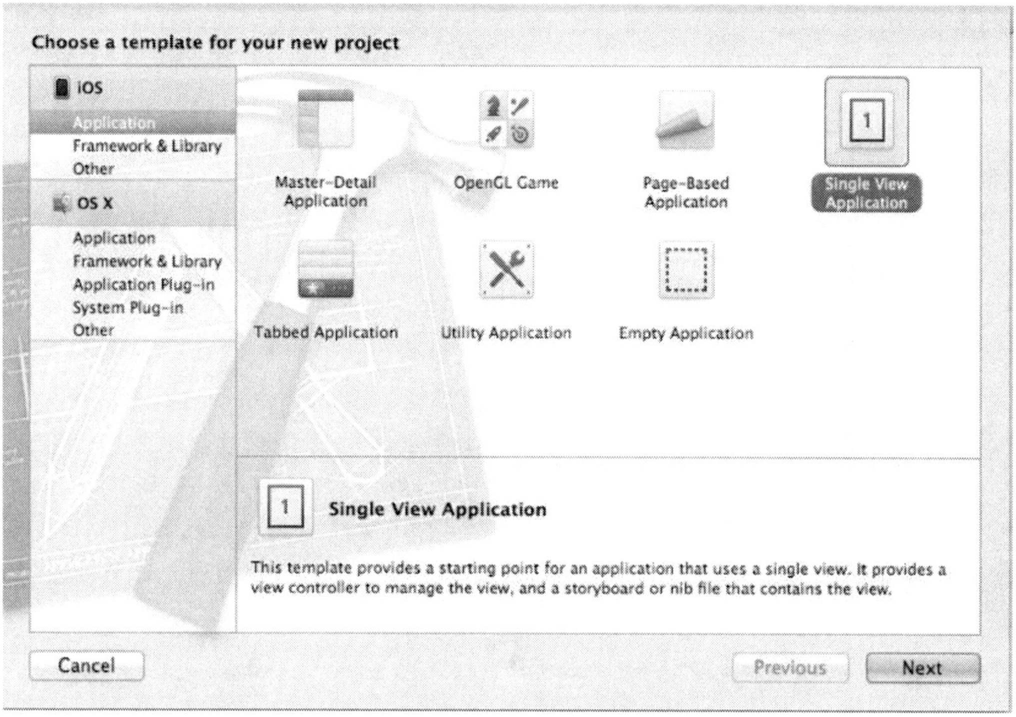

Figure 4-5. *Tap ⌘ + ⇧ + N and select Single View Application from the New Project window*

You may be thinking that a View-Based Application Template is normally used to help you design an application with a single view and that you should pick another option—because you've just made two views, the image of the stairs and the modified image of the stairs with Immanuel Kant in it. This reasoning would appear to be sound except that this is actually not the case here—it really still is a single view. Think of it this way: You'll be dealing with only one perspective, onto which you'll superimpose an image, not a view. If you were going to have portions of your code in one navigation pane and other portions in other navigation panes, then you'd probably choose a Navigation-Based Application. In this current project, though, you're going to manipulate one view in which you'll superimpose images rather than navigate from one pane to another. In essence, you'll be playing tricks with a single view.

6. Because this is the fourth `helloWorld`, name it `helloWord_04`, as shown in Figure 4-6.

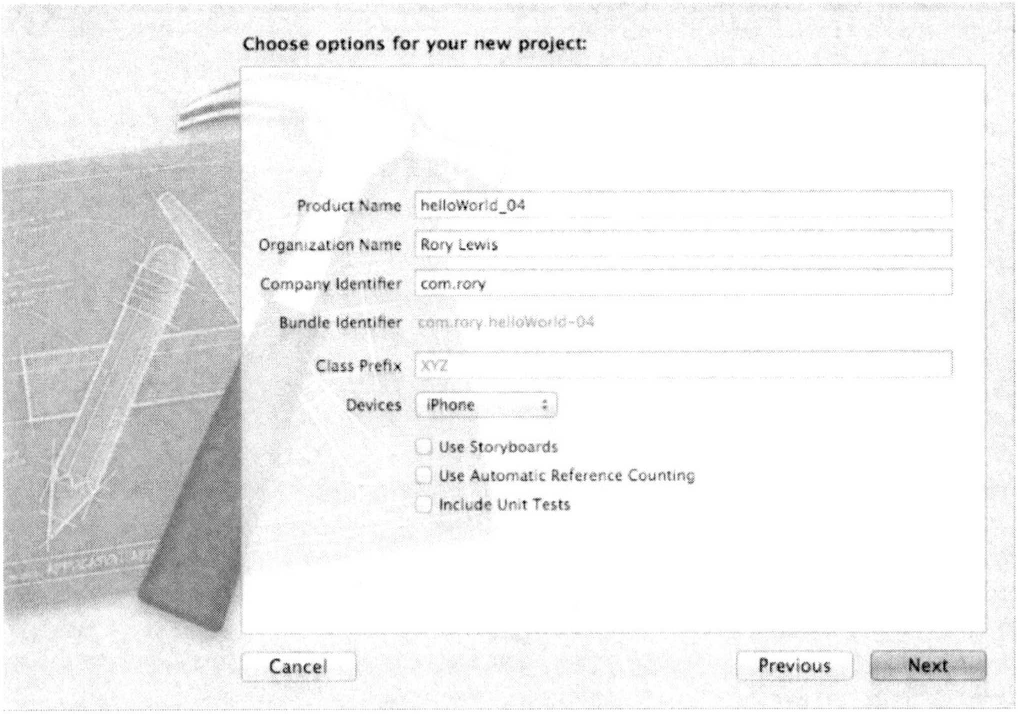

Figure 4-6. *Name your project and define it as an iPhone project*

7. Save your View-Based Application to your desktop as helloWorld_04
    (as shown in Figure 4-7). This will be the last of your Hello World apps.
    Once you've completed this program, save all of them in a Hello World
    folder inside your Code folder. You'll probably find yourself going back to
    these folders at some point to review the code.

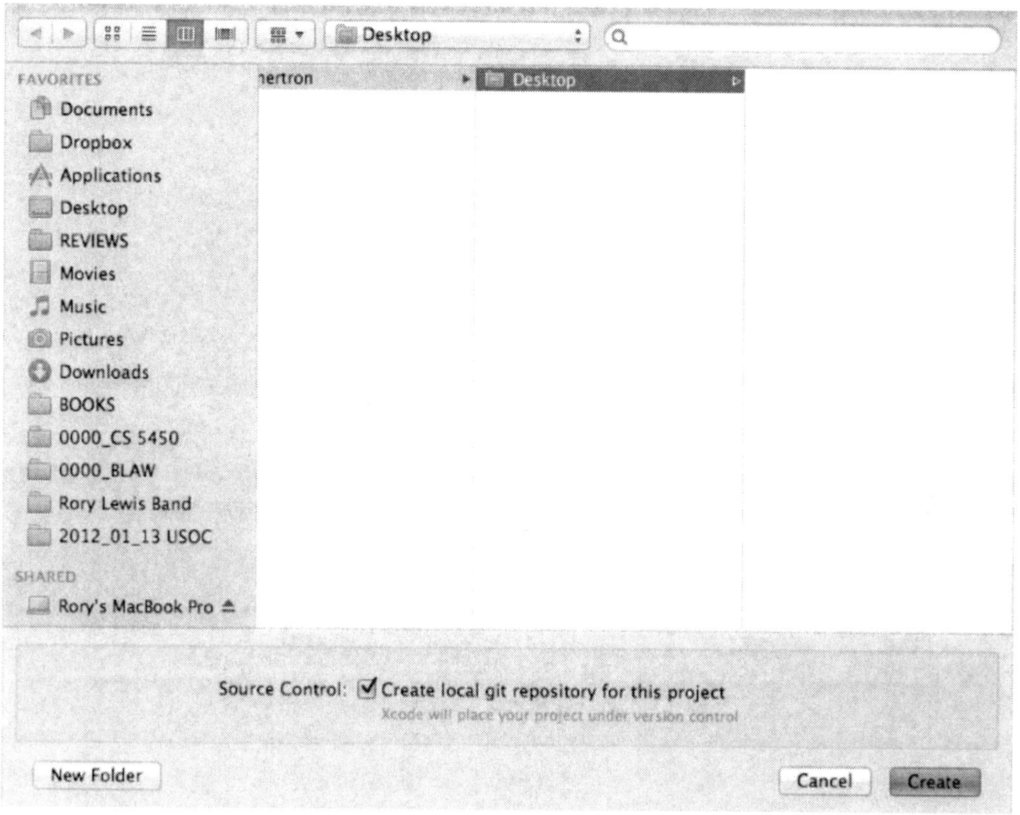

Figure 4-7. Save it to your desktop

Later in the book, when I go into the details of Objective-C and Cocoa, there is a good chance that you'll scratch your head and say, "Damn—that sounds complicated, but I *know* I did this before. I want to go back and see how I connected these files in those Hello World exercises I did at the beginning of this book."

8. First, you'll drag icons into the project. Select your 57 × 57 icon.png file and place it into the slot immediately to the left of the Retina Display icon slot. Then drag your 114 × 114 icon.png and place it into the Retina Display slot. Figure 4-8 shows the 57 × 57 icon.png in its place next to the 114 × 114 icon.png being dropped into position.

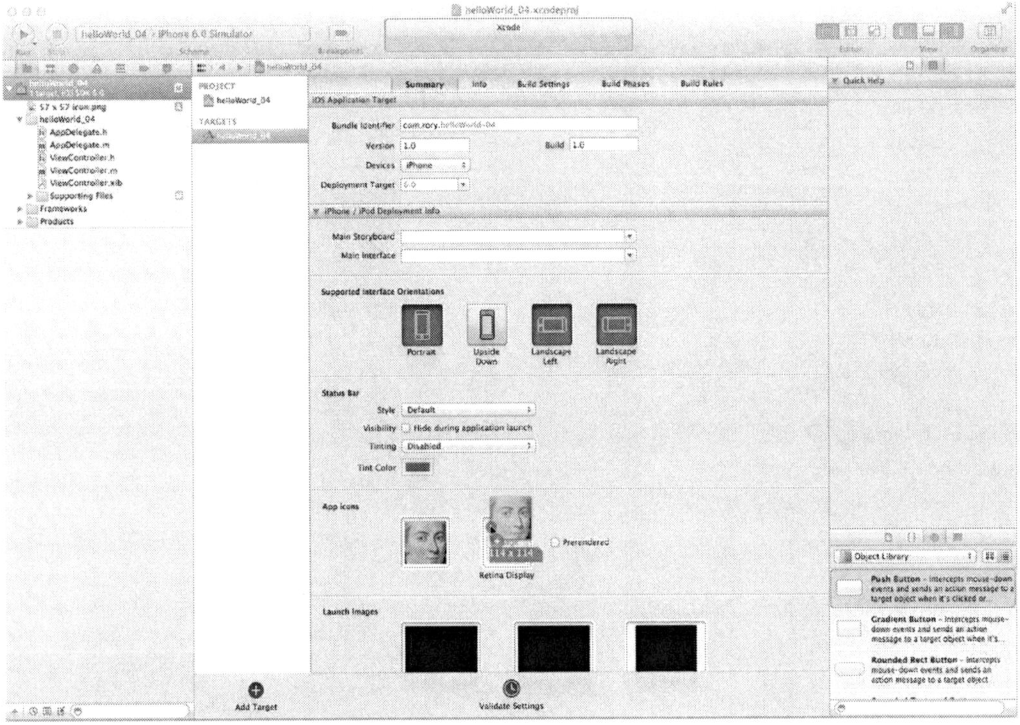

Figure 4-8. Drag your three icons into the project

9. Now drag your two images (KANT.png and STAIR.png) into your Supporting
   Files folder. As you probably know by now, Xcode has instantiated a project
   named helloWorld_04, as shown in Figure 4-9. Note that when the folder
   highlights, it means that the object is selected. Focus on where your mouse
   pointer is—that's the point at which the folder will react. Once it highlights,
   drop the object in by releasing the mouse button. Sometimes students get
   confused because it seems that the images should be able to drop into the
   folder, but it won't highlight. This's because the folder opens, or highlights,
   only when your mouse pointer carrying all the pictures hovers over the folder.
   So, remember that when you're dragging objects over to the folders, focus
   on where your mouse pointer is and ignore everything else.

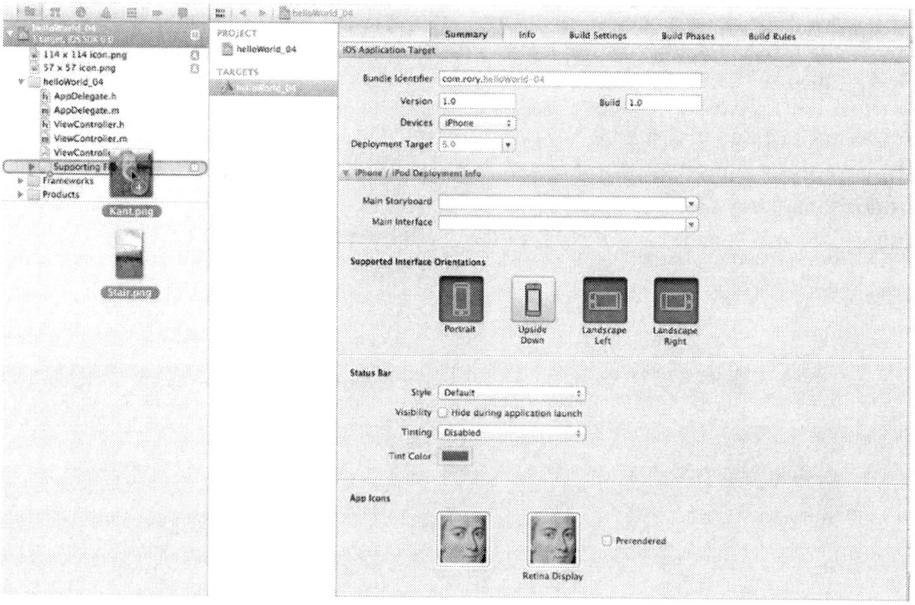

Figure 4-9. Drag your two images into the project

10. After dropping the image into the Resources folder, you're prompted to define whether the image will always be associated with its position on your desktop or whether it will be embedded with the code and carried along with the application file, as shown in Figure 4-10.

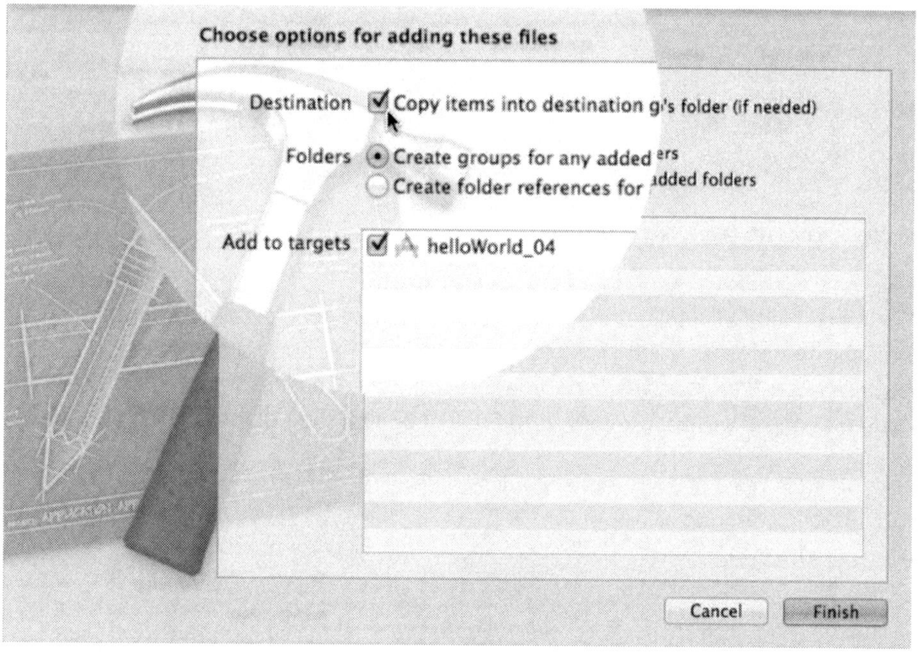

Figure 4-10. Check the "Copy items into the destination group's folder" box

You want it to be embedded, of course, so click the "Copy items. . ." box. Also check the "Create groups for any added folders" box. Then click Finish (or tap Enter).

11. Icons are housed in the blue helloWorld_04, 1 target iOS SDK 6.0 folder at the top of the page. You want to get into the habit of making sure that all your images all always in the Supporting Files folder, so drag them from the blue folder into the Supporting Files folder, as shown in Figure 4-11.

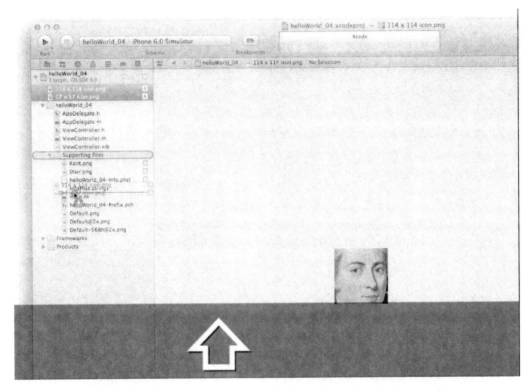

Figure 4-11. Drag icons into the Supporting Files folder

12. Click your nib file, as illustrated in Figure 4-12, because it's time to start building the objects you'll need for your project. You should be seeing a pattern now: first you dump our images into the Resources folder, then you drag our objects onto the view, and finally you link the objects up with code.

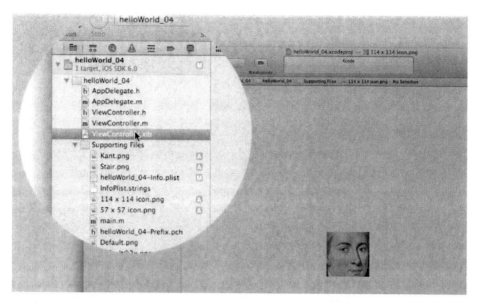

Figure 4-12. Open your nib file

13.   Your top layer image will be placed over the base layer when the user taps
      the button. Therefore, you want to handle the base layer in the same manner
      as you have in the past. Scroll down in your Library to the Cocoa Touch
      objects folder and locate the Image View icons. Drag one onto your View
      frame, as illustrated in Figure 4-13.

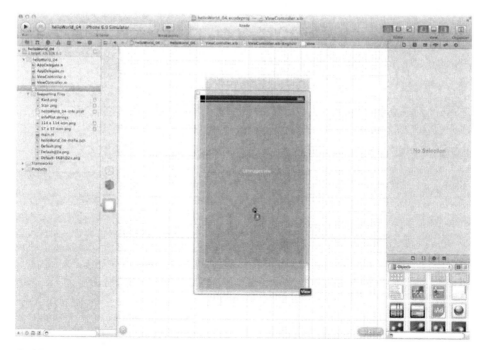

Figure 4-13. Position the UIImageView onto the View screen, flush with the bottom

14. You want to connect the 640 × 1096 STAIR.png to your Image View so that it
     will appear. Go to the Information tab of the Image View Attributes window,
     open the drop-down window, and select the image, as shown in Figure 4-14.

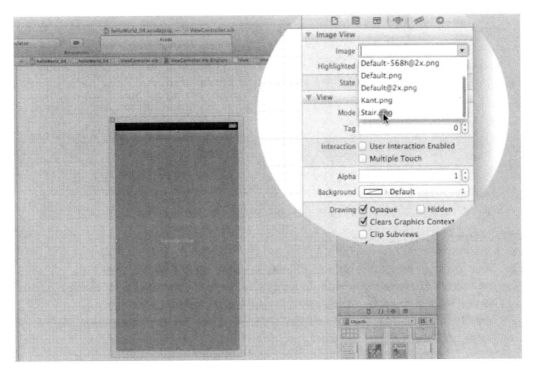

Figure 4-14. Associate an image with UIImageView, which you've just dragged onto the View screen

15. Earlier, I said that when the user taps the button, Immanuel Kant should
     appear and announce, "Hello World I'm back!" The method you'll employ
     here will be a *label instance variable*—with a text property assigned with
     "Hello World I'm back!" So, drag out a label that will be your instance variable
     (see Figure 4-15), and you'll assign the text "Hello World I'm back!" onto the
     base view later. When you put the label onto the view, repeat the way that
     you adjusted the size in the earlier assignments; that is, widen it so it can fit
     this text.

Figure 4-15. Drag a label onto the view

16. Just as you've done before, center the text, change its color to white in the Properties frame, and delete the default text "Label." In Figure 4-16, note that the center text has been selected and I am just about to change the black text.

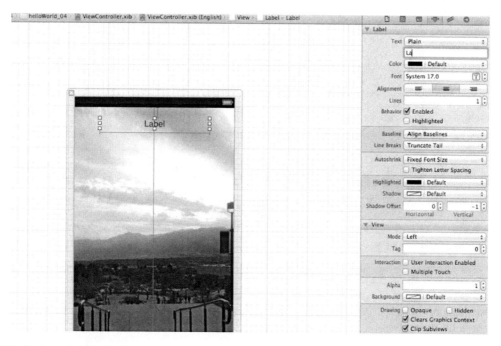

Figure 4-16. Center and delete the text

17.   You want the picture and the text to appear when a button is tapped, which
      means you need a button. Go ahead and drag one onto your base layer, as
      shown in Figure 4-17, and in its Title field enter *Guess who's back in town?*
      When users see a button asking this question, they will be compelled to tap it.
      When they do, you want Immanuel Kant to appear, saying, "Hello World, I'm
      back!" You may want to adjust the size of the button as you've done before.
      If you're inclined to make your button fancier than the one I created in the
      video, you may want it to show some of the underlying image. While still in
      the Image View Attributes window, scroll down and shift the Alpha slider to
      about 0.30. Jumping ahead, you may want to start thinking about what you're
      doing in terms of the code you'll soon write. We're looking at two IBOutlets: a
      label and the underlying base image. Each category "whispers" something to
      Interface Builder. One says that you want a UILabel class to use text that the
      pointer *label points to; the other says that the UIImageView class will put up
      an image located at a place the pointer *uiImageView points to.

Figure 4-17. Drag a button onto your base layer

Well, what have you done so far in Interface Builder? You've installed the background image and
inserted a button that will trigger these two IBOutlets. Now, while still taking a minute to think ahead
about what happens each time you drag outlets onto your header file, let's take a high-altitude view
of what you'll be doing here:

```
- (IBAction)someNameWeWillGiveTheButton:(id) sender
```

That line, in fact, invokes your two friends—the two IBOutlets for the label and background image—for the label, with

```
label.text = @"Hello World, I'm back!";
```

and the image, with

```
UIImage *imageSource = [UIImage imageNamed: @"Kant.png"];
```

To make all that work in the implementation file, you need to perform some action on the header file. You have to set the label and the image up—which is called *declaring* them.

You'll declare the label with this:

```
IBOutlet UILabel *someNameWeWillGiveTheLabel
```

And you'll declare the image with this:

```
IBOutlet UIImageView * someNameWeWillGiveTheImageView
```

Okay, that was a quick mental journey into the future. Now you're ready for action. You've created a button that will call your two friends; all you need to do now is create the image and the label and then associate them with the appropriate pieces of code.

18. You need the button to entice the user to tap it. So you'll ask the user "Guess who's back in town?" by double-clicking the button and writing the text in it. You may notice that the button cleverly adjusts its size to accommodate the text width (Figure 4-18).

Figure 4-18. Write the button text

19. Think about this for a second now. When the button is tapped, you want the kantStair.png image to appear on top of the background, STAIR.png. How does it get there? It's carried onto the screen by way of an Image View. Therefore, drag an Image View onto the screen, as shown in Figure 4-19. Then place it flush to the bottom edge of the iPhone/iPad screen. You don't want the image floating in the middle of the screen, but rather appear as if it's projecting from the bottom. Once you've dragged the image to the screen, just let it go. You haven't configured its size or placement. That's next.

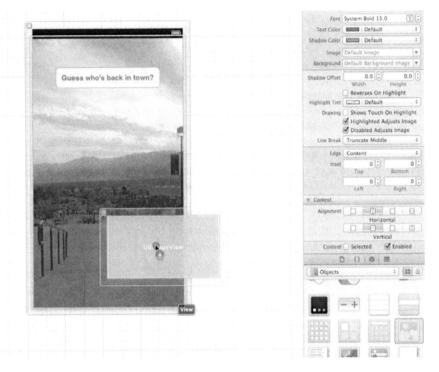

Figure 4-19. Drag the second image view onto the view

20. In the Image View Attributes Inspector, click the View tab. The View mode Scale to Fill is selected by default. You want to change that to Bottom, as illustrated in Figure 4-20. Before moving on to the next step, take a minute to align the label and button with each other, and in context with the center of the screen, as depicted in Figure 4-20.

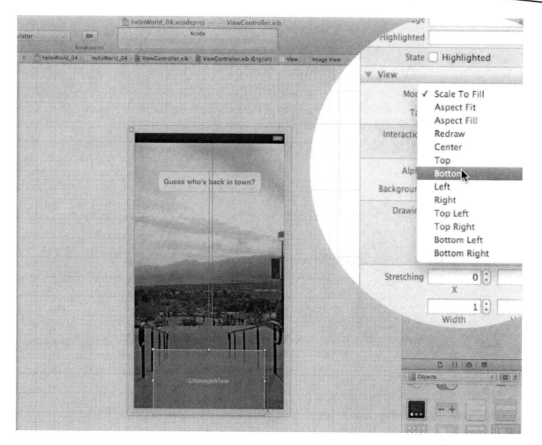

Figure 4-20. Adjust the location of the second Image View

You're now done with dragging items out onto the View. You have your label, a button, and two Image Views. Now save everything, and you'll start putting some code behind these items you've dragged onto the view.

21.   You now want to start tweaking your screenview to accommodate code.
As in the three earlier apps, you'll start moving from the Interface Builder
View to our Coding View by clicking the Assistant, as depicted in Figure 4-21.

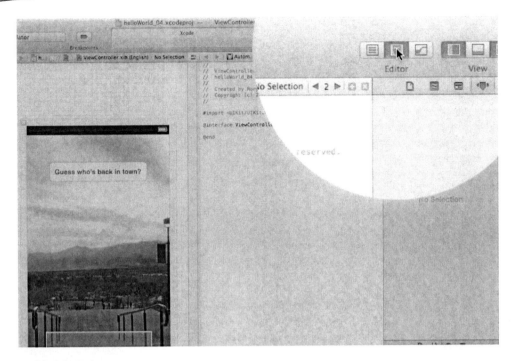

Figure 4-21. Click the Assistant

22. Select the button in preparation for Control-dragging it over to the header
     file (see Figure 4-22). Don't drag it yet; you have to look at IBOutlets and
     IBActions a little more first.

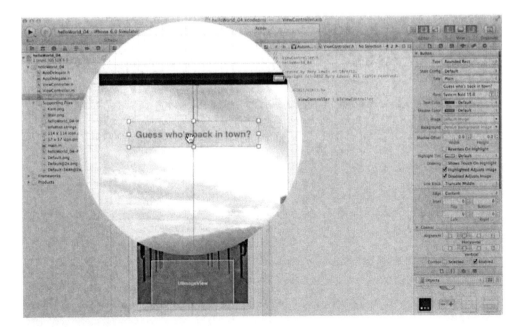

Figure 4-22. Select the button

Understanding IBOutlets and IBActions

In previous chapters, I discussed the .m and .h extensions in detail. You've been doing what most Cocoa and Objective-C programmers do: Start off by programming the header files. In geekspeak, you'd say, "After dragging out objects onto the view, I opened the header and Control-dragged the IBOutlets and IBActions into the header file." If anybody were to ask you on a forum to explain, you may tell them, "Click the disclosure triangle in your Classes file and open the ViewController.h file."

You've already programmed three previous header files, so you should be accustomed to just flying over this portion of your code. But this time you're going to hit the brakes and think about what you're doing. For all your previous examples, you've only had to use one IBOutlet, a thing that allows you to interact with the user. Let's get more technical and specific and dig deeper into what an IBOutlet is so that when you get to the "Digging the Code" section, you'll be able to really understand it. But before digging the code, you need to hook up your IBActions and IBOutlets knowing that you'll go deep into the code that Xcode instantiates for you as you connect the labels and buttons to your header file.

23. Control-drag your button to the area below the @interface directive, as shown in Figure 4-23.

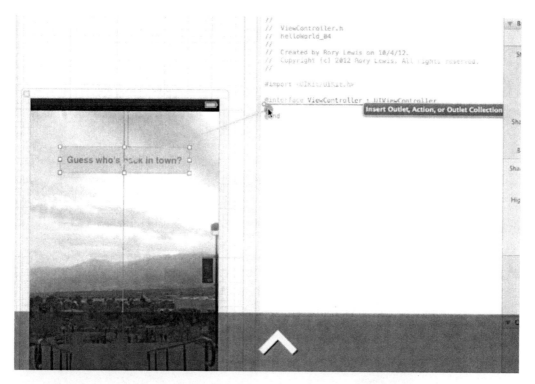

Figure 4-23. Control-drag a connection from your button in Interface Builder into your header file

24. Change the connection type in the top drop-down menu in the dialog box from Outlet to Action, as shown in Figure 4-24.

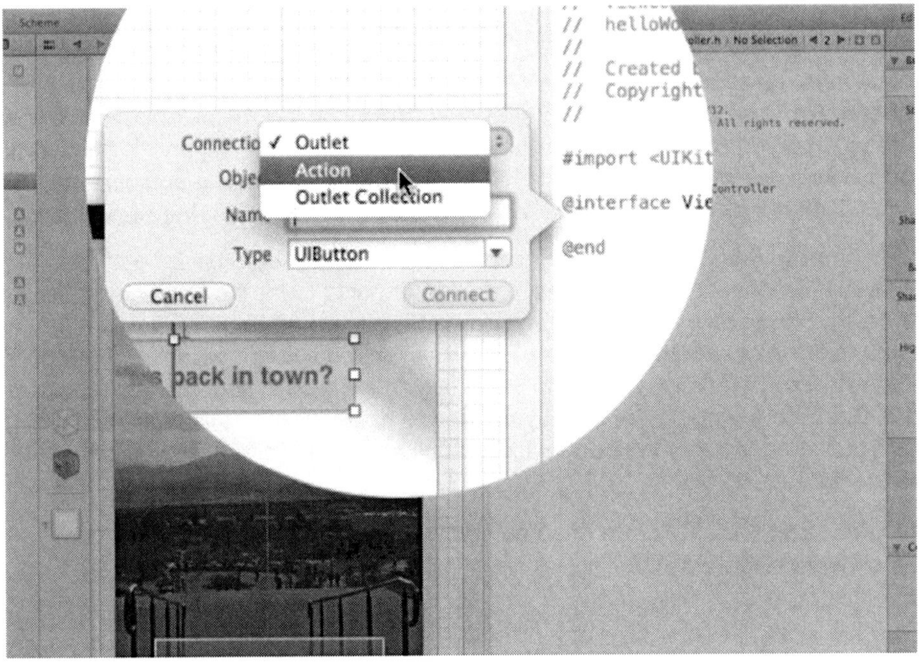

Figure 4-24. *Open the drop-down menu and change the type of connection to Action*

25. You now need to name this action. You could name it monkey or anything you like, but call it button, as shown in Figure 4-25.

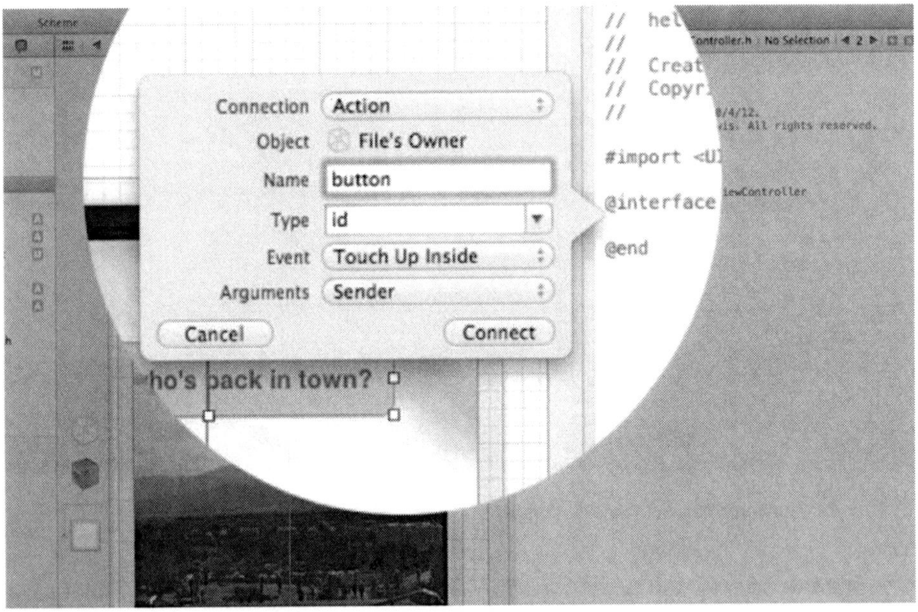

Figure 4-25. *Name the Action type button*

26. As shown in Figure 4-26, after clicking the label once in Interface Builder, Control-drag it into your header file. Make sure you keep on Control-dragging until you see the insertion indicator, as shown in Figure 4-26.

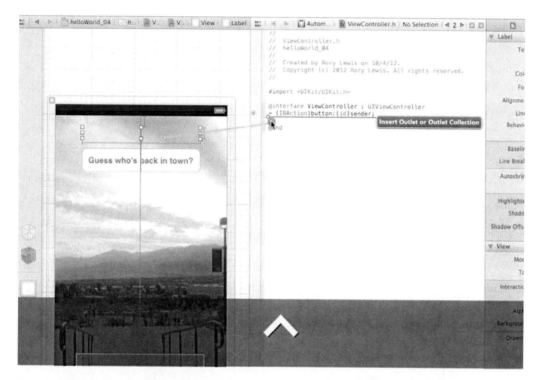

Figure 4-26. Control-drag from the label to your header file

27. As shown in Figure 4-27, when you've Control-dragged your label out to the @interface directive, drop it there, call it label, and leave the Connection type as Outlet.

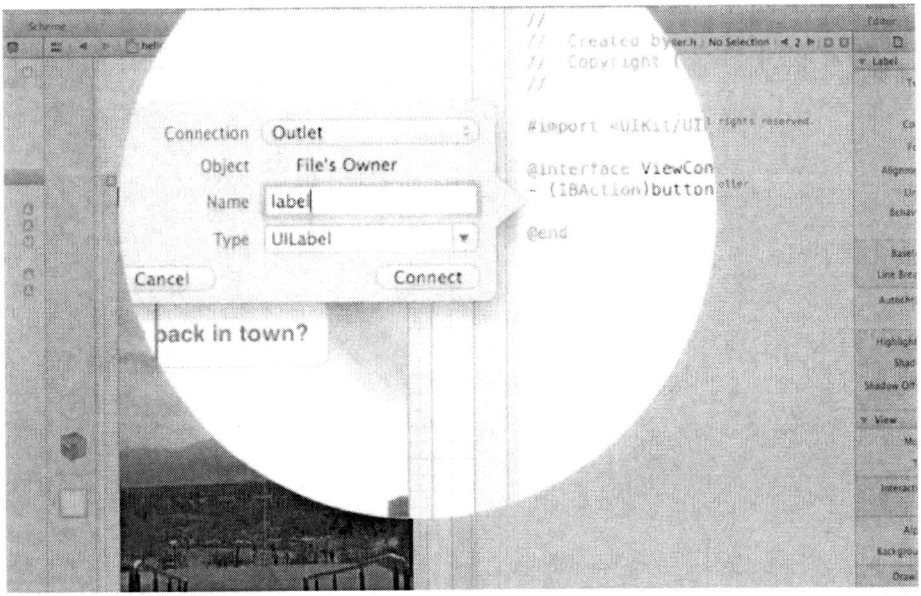

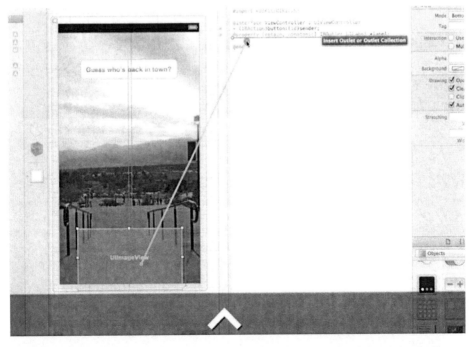

Figure 4-27. Let's name the label outlet "label"

28.   After clicking the second `UIImageView` in Interface Builder, Control-drag it until you see the insertion indicator, as shown in Figure 4-28. Make sure that when you Control-drag into your header file, you go directly under the `label` outlet you just created.

Figure 4-28. Control-drag a connection from your second UIImageView in Interface Builder into your header file

29. As shown in Figure 4-29, when you've Control-dragged from the second
     UIImageView out to the @interface directive, drop it there, call it kant, and
     leave it as an Outlet Connection type.

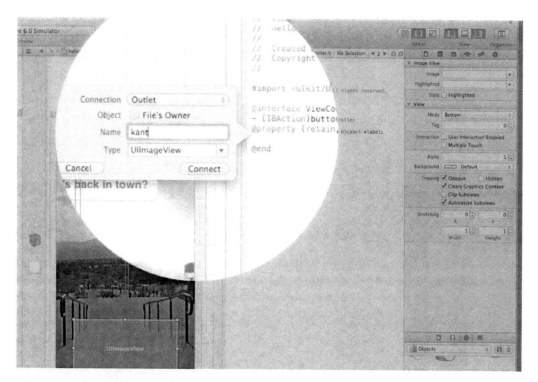

Figure 4-29. Name the second UIImageView outlet kant

30. The following is the code in your header file (Figure 4-30 shows it in context).
     You seek a deeper understanding of these elements:

```
#import <UIKit/UIKit.h>
@interface ViewController : UIViewController
- (IBAction)button:(id)sender;
@property (retain, nonatomic) IBOutlet UILabel *label;
@property (retain, nonatomic) IBOutlet UIImageView *kant;
@end
```

Figure 4-30. Save your work

Let's start with the first line:

```
#import <UIKit/UIKit.h>
```

This is what permits you to use the IBOutlet keyword. You use #import to import the UIKit, which is the user interface (UI) framework inside the huge body of core chunks of code called IPhoneRuntime, which is a stripped-down version of the OS X operating system found on a Mac. Of course, IPhoneRuntime is smaller so it works on an iPhone or an iPad.

When you import the UIKit framework, it gives you the ability to use tons of code Apple has already written for you—called *classes*—one of which is the very cool and popular class you've already used: IBOutlet. The IBOutlet keyword is a special directive for what's called an *instance variable*; this directive tells Interface Builder to display items that you want to appear on the iPhone or iPad. In turn, Interface Builder uses these "hints" to tell the compiler that you'll be connecting objects to your .xib files. Interface Builder doesn't connect these outlets to anything, but it tells the compiler that you'll be adding them.

Here's an inventory of what you'll be using:

- The background image of the stairs
- The top-layer image of Kant
- The text of what he will say upon his return to the campus

In the next exercise, you'll be using two IBOutlets—one dealing with the text in the label where Kant says "Hello World, I'm back!—and the other with your second view where Kant magically appears. Knowing that you need two IBOutlets, you can visualize how it will look. The IBAction and IBOutlets are in bold. Start by focusing on the code that follows @interface ViewController : UIViewController. Your code will need to appear as follows:

```
#import <UIKit/UIKit.h>
@interface ViewController : UIViewController
- (IBAction)button:(id)sender;
@property (retain, nonatomic) IBOutlet UILabel *label;
@property (retain, nonatomic) IBOutlet UIImageView *kant;
@end
```

You know that when you shoot text onto the iPhone or iPad screen, you use the UILabel class. This class draws multiple lines of static text. Now, consider what you'll need for the second IBOutlet. You know you want to impose the top layer image, as shown in Figure 4-3. A good idea here would be to use the UIImageView class because it provides you with code written by Apple that can display either single images or a series of animated images. As you can see, it now makes sense to say you have two IBOutlets:

- Let one call the UILabel class to control the text.

- Let the other call the UIImageView class to control the second image.

```
#import <UIKit/UIKit.h>
@interface ViewController : UIViewController
- (IBAction)button:(id)sender;
@property (retain, nonatomic) IBOutlet UILabel *label;
@property (retain, nonatomic) IBOutlet UIImageView *kant;
@end
```

Using pointers

Now that you have the means to push text and an image to the screen, you need to specify which text and which image. You can use predefined code, created by the folks at Apple, which does what it does by virtue of referencing or *pointing* to your *resources*—that is, your text and images. This is the context in which you'll be using pointers.

In previous examples, I told you not to worry about that star thing (*) yet. Well, now it's time to take a look at it. Let's focus for a moment on how these (*) things—*pointers*—do what they do. You need an indirect way to get your text and picture onto the screen because you won't be writing the code to do it—you'll use Apple's code to do it. You call up pre-existing classes, and these classes call up your text and your image. That's why I say it's an *indirect* means of obtaining your stuff.

Consider this little analogy: suppose you make a citizen's arrest of a burglar who breaks into your house. You call the police and, when they arrive, you point to the criminal and say, "Here's the thief!" Then the policeman, not you, takes the criminal away to be charged.

Now, you want to display text on your iPhone/iPad. You call UILabel, and when it "arrives," you point to your words and say, "Here's the text." Then the UILabel, not you, deals with the text.

You do likewise when you want to display an image. You call UIImageView, and when it "arrives," you point to your image and say, "Here's the image." Then the UIImageView code, not you, deals with the picture.

What are these pointers called? You can give them whatever names you want. Let's point the UILabel to *label and the UIImageView to a pointer called *kant. Look at the code you've just written:

```
#import <UIKit/UIKit.h>
@interface ViewController : UIViewController
- (IBAction)button:(id)sender;
@property (retain, nonatomic) IBOutlet UILabel *label;
@property (retain, nonatomic) IBOutlet UIImageView *kant;
@end
```

Some of the clever people at Apple describe their reasoning for creating and coding IBOutlets as giving a hint to Interface Builder into what it should "expect" to do when you tell it to lay out your interface.

- One IBOutlet whispers into Interface Builder's ear that the UILabel class is to use text indicated by the *label pointer.

- The other IBOutlet whispers into Interface Builder's ear that the UIImageView class is to use the image referenced by the *kant pointer.

You're not done yet. After you tell Interface Builder what to expect, you need to tell your Mac's microprocessor—through the compiler—that an important event is about to descend upon it. Your compiler always wants to know when an object is coming its way. That's because objects are independent masses of numbers and symbols that put significant demands on the microprocessor, and the processor needs to be told by you—the programmer—when it needs to catch the object and put it into a special place in memory.

Objects can come in a wide variety of flavors, as conceptually different as *bird*, *guru*, *soccer*, and *house*. To enable the processor to handle its job when the time comes, you need to tell it that each object you'll be using in your code has two specific and unique parameters, or features: they're called *property* and *type*.

Don't freak out! Providing this information is really easy. It consists of two steps.

The first step is what you just read about: you give the compiler a heads-up about the objects you'll be using by defining their property and type. The second step that when the microprocessor receives this data, it utilizes this information by *synthesizing* it.

To summarize:

- First you declare that your object has a property with a specific *type*.

- Second you instruct the computer to implement—or *synthesize*—this information.

You tell the compiler about your object by *declaring* it, including giving the specific descriptive parameters of its properties. Then you give the compiler the go-ahead to implement your object by telling it to synthesize it.

How do you do this declaring and implementing? Using tools in your code called *directives*. You signal directives by inserting @ before stating your directive. You put the @ symbol in front of the word property to make it a property directive: @property.

Easy, huh? Just two more points now, and then you'll get back to your code.

Properties: Management and Control

You also need to specify whether a property will be *read-only* or *read-write*. In other words, you need to specify whether it will always stay the same or whether it can mutate into something new. In geekspeak, we call this *mutability*. For the most part, you'll use Apple code to handle the mutability of properties with respect to your objects.

To instruct the Apple code to handle the mutability property, you designate the property as *nonatomic*. *Atomic* implies the ability to go into the microscopic world and effect change. *Nonatomic* must mean not-so-powerful, more superficial, and unmanipulable.

If you designate a property (such as mutability) as *nonatomic*, you're basically saying, "Apple, please handle my mutability and related stuff—I really don't care. I'll take your word for it." At a later date, you may want to take direct control of this property, and then you'd designate it as atomic. Right now, though, you'll use the more relaxed approach and let Apple handle the microscopic business. So, when it's time to choose one designation or the other, just use nonatomic.

The other point I want to make deals with memory management. You need to address the issue of how to let the iPhone/iPad know, when you store an object, whether it is *read-only* or *read-write*. In other words, you need to tell the computer the nature of the memory associated with an object— who gets to change it, when, and how. Generally speaking, you want to control and keep this information—that is, *retain* it. As you move through the remaining exercises in this book, you'll keep the code in your own hands and retain the right to manage your memory.

```
#import <UIKit/UIKit.h>
@interface ViewController : UIViewController
- (IBAction)button:(id)sender;
@property (retain, nonatomic) IBOutlet UILabel *label;
@property (retain, nonatomic) IBOutlet UIImageView *kant;
@end
```

To summarize, the `@property (nonatomic, retain)` directive says the following:

- Mutability should be nonatomic. Apple, please handle this!

- Memory management is something you want to retain. You will maintain control.

Remember IBOutlets? Oh yeah—let's return to that part of your program. The IBOutlet for the text is UILabel with pointer *label, so you created the code to control the text for the label as follows:

```
#import <UIKit/UIKit.h>
@interface ViewController : UIViewController
- (IBAction)button:(id)sender;
@property (retain, nonatomic) IBOutlet UILabel *label;
@property (retain, nonatomic) IBOutlet UIImageView *kant;
@end
```

The IBOutlet for the picture is UIImageView with the pointer *kant, so enter the code for the picture:

```
#import <UIKit/UIKit.h>
@interface ViewController : UIViewController
- (IBAction)button:(id)sender;
@property (retain, nonatomic) IBOutlet UILabel *label;
@property (retain, nonatomic) IBOutlet UIImageView *kant;
@end
```

Are you done with the header file yet? Not quite. You need to look at your IBActions. You've analyzed both your IBOutlets, but now you're going to analyze the IBAction you used for your . . . can you guess?

Adding IBActions

Yes, you needed a button! So you made an IBAction for your button, as shown in Figure 4-25. We could "go deep" again, into the code for the IBAction, but this has been a challenging section. Let's save the technical part of this element for the "Digging the Code" section. Meanwhile, just enter the new code that's highlighted here. See if you can anticipate the functions of the different pieces—or parameters—and you'll see how close you are later.

This is what you'll be focusing on:

```
#import <UIKit/UIKit.h>
@interface ViewController : UIViewController
- (IBAction)button:(id)sender;
@property (retain, nonatomic) IBOutlet UILabel *label;
@property (retain, nonatomic) IBOutlet UIImageView *kant;
@end
```

GO OUT NOW AND TAKE A BREAK

---

31.   Right now, the Interface Builder is showing your nib file. Save everything, go to your Navigator, and click the implementation file (.m), as shown in Figure 4-31.

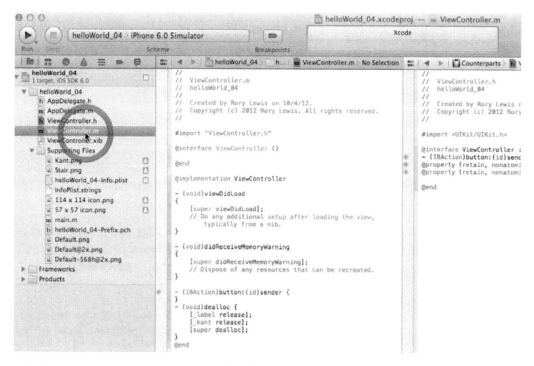

Figure 4-31. Save your work and open the implementation file

32. Look at the code Apple has instantiated for us (see Figure 4-32 to see where it appears). Look at these three lines in bold first:

Figure 4-32. With the implementation file open, you can now code

```
#import "ViewController.h"
@interface ViewController ()

@end

@implementation ViewController

- (void)viewDidLoad ...
- (void)didReceiveMemoryWarning ...
- (IBAction)button:(id)sender {} ...
- (void)dealloc {} ...

@end
```

You can see that the implementation file first imports all the code of the iBOutlets and IBActions you created from your header file using the #import "ViewController.h" statement. Next you'll see the @interface ViewController () and, of course, you'll ask why do you see @interface twice—once inside the header .h and then again inside the .m over here? This is going a little deep here—don't worry if you don't understand it; just let it drift through your brain: This @interface in your .m file is something called a *class extension*. In other words, your class implementation is identified by two compiler directives—here, @implementation (for the View Controller) and @end. These directives provide extra information the compiler needs to associate the enclosed methods with the corresponding class. But as I said, don't worry about this now—Apple just does it for you.

Let's quickly review what else you have by looking at the two methods (void)viewDidLoad and - (void)didReceiveMemoryWarning. Refer to Apple's comments for each of these. - (void)viewDidLoad is the place to code any additional setup after loading the view, typically from a nib, and - (void)didReceiveMemoryWarning is the place where you dispose of any resources that can be re-created:

```
#import "ViewController.h"
@interface ViewController ()
@end
@implementation ViewController

- (void)viewDidLoad
{
    [super viewDidLoad];
        // Do any additional setup after loading the view, typically from a nib.
}

- (void)didReceiveMemoryWarning
{
    [super didReceiveMemoryWarning];
    // Dispose of any resources that can be recreated.
}

- (IBAction)button:(id)sender {} ...
- (void)dealloc {} ...

@end
```

I'll focus on the method that controls what happens when the user taps the button you created, - (IBAction) button:(id)sender. The -(void) dealloc method just deallocates the memory you need to use to run what's inside it: _label, _kant, and super (everything we missed). Note that adding an underscore (_) to an instance variable name is a common convention in Objective-C. Figure 4-32 shows me typing in the first word in this section, label, in anticipation of the next step.

```
#import "ViewController.h"
@interface ViewController ()
@end
@implementation ViewController

- (void)viewDidLoad ...
- (void)didReceiveMemoryWarning ...

- (IBAction)button:(id)sender {}

- (void)dealloc {} ...
@end
```

33. As indicated in Figure 4-33, you're now ready to program the code that will execute when the user taps the button. In other words, you're ready to program the button's code. Scroll down until you get to the button method that exists but is currently empty.

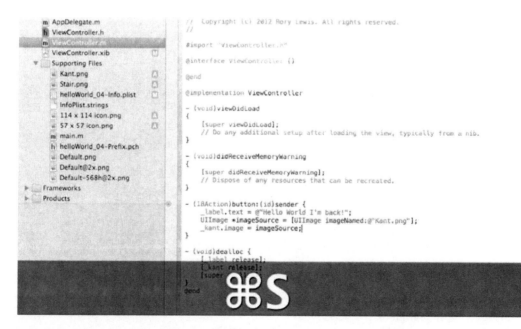

Figure 4-33. Write the first two lines of the button method

When the user runs this app and taps the button, the image of Kant will appear instantly on top of the background staircase. He's going to "say" something via the embedded text. As noted earlier, let's go with, "Hello World I'm back!" To accomplish this, you need to associate the label instance variable with a text property assigned with your desired text, as follows:

```
#import "ViewController.h"
@interface ViewController ()
@end

@implementation ViewController
- (void)viewDidLoad {[super viewDidLoad];}

- (void)didReceiveMemoryWarning {[super didReceiveMemoryWarning];}

- (IBAction)button:(id)sender {
    _label.text = @"Hello World I'm back!";
    UIImage *imageSource = [UIImage imageNamed:@"Kant.png"];
    _kant.image = imageSource;
}

- (void)dealloc {[_label release]; [_kant release]; [super dealloc];}
@end
```

> **Note** When reading declarations, the : is shorthand for *subclasses*, and the <> is shorthand for *implements*.

Having completed the task of coding for the text, you now need to add the code that will cause the image of Kant to appear. For that, you'll use a class method called imageNamed that will display the kant.png image, the top-layer photo you prepared at the beginning of this project. Enter the line in bold in the following code immediately under the code you just entered for the text:

```
#import "ViewController.h"
@interface ViewController ()
@end

@implementation ViewController
- (void)viewDidLoad {[super viewDidLoad];}

- (void)didReceiveMemoryWarning {[super didReceiveMemoryWarning];}

- (IBAction)button:(id)sender {
    _label.text = @"Hello World I'm back!";
    UIImage *imageSource = [UIImage imageNamed:@"Kant.png"];
    _kant.image = imageSource;
}

- (void)dealloc {[_label release]; [_kant release]; [super dealloc];}
@end
```

Your pointer's name for the image is Kant, but right now the `kant.png` image file is in `UIImage`'s assigned pointer called `imageSource`. You need to assign this automatically assigned pointer `imageSource` to the image of Kant, as shown in the following code:

```
#import "ViewController.h"
@interface ViewController ()
@end

@implementation ViewController
- (void)viewDidLoad {[super viewDidLoad];}

- (void)didReceiveMemoryWarning {[super didReceiveMemoryWarning];}

- (IBAction)button:(id)sender {
    _label.text = @"Hello World I'm back!";
    UIImage *imageSource = [UIImage imageNamed:@"Kant.png"];
    _kant.image = imageSource;
}

- (void)dealloc {[_label release]; [_kant release]; [super dealloc];}
@end
```

If that doesn't quite make sense at the moment, that's okay. There sure are a lot of entities with *image* as part of their name, object, or association, and it's confusing. You'll be examining this topic more thoroughly as you move forward, so, right now, don't lose any sleep over it. Figure 4-33 illustrates how your code should appear at this point. Now save your work by pressing ⌘+S and give yourself a pat on the back. You've worked through the header and implementation files at a much deeper level than in previous chapters. Even though you've walked through some of these technical functions before, you braved them again while remaining open to a deeper understanding.

34.   Now that you're through writing your code, run it and see if you have any errors (Figure 4-34).

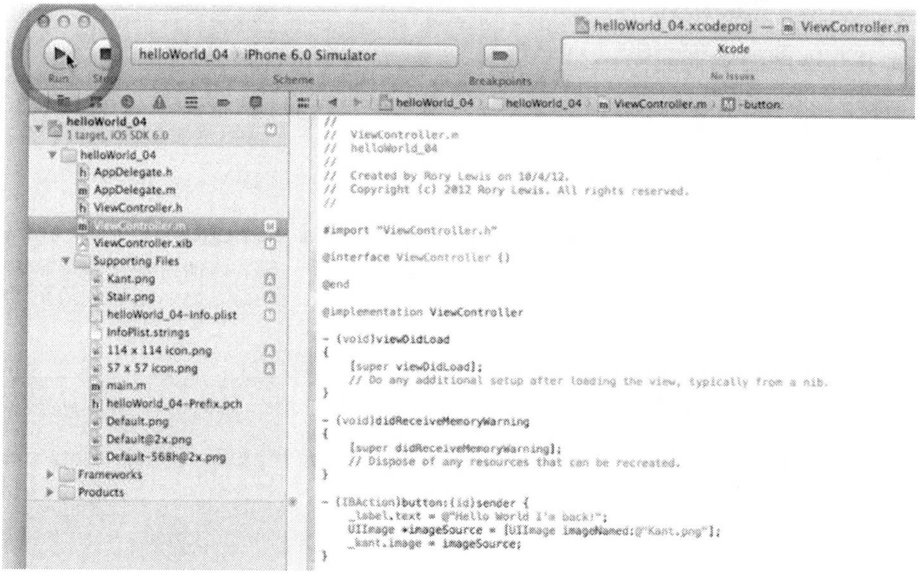

Figure 4-34. With the code all written, let's run it

35.   Figure 4-35 illustrates the two views of helloWorld_04. Your images will be different, of course, if you used your own. The first view is what the user sees when the app first opens. The second image is what appears when the button is tapped. The label text appears, and the second image is superimposed on top of the underlying image.

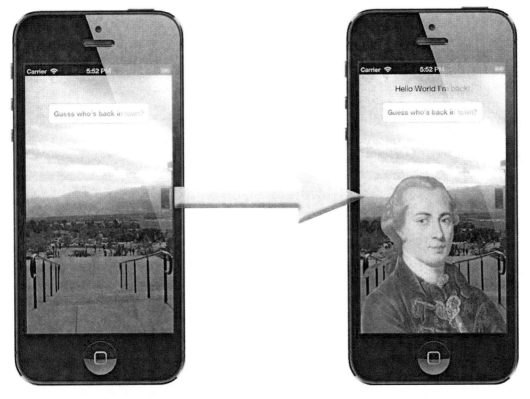

Figure 4-35. The two helloWorld_04 views

Digging the Code

In this section, let's zoom in on some of the key components you encountered earlier in this chapter. I want to talk a little more about IBOutlets and IBActions–specifically, how they include keywords and even *quasi*-keywords. I also touch on pointers and their relationship to addresses in the code.

IBOutlets and IBActions

Earlier, you worked with IBOutlet and IBAction keywords. Now I'm going to talk about a couple related concepts.

The Appkit of Objective-C converts original C language preprocessor directives such as #define (pronounced "pound define") into usable preprocessor directives.

> **Note**   In the United States, the # sign is often called the *pound sign*, especially in Objective-C and other programming contexts. In the United Kingdom, it's referred to as the *hash character*. Many iPhone/iPad developers refer to the #define preprocessor directive simply as the *define directive*.

The #define preprocessor directive tells the computer to substitute one thing for another. That's an easy concept, right? For example, if I program the computer to substitute 100 every time it sees an instance of your name, the code in C would look like this:

```
#define yourName 100
```

This would tell the computer to substitute 100 each time it processes yourName—a variable that recognizes instances of your actual name.

Back to Xcode now, and our topic. In this context, the IBOutlet and IBAction quasi-keywords aren't really defined to be anything. In other words, they don't do anything substantial *for the compiler*, which is the core of the computer.

Quasi-keywords are flags, though, and they're important to communication with the Interface Builder. When the Interface Builder sees the IBOutlet and IBAction quasi-keywords, it gets some of its internal code ready to perform specific tasks. It gets itself ready to deal with instance variables and all the hooks and connections that we make in that programming arena.

More About Pointers

Understanding the concept of *pointers*—also sometimes known as the concept of *indirection*—is difficult for many programming students. Explaining the idea isn't easy because it's one of the most sophisticated features of the C programming language.

Earlier in this chapter, I presented the analogy of seeing a criminal doing something and then calling the police and pointing the police to where he is—so they, not you, can arrest the criminal. The analogy works for many students, but now let's go a little deeper.

If you ask a computer science professor what a pointer is, he'll probably say something like, "Pointers hold the address of a variable or a method."

"The *address*?" you ask. Well, consider this new analogy. Have you ever seen a movie in which a character is traveling all over the place, looking for clues to the treasure map, or the missing painting, or the kidnapped daughter? Sometimes they spot a clue—a fingerprint, receipt, or envelope containing a cryptic message—and these take the people one step closer to their goal of finding the missing objects themselves.

We can call these clues *pointers*; they point to the next place to go for the solution of the given problem. They don't necessarily give the ultimate address where everything is handled and resolved, but they give intermediate addresses or places to continue our work.

Thus, what the professor of computer science means is that pointers do not actually contain the items they direct us to; they contain the locations within the code—the addresses—of the desired objects or actions or entities. This important feature makes the C family of languages very powerful.

This simple idea makes turning complex tasks into easy ones very efficient. Pointers can pass values to types and arguments to functions, represent huge masses of numbers, and manipulate how to manage memory in a computer. You may be thinking that pointers are similar to variables in the world of algebra. *Exactly!*

In our first analogy, a pointer enabled an unarmed citizen to arrest a dangerous criminal by using indirection—that is, by calling the police to come and solve the problem.

Consider an example where a pointer directs us to your bank balance. To do this, define a variable called bankBalance as follows:

```
int  bankBalance = $1,000;
```

Now, let's throw another variable into the mix and call it int_pointer. Let's also assume that, for argument's sake, you've declared it. This lets you use indirection to indirectly connect to the value of bankBalance by this declaration:

```
int  *int_pointer;
```

The *, or asterisk, tells the family of C languages that your variable int_pointer is allowed to indirectly access the integer value of the amount of money in your variable (placeholder): bankBalance.

I want to remind you that our digging around here is not an exhaustive or rigorous exploration into these topics. It's just a fun tangent into some related ideas. At this point, there's no reason for you to be bothered if you don't fully understand pointers. Seeds have been planted, and that's what counts for now!

Model-View-Controller

As mentioned previously, the programmers who developed Cocoa Touch used a concept known as the Model-View-Controller (MVC) as the foundation for iPhone and iPad app code. Here is the basic idea:

- *Model*: This holds the data and classes that make your application run. It's the part of the program where you might find sections of code I told you to ignore. This code can also hold objects that represent items you may have in your app (for example, pinballs, cartoon figures, names in databases, or appointments in your calendar).

- *View*: This is the combination of all the goodies users see when they use your app. This is where your users interact with buttons, sliders, controls, and other experiences they can sense and appreciate. Here you may have a Main View that's made up of a number of other views.

- *Controller*: The controller links the model and the view together while always keeping track of what the user's doing. Think of this as the structural plan—the backbone—of the app. This is how you coordinate what buttons the user taps and, if necessary, how to change one view for another, all in response to the user's input, reactions, data, and so on.

Consider the following example that illustrates how you can use the MVC concept to divide the functionality of your iPhone/iPad app into three distinct categories. Figure 4-36 shows a representation of your app. You can see that the VIEW displays a representation—a label—of "Your very cool fantastic App Includes 3 layers: A, B and C."

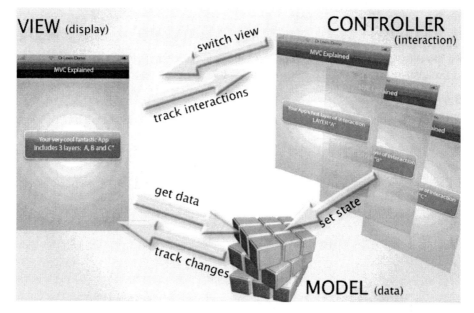

Figure 4-36. The Model-View-Controller (MVC)

In the CONTROLLER section of the app, you see the three individual layers separated out: Layer "A," Layer "B," and Layer "C." Depending on which control mechanism the user taps in the VIEW domain, the display the user sees, the CONTROLLER returns the appropriate response—the next view from the three prepared layers.

Your app will probably utilize data of some type, which is stored in the MODEL section of your program. The data could be phone numbers, players' scores, GPS locations on a map, and so on.

As the user interacts with the VIEW section, the app may have to retrieve data from your database. Let's say your data contains the place where your user parked her car. When the user taps a particular button, the app may retrieve the GPS data from the MODEL. If it's a moving target, it may also track changes in the user's position in relation to a car in the parking lot. Lastly, the CONTROLLER may change the state (or mode) of your data. Maybe one state shows telephone numbers, and another shows GPS positions or the top ten scores in a game. The CONTROLLER is also where animation takes place. What happens in the animation can affect and perhaps change the state in your MODEL. You could do this by using various tools, such as UIKit objects, to control and animate each layer, state, and so on.

If this sounds complicated, bear in mind that you've already done much of this without even knowing it! In the first app, you had the user tap a button, and up popped a label saying "Hello World!" See? You've already built an interaction with a ViewController. We'll be delving further into these possibilities, of course.

I'll do my best to keep you focused on the big picture when it comes to interactions . . . via navigation. Our goal will be to have the user move from less specific information to more specific information with each new view.

Chapter 5 moves to the next level of complexity: Switch View Applications. You'll see how a team of characters or roles within your code work together to direct an outcome, or series of outcomes, that gives the user the sense of seamless flow.

You'll learn about delegators and Switch View Controllers, classes and subclasses, and *lazy loads*. You'll get into the nitty-gritty of the xib files, examine the concept of memory deallocation, and learn about imbedded code comments. It's getting curiouser and curiouser. . .

Onward to the next chapter!

Chapter 5

Touches

Here in your fifth app, you take a giant leap forward and really program some code. I want to say this right now: even though this is a big leap forward, there is always an easy way out. Yes, some of you will use DemoMonkey, and some will type in the all the code as you diligently follow the steps. Either way, I want you to carry on when you feel like giving up; but first, I want to clarify something with you, as I do with my students.

Redefining "Giving Up"

I need to talk about this for one page and I want you to read through this in order to prepare yourself for this chapter. In the past, you may have associated *giving up* with totally relinquishing a dream you had. So, let me share with you my outlook on three terms: giving up, dreams, and goals. I want to talk about these terms in the context of the following four points:

- A person can have a dream until the day she dies. For example, one could dream of being a supernova geek who programs phenomenal multimillion dollar apps. A person could have that dream until the day she dies, even if she had never even touched an iPhone or knew what the word *Xcode* meant. That's because the equation that makes up a dream has *no element of time*.

- A goal, however, is a dream *with an added element of time*. Think about it. When the element of time in your goal's equation runs out, you FAIL! It's really simple. If you plan to sell a million apps within 12 months, and you can't compile Hello World after 12 months, then you've FAILED!

- *The more you accomplish goals within your time constraints, the more confident you become*. That's why a good professor sets up baby steps along the way to ensure that his students accomplish goals and feel really good about themselves. And that's why a good professor makes little programs that move students a little closer to their ultimate goals. Each week, my students need to finish a set goal by programming an app. If they don't send me that completed app within the time limit, I fail them for that assignment. But that's rare, because rather than give up when it gets really hard, I have some backup angels that help my students succeed and meet their goals in time.

- Rather than *give up* when the going gets tough, you can do the following:

  - First, *watch* me program this code in the video at `http://www.rorylewis.com/docs/02_iPad_iPhone/06_iphone_Movies/iPhone%205%20iOX6%20Movies/005_touches.html` and simply follow along. I go a little fast to keep the video short, but you can always pause it. In June 2011, the average viewer paused the video 28.5 times. The average student of mine paused the video 11.3 times.

  - Second, if watching the video doesn't result in total success, you can download my code for this program from `http://bit.ly/ReiQ1k`. That way, you can visually compare your code with mine. I tell students to try visually comparing first; if that doesn't work, I have them paste my code into either Pages or Word and then paste their code into another similar document. After this, they should go away from their computers and check my code line by line against theirs.

  - Third, if the preceding steps don't work, you still shouldn't give up. Instead, paste my code into your code after you've dragged your icons from the nib file into your header file. This means that you still do steps 1 through to 30, which involve mostly dragging and dropping. Then paste the implementation code into your implementation. When it compiles, I want you to try it again on your own before moving on to the next chapter.

The preceding steps eliminate the possibility of your giving up on being a supernova geek. I *love* receiving emails from students and readers telling me how proud they are of being geeks, and how they cannot believe that so many people are downloading and buying their apps. I especially love it when they tell me that they never programmed before in their lives, and how my book showed them that they could program apps and not give up. A wife and mother of four in Helena, Montana brought me to tears when she told me that when her husband lost his job as a boilermaker, she bought my book and never gave up—she supported her family for over a year and has continued to program and sell apps since her husband found another job.

Essentially, first try to do it by just reading the chapter. When you get stuck, check out the video. If the video doesn't help, download the code, move away from your computer, and check your code visually, line by line. As a last resort, paste my code into yours after you drag-and-drop the other elements into your code.

OK—let's do it.

Roadmap Recap

To return to the car mechanic analogy from Chapter 4, remember that nowadays, car mechanics are very specialized: only a handful know how to completely disassemble and rebuild any specific car. So far, you've been peering over the shoulder of one such car mechanic as he's changed and swapped specific components inside the engine. Today, you'll build a very basic lawnmower engine. It will involve more steps than you've had to take thus far, but by the end of this chapter, you'll have taken a huge leap forward.

As you build your lawnmower engine, you may look down and see a bigger mess of tools, nuts, and bolts than you've ever seen before. But hang in there. Follow me as I ask you to stand up from time to time and look at that "mess" from my point of view, not yours, and it will all make sense to you.

Touches: A View-Based Application

The touches app initially looks like the cover of this book. You can move the lulu fruit around with your fingertips after you touch it. There are also three buttons on the top called Shrink, Hide, and Change. The Shrink button is a special button; after you tap it, the lulu fruit icon shrinks, and the text inside the button automatically changes to *Grow*. When you tap the Grow button that used to be the Shrink button, the lulu fruit grows back to its original size. If you like, you can quickly have a look at Figures 5-36, 5-37, and 5-38. You can also see the app working right at the beginning of the video here: http://www.rorylewis.com/docs/02_iPad_iPhone/06_iphone_Movies/iPhone%205%20iOX6%20 Movies/005_touches.html. Only look at the app working though—don't follow the video through the code, because I want to explain the code to you in a specific way.

CGAffineTransform Structs

You'll also be working on animation code that the clever people at Apple wrote into a bundle called a *data structure*. This is a critical tool that coders use to animate their objects. The data structure can shrink an object, change its angle, move it, tilt it, and make it do all sorts of other cool animations. All the code that Apple uses to perform these animations is kept in vaults located in core animation data structures called *structs*. Apple explains this by saying that the "CGAffineTransform data structure represents a matrix used for *affine* transformations." Huh? What does that mean? It means that the CGAffine transforms all the critical points of an object you want to animate into a property called a *transform*. This transform property is simply a matrix. Once the object you want to animate is in this matrix, CGAffine obeys you when you instruct it to change your object's position, angle, shape, scale, and so on. This is what you'll do to the lulu fruit icon.

1.   Do I even need to say this? Close all programs, delete all trash, and drag all your important files and folders to their proper destinations so that you have a perfectly clean desktop. Download the DemoMonkey file and images from http://bit.ly/ReiGqK and upon unzipping the downloaded file, you'll see one demoMonkey file and eight images on your desktop. The five background images are various versions of the front cover of this book. The first image is the center one in Figure 5-1, the cover without the lulu fruit icon. You can see that the three lulu fruit icons are separate from the backgrounds. The largest lulu fruit icon is the one that will appear on the user's screen, and you'll animate it using CGAffineTransforms to impose transforms. The two smaller lulu fruit icons are 57 x 57 icon.png and 114 x 114 icon.png, the latter being the Retina version. The Change button will scroll through all five background images. The Shrink and Hide buttons will use CGAffine structs to animate the lulu fruit icon.

Figure 5-1. *The five background images, demoMonkey file, and three lulu fruit icons downloaded from the repository*

Note   You can, of course, use your own images and icons. But this is a long chapter even without spending resources on creating your own images. In class, I tell students to hand in this homework assignment using my icons first. Later, if done on time (within three days), they can hand in their homework again with their own icons for extra credit. No students have done this yet.

2.   Your desktop should look similar to Figure 5-2, with nothing but the eight icons, the DemoMonkey file, and your Mac hard drive on your desktop. Once everything is clean and your images are stacked up and ready to go, you're ready to blast off.

Figure 5-2. The eight images and DemoMonkey file on the desktop, ready to launch into Xcode

As you have done before, launch Xcode and open a new project using your keyboard shortcut ⌘+⇧+N. When you see the New Project wizard as depicted in Figure 5-3, click the Single View Application template. Press Return (Enter) or click the Next button.

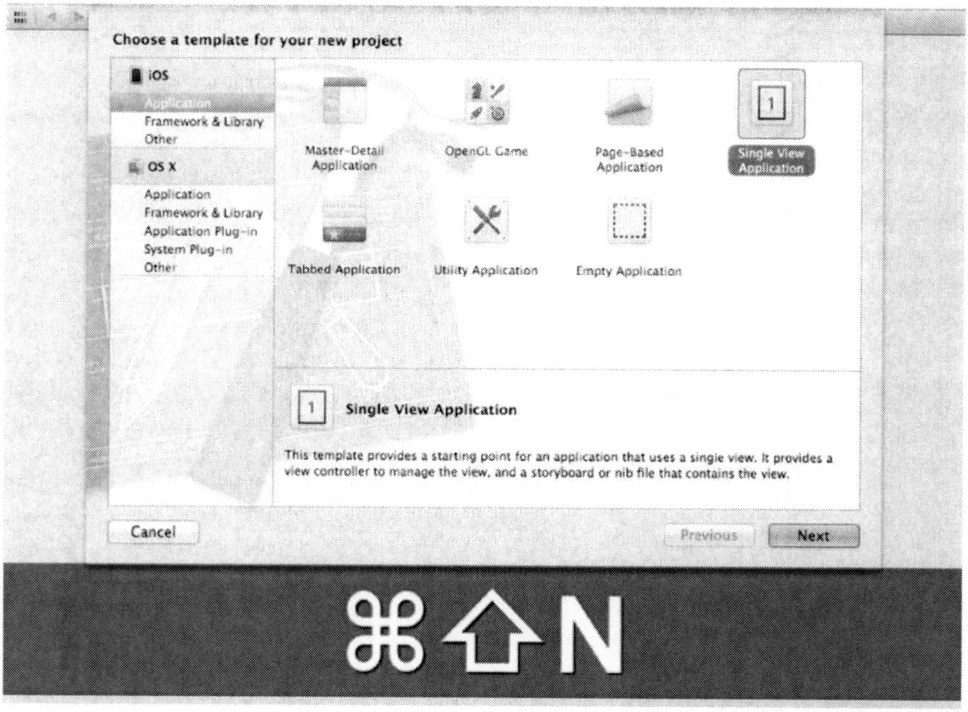

Figure 5-3. Press ⌘+⇧+N. Xcode 4.5 provides the option for a Single View Application, which is the same as the older versions of View-Based Application

3. Call your project touches and, most importantly, remember to deselect the Use Storyboards option, as shown in Figure 5-4. Press Return or click Next.

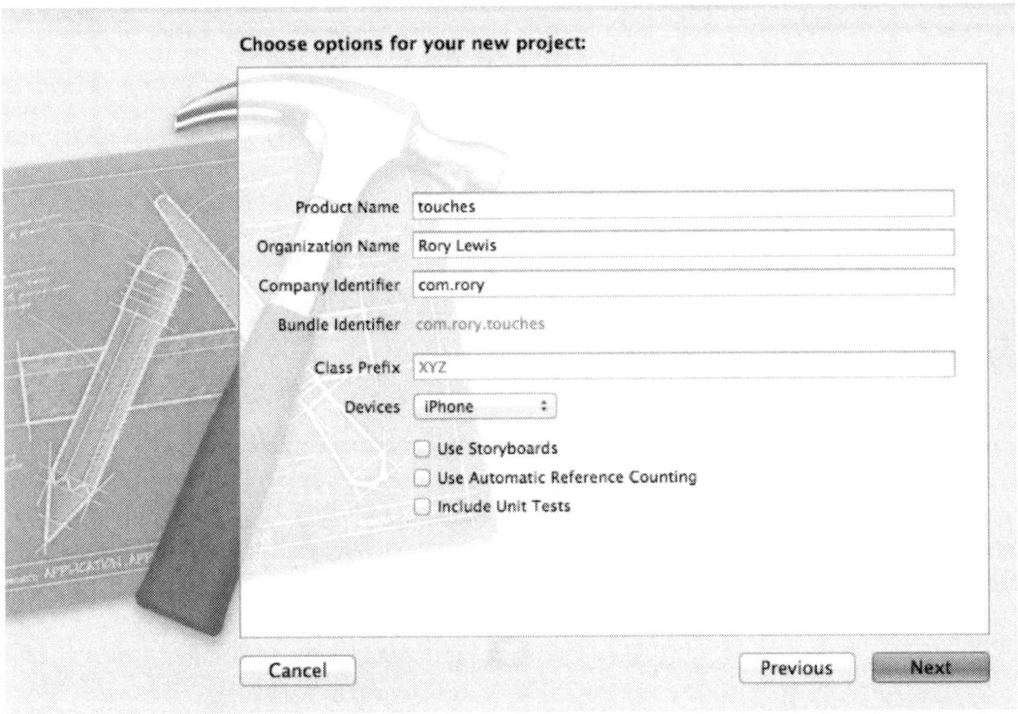

Choose options for your new project:

Product Name	touches
Organization Name	Rory Lewis
Company Identifier	com.rory
Bundle Identifier	com.rory.touches
Class Prefix	XYZ
Devices	iPhone

◯ Use Storyboards
◯ Use Automatic Reference Counting
◯ Include Unit Tests

Cancel   Previous   Next

Figure 5-4. Call your project touches

Save your project to your desktop. You can probably guess by now that you always make sure your current project is located on the desktop. After you're done with it, you'll place it an appropriate folder. I have kept the "Create a Git Repository For Your New Project" option checked so that when you go to an interview to become a code programmer, or if you happen to work with some friends on a project, you'll sound really smart if you say that you're familiar with *software control management* (SCM), which keeps track of changes in the code and coordinates work groups. SCMs save all your many versions of each file of Xcode on disk, storing metadata about each version of each file in a location known as an SCM repository.

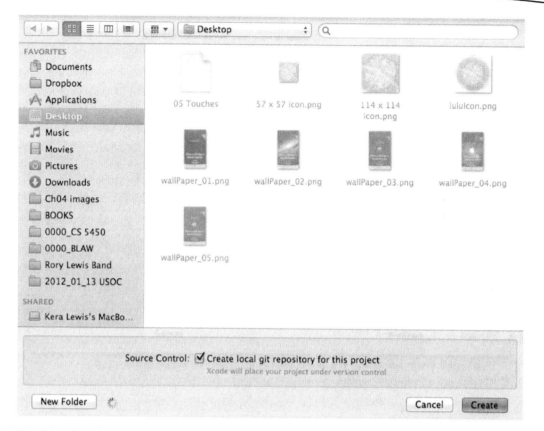

Figure 5-5. *Select the option to save your project to your desktop*

4. Initially, when Xcode instantiates itself, it creates a large window that nearly
    covers your entire desktop. Grab the bottom right-hand corner and shrink
    the window just enough to see the seven images you downloaded from
    the repository at http://bit.ly/ReiGqK. Drag 57 x 57 icon.png into the
    left-hand App Icons slot and then drag 114 x 114 icon.png into the Retina
    Display App Icons slot, as shown in Figure 5-6.

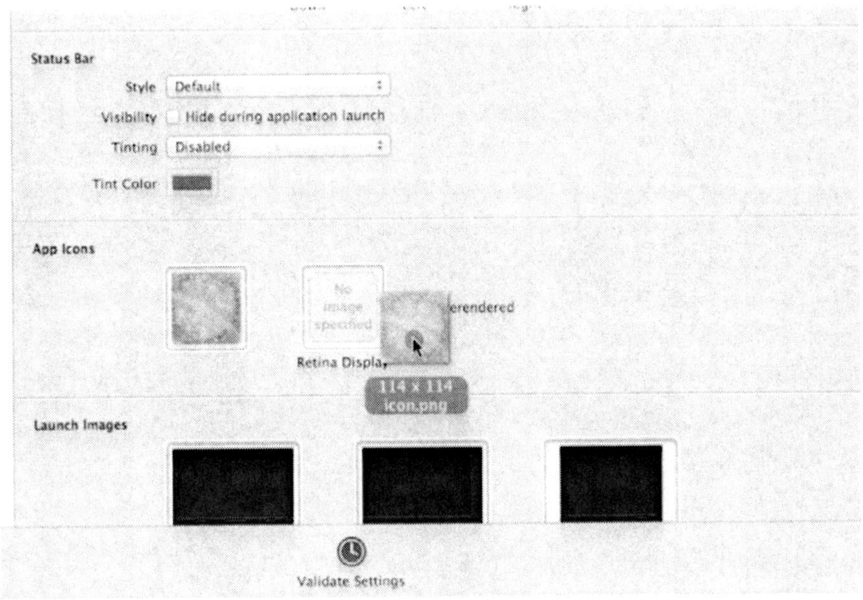

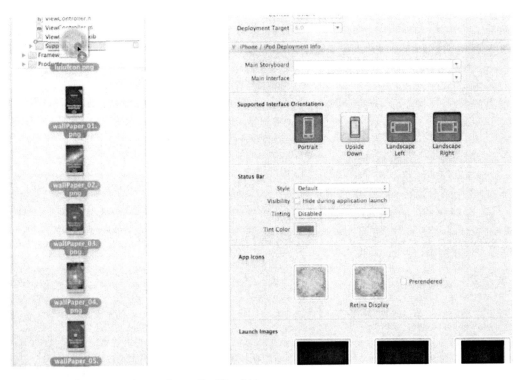

Figure 5-6. *Drag your icons into the App Icon slots*

5. Then grab your remaining 6 images and drag them into your Supporting
    Files folder in Xcode, again, as shown in Figure 5-7.

Figure 5-7. *Drag your images over to your Supporting Files folder*

6. After dropping the image into the Resources folder, you're prompted to
    define whether the image will always be associated with its position on your
    desktop or embedded with the code and carried along with the application
    file, as shown in Figure 5-8. You want it to be embedded, of course, so click
    the "Copy items into destination group's folder (if needed)" box. Also, if not
    already checked by default, select the "Create groups for any added folders"
    radio button. Then click Finish or press Enter.

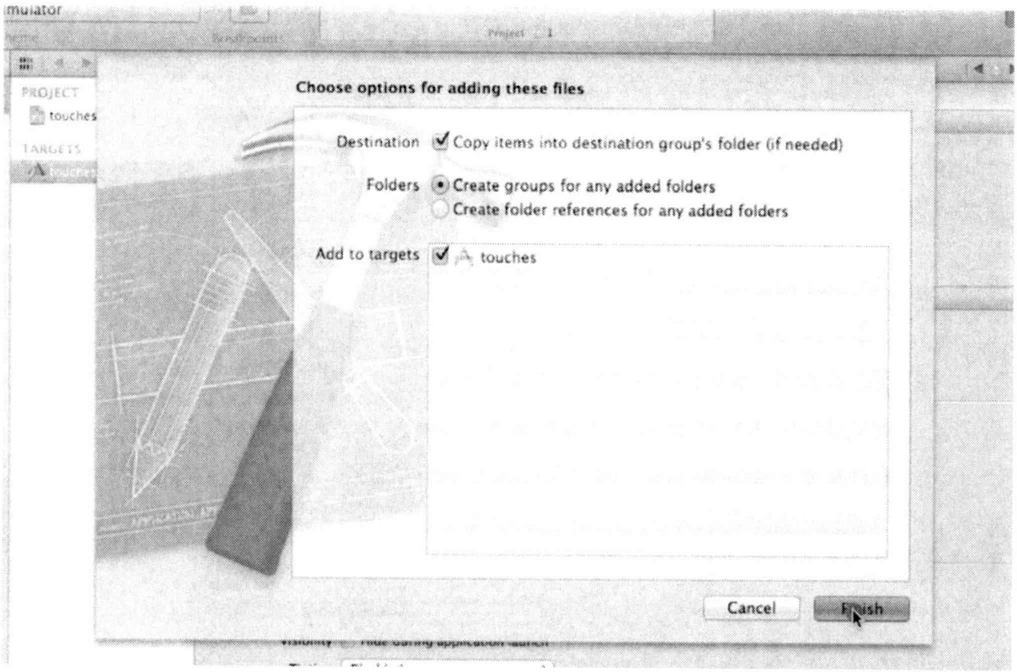

Figure 5-8. Check the "Copy items into the destination group's folder (if needed)" box

7. You now need to do a little housekeeping. Notice how the two icon files are
    in the root directory of touches? You don't want them there, so drag them
    over to your Supporting Files folder, as shown in Figure 5-9.

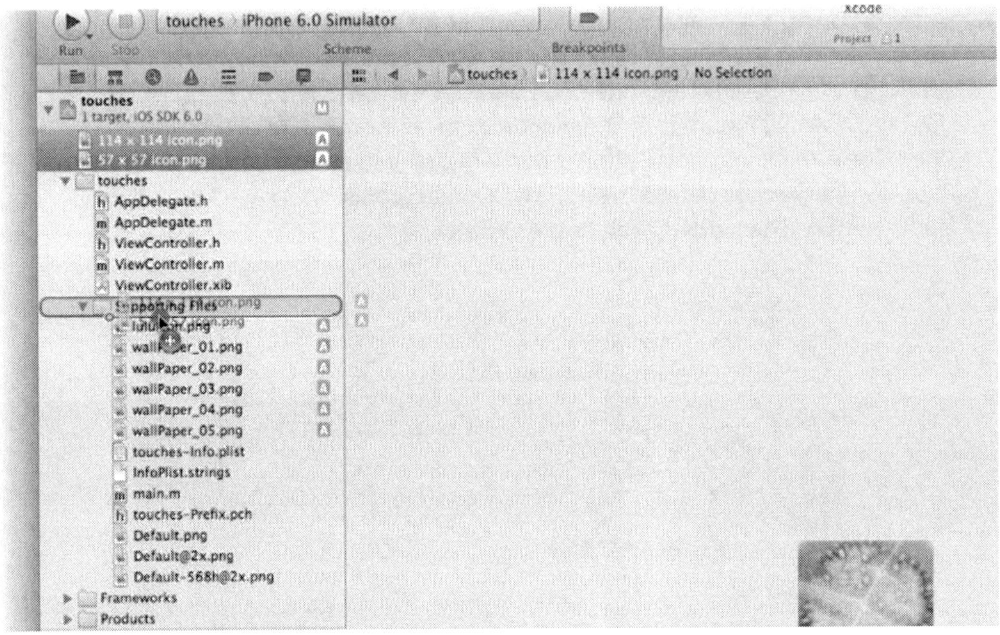

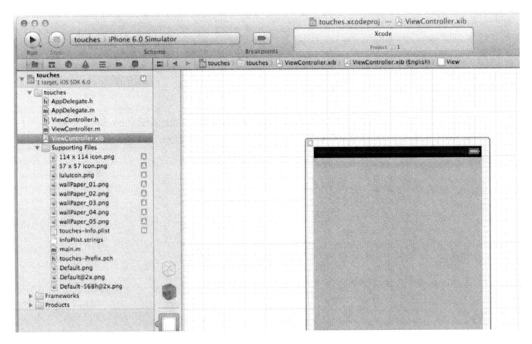

Figure 5-9. Drag icon files into the Supporting Files folder

8.   Now you want to open your `nib` file, as shown in Figure 5-10. You need more space, so, as you've done before, open the Utilities View so you can see the tools and icons you need to dress up the View Design area.

Figure 5-10. Click your nib file, open up the Utilities View, and close the Navigator View

9. With your Utilities pane open, drag a UIImageView onto your View Design area, as shown in Figure 5-11. The UIImageView will hold the current backgrounds you downloaded, named wallPaper_01 to wallPaper_05. Later, I explain how you'll write code that will determine which of the five background images will be housed on this UIImageView at any particular time. But you do know that the Change button will fire up the code that will switch the background, so you can guess that the next thing you need to do is drag some buttons onto the View Design area.

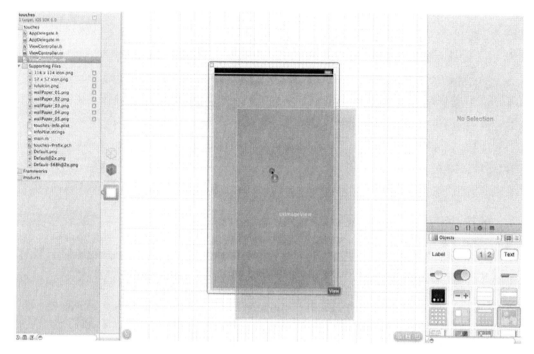

Figure 5-11. *Drag a UIImageView onto your View Design area*

> **Note**   Xcoders also call the View Design area the View screen or View frame. All those terms mean the same thing. I purposefully use the three terms interchangeably throughout this book.

10. As shown in Figure 5-12, start dragging the first of your three buttons onto the top of your View frame.

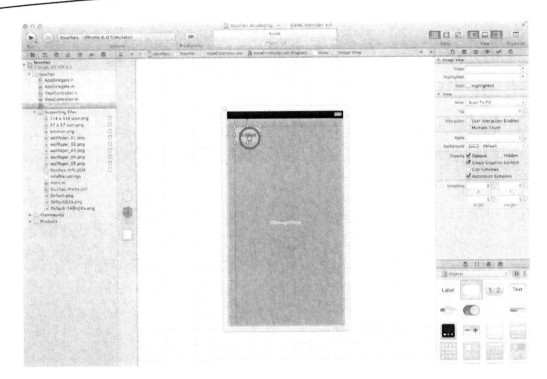

Figure 5-12. Drag the first of your three buttons onto your View Design area

11.   You'll want to keep the buttons in line with one another. Keep the outer two
buttons lined up with the outer margins and keep the center button centered
on the screen. The blue indicator lines will tell you when you move your
button close to the range of each of the respective boundaries. Once you've
positioned your three buttons onto your View frame, click the buttons and
name them Shrink, Hide, and Change, as illustrated in Figure 5-13.

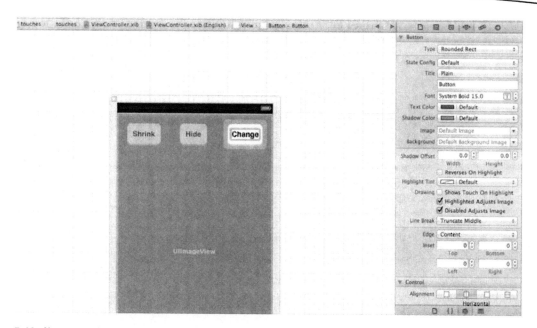

Figure 5-13. Name your three buttons Shrink, Hide, and Change

12. To associate the first wallpaper with the first UIImage you just brought in (your background image), click once on your background (UIImageView) and then go to the Image View and select wallpaper_01.png from the drop-down menu, as shown in Figure 5-14.

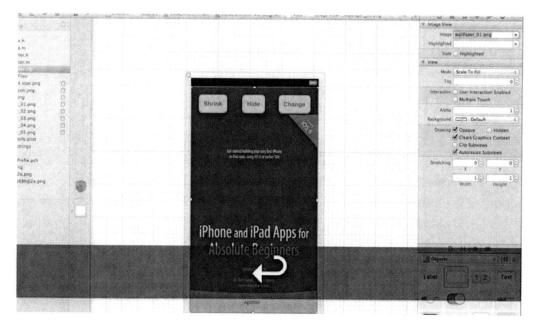

Figure 5-14. Associate your background image with wallPaper_01.png

13. You need another UIImageView to hold the lulu fruit icon that can be moved around with a finger, scaled with a button, and hidden with a button, so add another UIImageView onto your View frame, as shown in Figure 5-15.

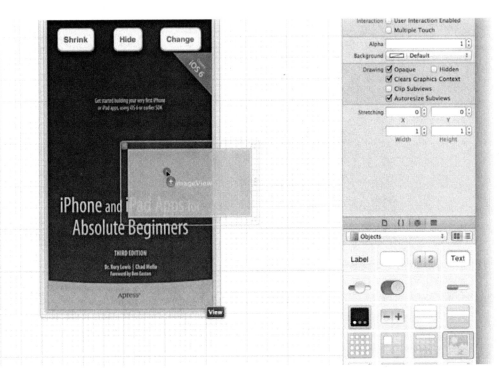

Figure 5-15. *Drag a second UIImageView onto your View Design area*

14. After the UIImageView frames appear, leave the Attributes dialog in your Utilities pane and click the Size Inspector (⌘⌥5); make the width of the lulu icon a square consisting of 112 × 112 pixels. Also, set the x-axis at 160 pixels from the left (centered) and the y-axis height to be 314 pixels down from the top of the View pane. You can either center the icon manually (as I do) or do it in the x-axis box. This is illustrated in Figure 5-16.

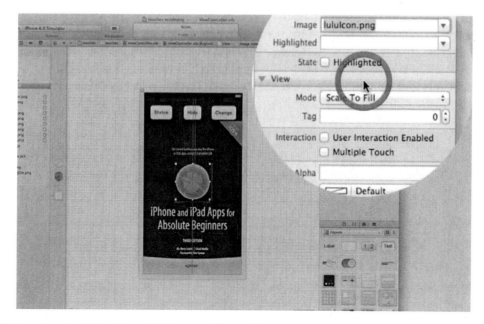

Figure 5-16. Size and locate luluIcon.png

15. With the second UIImageView selected, go to the Image drop-down menu in the Attributes dialog in your Utilities pane, as shown in Figure 5-17. Select the luluIcon.png to associate it with your second UIImageView.

Figure 5-17. Associate the lulu fruit icon with the second UIImageView

16. You're done dragging and positioning all the items necessary onto your nib. Now you need to connect these items to your code, as you've done before. You'll work on the ViewController header file. Open the Assistant and close the Inspector (arrows 1 and 2 respectively in Figure 5-18). Your screen will look similar to Figure 5-18.

Figure 5-18. Click the Assistant to bring up your touchesViewController header file

17. Before you bring in your outlets and actions, you need to create an array that will hold the background images. First, add curly brackets to the @interface directive and then drag in the first DemoMonkey file, named 01 ViewController.h @interface. As you drag it in-between the two curly brackets and let it go, there you'll see the code I typed in magically appear, as illustrated in Figure 5-19.

Figure 5-19. *Create two curly brackets and drag the array code from DemoMonkey*

> **Note**   If you've not already installed DemoMonkey, go back to the Chapter 1 section called "Installing DemoMonkey," located near Figure 1-17.

Now, in the DemoMonkey code you brought in (and as shown below), the NSArray brings in an *array*, a list of things that right now is empty and unnamed. You want the array to store the background images. You could give it any name you like, so let's call it something that denotes background images, such as bgImages. You need this array to be a pointer in the sense that it points to the address in memory where this list storing all your wallpapers is stored. So, add a star (*) there to call it a pointer. I go into this in more detail later, but for now, this is just perfect. Rename bgImages to *bgImages.

```
@interface ViewController : UIViewController{
    NSArray *bgImages;
    int currentBackground;
    bool hasMoved;
    bool hasShrunk;

    CGAffineTransform translate;
    CGAffineTransform sizeShrink;
    CGAffineTransform sizeGrow;
}
```

You also need to keep track of which background image is currently being displayed. For example, say that the third background in the sequence is currently the background image being displayed. Now say the user taps the Change button to see the next image. Because you know that background image number three is currently on the screen, you go to your array and get the next number background—background number four (that's why we make it an integer). It grabs that fourth background from NSArray *bgImages and puts it onto the screen. To do this you need an item that you'll call currentBackground (you could call it whatever you like, but let's call it that). Make it of type integer Int:

```
@interface ViewController : UIViewController{
    NSArray *bgImages;
    int currentBackground;
    bool hasMoved;
    bool hasShrunk;

    CGAffineTransform translate;
    CGAffineTransform sizeShrink;
    CGAffineTransform sizeGrow;
}
```

You also need to keep track of whether your icon moved or shrunk—yes or no, has it moved or shrunk? This is Boolean. You can give either of these Boolean types any name you like, but let's call them hasMoved and hasShrunk and make them of the Boolean type bool:

```
@interface ViewController : UIViewController{
    NSArray *bgImages;
    int currentBackground;
    bool hasMoved;
    bool hasShrunk;

    CGAffineTransform translate;
    CGAffineTransform sizeShrink;
    CGAffineTransform sizeGrow;
}
```

You also need to have three means of manipulating the lulu fruit icon. One to translate it, one to shrink it, and one to grow it. You'll use CGAffines, as explained at the beginning of the chapter. As you manipulate it in your implementation file, this will all make more sense. For now though, move on and create your outlets and actions.

```
@interface ViewController : UIViewController{
    NSArray *bgImages;
    int currentBackground;
    bool hasMoved;
    bool hasShrunk;

    CGAffineTransform translate;
    CGAffineTransform sizeShrink;
    CGAffineTransform sizeGrow;
}
```

18. Before, when you've reached this juncture, I've instructed you to just blindly start Control-dragging outlets and action into your header file. This time, I want you to think about what you're going to do, so you can fuse synapses in your brain and understand how to create a robust header file. To recap what you've done in the past, I fed you a ration of outlets and actions using the following very broad criteria:

    ▦ Outlets to connect nib file members with your UIImageView's code, which the clever people at Apple wrote for you

    ▦ Actions to connect your buttons with code you write in the implementation file

Now, it's time to grow up and move on. Remember how I mentioned that when you tap the Shrink button, it shrinks the lulu fruit icon and the text inside it changes to *Grow*—and then when you tap the button again, the icon grows? Well, you'll use the code the folks at Apple wrote that allows you to do cool things like change the colors, text, and other appearances inside a button.

Note   This code provided by Apple is located in a class called UIButton. When you use this code, we say you're using an *instance of* UIButton. In short, you need an outlet for your Change button so you can change the text in it from *Shrink* to *Grow*.

You'll also need an outlet for the lulu fruit icon, of course, and the background that will hold whatever WallPaper_0x.png is being used. So, you'll need three outlets. You now have six items:

    ▦ An array you'll call bgImages

    ▦ A way to keep track of the currentBackground

    ▦ The state of hasMoved

    ▦ The state of Shrunk

    ▦ A way to transform translate (the position of the lulu fruit icon)

    ▦ A way to transform size (the size of the lulu fruit icon)

So how do you do this? Backtracking a little, after you've correctly Control-dragged your four outlets into the header, it will look something like this:

```
IBOutlet UIImageView *some variable name for our background;
IBOutlet UIImageView *some variable name for our icon;
IBOutlet UIButton *some variable name to change the text in the Shrink button;
IBOutlet UIButton *some variable name to change the text in the Shrink button;
```

Yup! You need to give each of these outlets variable names. Let's use myBackground for the background, myIcon for the icon, hideButton for the button that fades out and hides the lulu fruit icon, and shrinkButton for the button that shrinks the lulu fruit icon. You could use different names, but do that later. Just follow along with me now and remember that it will look something like the following once you drag and associate these outlets into the header file:

```
IBOutlet UIImageView *myBackground;
IBOutlet UIImageView *myIcon;
IBOutlet UIButton *shrinkButton;
IBOutlet UIButton *hideButton;
```

Insofar as the actions for the three buttons are concerned, they stay the same. You'll still have three actions for your three buttons sitting right after and outside the @properties directive, and the code will look something like this:

```
- (IBAction) some variable name for the Shrink button:(id)sender;
- (IBAction) some variable name for the Hide button:(id)sender;
- (IBAction) some variable name for the Change button:(id)sender;
```

Yup! You need to give each of these actions variable names. Let's use shrink for the Shrink button, hide for the Hide button, and change for the Change button. Again, you could use different variable names here, but for now just follow along with me. It will look like this:

```
- (IBAction)shrink:(id)sender;
- (IBAction)hide:(id)sender;
- (IBAction)change:(id)sender;
```

Let's get to it. Start off by Control-dragging from your background to the @interface directive, as illustrated in Figure 5-20.

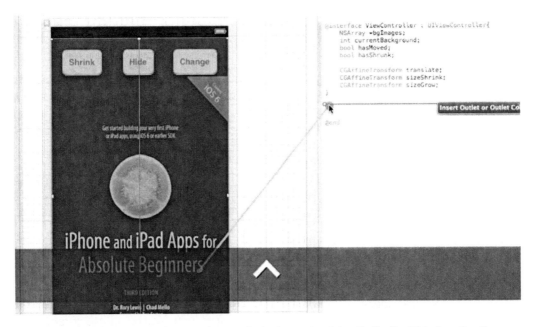

Figure 5-20. Control-drag a connection from anywhere on the background and drop it after the @interface directive

Note   You may have noticed that sometimes I say, *Control-drag a connection from _____ in Interface Builder into your header file*, and other times I say, *Control-drag a connection from _____ in Interface Builder into the View Design area*. This is not to confuse you; it's to let you know that they mean the same thing, and you may work for, hire, or meet people who use one or the other in their nomenclature.

19.   You need to connect the `UIImageView` you dragged into the View Design area after the `@interface` directive that has your array code in it. When you reel the fishing line into your `@property`, keep it as an outlet and name it `myBackground`, as shown in Figure 5-21.

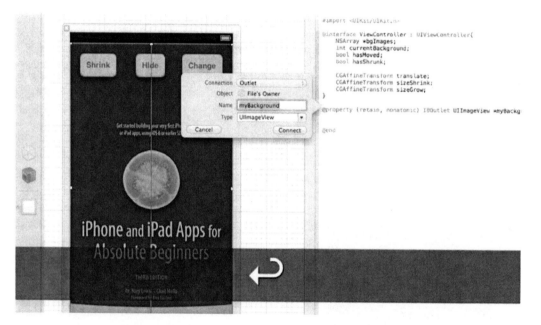

Figure 5-21. Name the outlet myBackground

20.   Control-drag from your icon to the View Design area, as shown in Figure 5-22. Keep it as an outlet and name it `myIcon`.

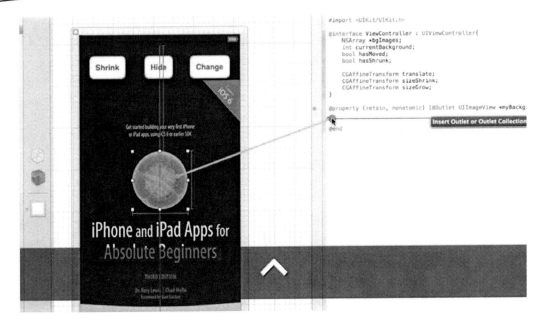

Figure 5-22. Keep the icon as an outlet and name it myIcon

21. As shown in Figure 5-23, after clicking the Shrink button in Interface Builder once, Control-drag into your header.

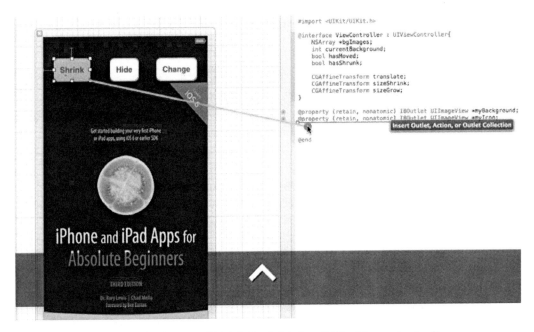

Figure 5-23. Control-drag a connection from your Shrink button in Interface Builder into your header file

Drop it and name it shrinkButton. Now, repeat that to enable you to also change the text in the Hide button.

22. Control drag from the Hide button and name it hideButton, as shown in Figure 5-24. You should have four outlets now as follows:

```
@property (retain, nonatomic) IBOutlet UIImageView *myBackground;
@property (retain, nonatomic) IBOutlet UIImageView *myIcon;
@property (retain, nonatomic) IBOutlet UIButton *shrinkButton;
@property (retain, nonatomic) IBOutlet UIButton *hideButton;
```

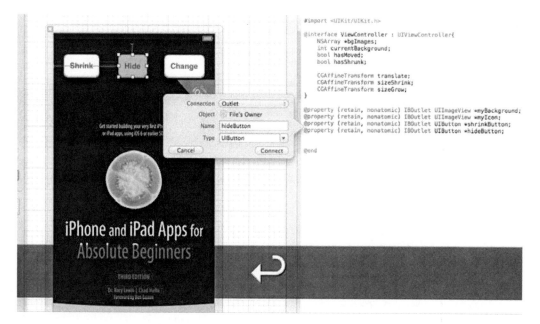

Figure 5-24. Finish outlets by naming the hideButton

23. Now you'll make three actions for your three buttons. Control-drag from the Shrink button to your header file, drop it in, and change it to an action by selecting Action from the Connection drop-down menu. Call it shrink, as shown in Figure 5-25. Repeat this for the Hide button: make it an action, name it hide, and then, as you did before, Control-drag in from the Change button.

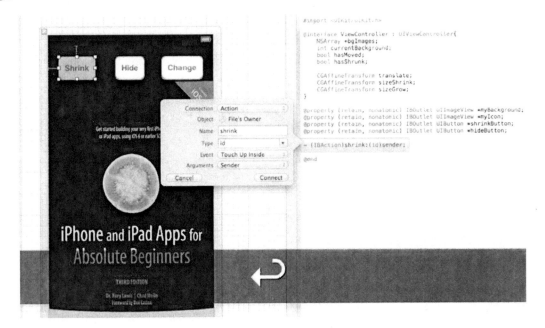

Figure 5-25. Now for the actions: Control-drag a connection from the Shrink button in Interface Builder into your header file

24. After you've Control-dragged into the header from the Change button and made it an action, name it change, as shown in Figure 5-26. You should have three actions as follows:

- (IBAction)shrink:(id)sender;
- (IBAction)hide:(id)sender;
- (IBAction)change:(id)sender;

Figure 5-26. *Name the Change button change*

With this done, you're now finished coding your header file. Before moving on to the implementation file, I strongly encourage you to check every letter, space, semicolon, empty line, and comma of your header code against mine. This is how your header file should look:

```
#import <UIKit/UIKit.h>

@interface ViewController : UIViewController{
    NSArray *bgImages;
    int currentBackground;
    bool hasMoved;
    bool hasShrunk;

    CGAffineTransform translate;
    CGAffineTransform sizeShrink;
    CGAffineTransform sizeGrow;
}

@property (retain, nonatomic) IBOutlet UIImageView *myBackground;
@property (retain, nonatomic) IBOutlet UIImageView *myIcon;
@property (retain, nonatomic) IBOutlet UIButton *shrinkButton;
@property (retain, nonatomic) IBOutlet UIButton *hideButton;

- (IBAction)shrink:(id)sender;
- (IBAction)hide:(id)sender;
- (IBAction)change:(id)sender;

@end
```

Once you're confident that every line of your code matches mine, you need to start getting your View area ready to do some huge coding.

Coding the Implementation File

The implementation file for this project has more code in it than all the code you've coded so far put together. So don't freak out. You'll code five things:

- The viewDidLoad and the array that holds your background images

- The code to move the icon around with your finger

- The code to make things shrink and grow

- The code that makes things fade and then come back

- The code that changes the backgrounds

25. Now and only now that you've correctly created and defined your variables do you open the implementation file, as shown in Figure 5-27.

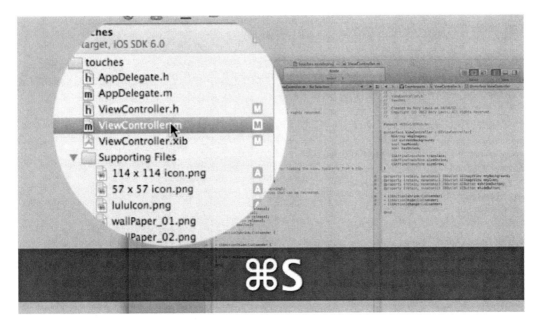

Figure 5-27. Open the implementation file

26. As shown in Figure 5-28, open the Standard editor. The first thing you'll code is the viewDidLoad method. You'll go through this meticulously, but first drag in the DemoMonkey code and make sure it's in the correct place. Then you'll go through each line of the code.

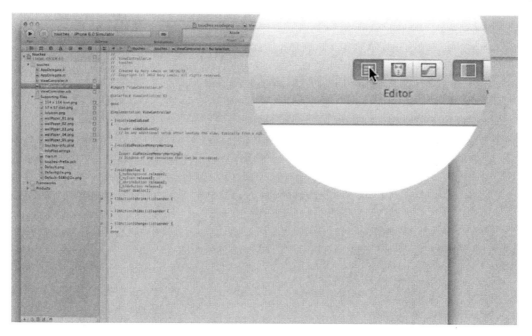

Figure 5-28. *Change to the Standard editor*

27. Once your view loads, you need to clean things up and insert your array. Go to the ViewDidLoad method right at the top of the implementation file. Delete the comment code that says Do any additional setup after loading the view, typically from a nib.

```
- (void)viewDidLoad
{
    [super viewDidLoad];
    // Do any additional setup after loading the view, typically from a nib.
}
```

In its place drag in the DemoMonkey file named 02 ViewController.m viewDidLoad, as shown In Figure 5-29.

```
- (void)viewDidLoad
{
    [super viewDidLoad];
    02 ViewController.m viewDidLoad.
}
```

```
@interface ViewController ()

@end

@implementation ViewController

- (void)viewDidLoad
{
    [super viewDidLoad];
    |        02 ViewController.m viewDidLoad
}

- (void)didReceiveMemoryWarning
{
    [super didReceiveMemoryWarning];
    // Dispose of any resources that can be recreated.
}

- (void)dealloc {
    [_myBackground release];
    [_myIcon release];
    [_shrinkButton release];
    [_hideButton release];
    [super dealloc];
}
- (IBAction)shrink:(id)sender {
}
```

Figure 5-29. Drag in the viewDidLoad code from DemoMonkey

28.   With your screen looking like Figure 5-30, let's look at what you did.

```
@interface ViewController ()

@end

@implementation ViewController

- (void)viewDidLoad
{
    [super viewDidLoad];
    hasMoved = NO;
    hasShrunk = NO;
    currentBackground = 0;

    bgImages = [[NSArray alloc] initWithObjects:
                [UIImage imageNamed:@"WallPaper_01.png"],
                [UIImage imageNamed:@"WallPaper_02.png"],
                [UIImage imageNamed:@"WallPaper_03.png"],
                [UIImage imageNamed:@"WallPaper_04.png"],
                [UIImage imageNamed:@"WallPaper_05.png"],
                nil];

    sizeShrink = CGAffineTransformMakeScale(.25, .25);
    sizeGrow = CGAffineTransformMakeScale(1, 1);

    _myBackground.image = [bgImages objectAtIndex:currentBackground];
}
```

Figure 5-30. *The array code in its correct place in viewDidLoad*

viewDidLoad

The code inside the viewDidLoad method runs after machine language code reserves some space in memory for your view. Notice that the first thing called inside viewDidLoad is its superclass, superviewDidLoad. Now, before you get nervous after reading the word *superclass*, think of it this way: just as rats are a subclass of rodents, viewDidLoad is a subclass of superviewDidLoad. So, the first thing viewDidLoad does is call all the code from its superclass. It's here, at this exact moment, that you need to perform five tasks:

```
- (void)viewDidLoad
{
    [super viewDidLoad];
```

Set all your button and backgrounds to the start state
Create an array with all *your* wallpapers inside of it
Set how much the *Shrink* button will shrink the lulu fruit icon
Set how much the *Grow* button will grow the lulu fruit icon
Set the background image to the current background image

```
}
```

Set Buttons and Backgrounds to the Start State: Setting all your buttons and backgrounds to their start state creates a clean slate before the program starts to run. To create a clean slate in code, you need to set your state-changing variables to 0 (zero or nil). You have three such variables that tell you whether a state has changed hasMoved, hasShrunk, and currentBackground. Remember that both hasMoved and hasShrunk are Booleans, so they can either be YES or NO. The obvious start state for these is that they have not been moved yet. So, you need to set both hasMoved and hasShrunk to NO. This leaves you with currentBackground, which keeps track of which one of your five wallpapers is currently in the background being viewed by the user. Recall that you assigned currentBackground to be of type integer. Easy: set it to 0 (zero). See the following bold section of code:

```
- (void)viewDidLoad
{
    [super viewDidLoad];
    hasMoved = NO;
    hasShrunk = NO;
    currentBackground = 0;

Create an array with all our wallpapers inside of it
Set how much the shrink button will shrink the lulu fruit icon
Set how much the grow button will grow the lulu fruit icon
Set the background image to the current background image
}
```

Create the Array with All Your Wallpapers Inside It: It's time to create an *array*, which is just a list of things, and fill it up with your wallpapers. The technical way to say that is *You need to create an* NSArray object *and initialize it with some objects of type* png. That's not too obtuse, is it? Recall that you did declare the array in your header file. Often, students are so fearful of arrays that they forget to declare them when they write their exam code. In the header file, you wrote NSArray *bgImages, so you've declared an array and called it bgImages. You need to write bgImages = (the stuff that will make your array come to life). There are many complex ways to use arrays, but you'll use the plain cheeseburger . . . or should I say Apple . . . methods using the NSArray initializers. They're pretty much the same as the factory methods, only you do the allocation yourself, which is in the form of NSArray:

```
name of your array = [[NSArray alloc] initWithObjects: @"your 1st object", @" your 2nd object ",
@" your 3rd object "... , @" your 2nd to last object ",@" your last object ", nil];
```

That looks all cluttered. At the end of it, you'll see that all your objects are separated by commas; then you tell the array it's ended by putting that nil at the end. Let's do two things here. First, plug the real name of your array—bgImages—into the template and then take the contents between these commas and place them onto their own separate lines and see if this makes more sense:

```
bgImages array  = [[NSArray alloc] initWithObjects:
@"your 1st object",
@" your 2nd object ",
@" your 3rd object ",
•
•
•
@" your 2nd to last object ",
@" your last object ",
nil];
```

Pretty cool, huh?! This really spooky code is actually making sense to you! Yeah! You're not quite there yet, though. You need to do one more thing before you bring this array to life. Wrap your head around the UIImage class reference, which is an object the folks at Apple wrote to display images. Your objects are images, but really, they're filenames that contain images. You need to use the UIImage together with a method called imageNamed that returns image objects connected to filenames. So, for each filename, you need to use UIImage imageNamed. I've illustrated this as follows:

```
name of your array  = [[NSArray alloc] initWithObjects:
[UIImage imageNamed:@ "WallPaper_01.png "],
[UIImage imageNamed:@ "WallPaper_02.png "],
[UIImage imageNamed:@ "WallPaper_03.png "],
[UIImage imageNamed:@ "WallPaper_04.png "],
[UIImage imageNamed:@ "WallPaper_05.png "],
nil];
```

With that code, you've created an array that contains your five images. All you need to do now is insert it into your code. See the following bold code lines:

```
- (void)viewDidLoad
{
    [super viewDidLoad];
    hasMoved = NO;
    hasShrunk = NO;
    currentBackground = 0;

bgImages = [[NSArray alloc] initWithObjects:
                [UIImage imageNamed:@ "WallPaper_01.png "],
                [UIImage imageNamed:@ "WallPaper_02.png "],
                [UIImage imageNamed:@ "WallPaper_03.png "],
                [UIImage imageNamed:@ "WallPaper_04.png "],
                [UIImage imageNamed:@ "WallPaper_05.png "],
                nil];

sizeShrink = CGAffineTransformMakeScale(.25, .25);
sizeGrow = CGAffineTransformMakeScale(1, 1);

_myBackground.image = [bgImages objectAtIndex:currentBackground];
}
```

Set How Much You'll Shrink the Lulu Fruit Icon: It's really easy to set how much you'll shrink the lulu fruit icon when the Shrink button is tapped. Remember from the beginning of this chapter how CGAffine is able to obey you when you instruct it to change your object's position, angle, shape, scale, and so on? Well, now you're going to use it. I've randomly decided to shrink the lulu fruit icon by 25 percent. This means you need to tell CGAffine two things: first, that you want to scale the image, and second, how much you want to scale it on the x- and y-axes. You want to use CGAffine to scale the stuff you use . . . hmmm . . . let's guess . . . Ah! How about CGAffineTransformMakeScale? Yes! You're correct.

Now for the next assignment. To scale the image by 25 percent, you need to scale both the x- and y-axes equally at 0.25; but before you enter this into the code, remember in your header file you created a variable called sizeShrink of type CGAffineTransformMakeScale. You'll we need to set the

sizeShrink variable equal to the 25 percent shrinkage you tell the CGAffineTransformMakeScale code
to perform. This is illustrated by the following:

```
- (void)viewDidLoad
{
    [super viewDidLoad];
    hasMoved = NO;
    hasShrunk = NO;
    currentBackground = 0;

bgImages = [[NSArray alloc] initWithObjects:
                [UIImage imageNamed:@ "WallPaper_01.png "],
                [UIImage imageNamed:@ "WallPaper_02.png "],
                [UIImage imageNamed:@ "WallPaper_03.png "],
                [UIImage imageNamed:@ "WallPaper_04.png "],
                [UIImage imageNamed:@ "WallPaper_05.png "],
                nil];

sizeShrink = CGAffineTransformMakeScale(.25, .25);
sizeGrow = CGAffineTransformMakeScale(1, 1);

_myBackground.image = [bgImages objectAtIndex:currentBackground];
}
```

Set How Much You'll Grow the Lulu Fruit Icon: This is really simple. After you shrink the icon, the text
in the button changes to *Grow*. You then tap the Grow button, and it goes from 25 percent back to
100 percent, or 1.

```
- (void)viewDidLoad
{
    [super viewDidLoad];
    hasMoved = NO;
    hasShrunk = NO;
    currentBackground = 0;

bgImages = [[NSArray alloc] initWithObjects:
                [UIImage imageNamed:@ "WallPaper_01.png "],
                [UIImage imageNamed:@ "WallPaper_02.png "],
                [UIImage imageNamed:@ "WallPaper_03.png "],
                [UIImage imageNamed:@ "WallPaper_04.png "],
                [UIImage imageNamed:@ "WallPaper_05.png "],
                nil];

sizeShrink = CGAffineTransformMakeScale(.25, .25);
sizeGrow = CGAffineTransformMakeScale(1, 1);

_myBackground.image = [bgImages objectAtIndex:currentBackground];
}
```

Set the Background Image to the Current Background Image: The last job we need to do in the viewDidLoad is set the background image to the current background image. What does that mean? You may be scratching your head, but think about it. You've created an array that holds your five images. You'll set each of those images with a number. When you tap the Change button, whatever number image is on your background will be replaced by the next one. You've set currentBackground to 0 (zero). So, the first time somebody taps the Change button, it uses the code (that you have yet to code) to change the currentBackground from 0 to 0+1, which means that the current background will now be the next background in the array. This is how to use it now and later on your own: your variable that contains your image will be equal to [bgImagesobjectAtIndex: your variable that in your case holds the background image]. Don't think about it too much. Just use it as illustrated in the following code. If you do want to think about this now, Dave, Jack, Jeff, and Fredrik explain this in their Apress book (*Beginning iOS 6 Development: Exploring the iOS SDK*):

```
- (void)viewDidLoad
{
    [super viewDidLoad];
    hasMoved = NO;
    hasShrunk = NO;
    currentBackground = 0;

bgImages = [[NSArray alloc] initWithObjects:
                [UIImage imageNamed:@ "WallPaper_01.png "],
                [UIImage imageNamed:@ "WallPaper_02.png "],
                [UIImage imageNamed:@ "WallPaper_03.png "],
                [UIImage imageNamed:@ "WallPaper_04.png "],
                [UIImage imageNamed:@ "WallPaper_05.png "],
                nil];

sizeShrink = CGAffineTransformMakeScale(.25, .25);
sizeGrow = CGAffineTransformMakeScale(1, 1);

_myBackground.image = [bgImages objectAtIndex:currentBackground];
}
```

Coding the touchesMoved Method

Now you're going to code the touchesMoved method. Yes, I know you don't even see it yet! What I want you to do after deleting the appropriate code in your viewDidload is scroll down through all the methods Apple instantiated for you. Now you'll see three methods for your three actions you created in the header file for your three buttons.

```
- (IBAction)shrink:(id)sender {
}
- (IBAction)Hide:(id)sender {
}
- (IBAction)change:(id)sender {
}

@end
```

This is really great because you'll place all your code inside these methods. But hold on—you're missing the method that will handle your touching and moving the lulu fruit icon with your fingertip. Yup, you need to create that from scratch.

29.   You now need to create a method that will allow the user to touch the lulu fruit icon and move it around the screen with their finger. Make some space between the end of the dealloc and shrink methods and drag the DemoMonkey file named 03 ViewController.m touches into that space you created, as shown in Figure 5-31. Okay—let's talk about coding the touchesMoved method:

```
- (void)dealloc {
    [_myBackground release];
    [_myIcon release];
    [_shrinkButton release];
    [_hideButton release];
    [super dealloc];
}

-(void) touchesMoved:(NSSet *)touches withEvent:(UIEvent *)event{
    UITouch *touch = [[event allTouches] anyObject];

    if (CGRectContainsPoint([_myIcon frame], [touch locationInView:nil]))
    {
        if (hasMoved == YES && hasShrunk == YES) {
            _myIcon.transform = CGAffineTransformTranslate(sizeShrink, 0, 0);
            hasMoved = NO;
        }

        if (hasMoved == YES && hasShrunk == NO) {
            _myIcon.transform = translate;
            hasMoved = NO;
        }

        _myIcon.center = [touch locationInView:nil];
    }
}

-(IBAction)shrink:(id)sender {
}
```

Figure 5-31. Make space for the touchesMoved method

Let's look at it from a high altitude to start off with. Also, pretend you're typing it from scratch, something many of my students do. With your code there, follow along and type the following underneath it. What do you want the touchesMoved method to do? Well, it may not seem obvious, but you simply want the touches method to do the following:

```
-(void) touchesMoved:(NSSet *)touches withEvent:(UIEvent *)event{
Grab code that can sense all touches on the screen
Check if a touch on the screen is on the lulu fruit icon. If yes then
Check if icon was hid and shrunk using buttons if yes then
Keep shrunk size and Hide icon to its position before Hide button
Check if icon was hid and not shrunk using buttons if yes then
Hide icon to its position before Hide button
Set icon to be at the current touch location
}
```

Part of my teaching method is that I don't always teach you everything. You've seen this already when you blindly coded the first couple of Hello Worlds. Now I'm going to teach you how to use certain tools to perform tasks. I won't teach you how all these tools work right now, but I will teach you what tool to grab. At this point, you need to get code that can sense all touches on the screen. Remember that when you want the user interface to do cool stuff with touches, you need to first call the code Apple wrote that senses and records all touches. So, type UITouches, and one of the options the code completion will present is UITouch *touch = [[event allTouches] anyObject]. That's the tool I want you to invoke before you do anything with touches. Don't think about how it works right now. Just know to call it at this point. See the bold code lines in the following example:

```
-(void) touchesMoved:(NSSet *)touches withEvent:(UIEvent *)event{
UITouch *touch = [[event allTouches] anyObject];
Check if a touch on the screen is on the lulu fruit icon. If yes then
Check if icon was moved and shrunk using buttons if yes then
Keep shrunk size and move icon to its new position
Check if icon was moved and not shrunk using buttons if yes then
move icon to its new position
Set icon to be at the current touch location
}
```

Now you need an if statement to check whether a touch on the screen is on the lulu fruit icon. You need to know that the iPhone looks at the rectangle that your object fits into and check whether the person's finger is within that rectangle. To do that, you use if (CGRectContainsPoint([myIcon frame], [touch locationInView:nil])). You only need to type in if and CGRect, and then *touch and code completion* will fill in the rest. You'll nest two more if statements inside this if statement. Notice how your road map tasks are nested inside this if statement, as illustrated in the following:

```
-(void) touchesMoved:(NSSet *)touches withEvent:(UIEvent *)event{
UITouch *touch = [[event allTouches] anyObject];
    if (CGRectContainsPoint([myIcon frame], [touch locationInView:nil]))
    {
Check if icon was moved and shrunk using buttons if yes then {
Keep shrunk size and move icon to its new position
}

Check if icon was moved and not shrunk using buttons if yes then {
move icon to its new position
}
Set icon to be at the current touch location
}
}
```

At this point, you need to insert two nested conditions inside the if statement you just created. But think about this. All you want to do is test to see whether the lulu fruit icon has been moved by the buttons, and if it has, regardless of whether it's been shrunk, you need to reset whether it was moved back to a state in which it hadn't moved. The two conditions that would have moved the lulu fruit icon are:

- When you moved it and shrank it
- When you moved it and didn't shrink it

Either way, you want to change the state to not being moved so that when the user's finger touches the lulu fruit icon, you can say, "You were not moved but now you are being moved." You can't say, "You were moved and now you're being moved again."

```
-(void) touchesMoved:(NSSet *)touches withEvent:(UIEvent *)event{
UITouch *touch = [[event allTouches] anyObject];

    if (CGRectContainsPoint([myIcon frame], [touch locationInView:nil]))
    {
        if (hasMoved == YES && hasShrunk == YES) {
            _myIcon.transform = CGAffineTransformTranslate(size, 0, 0);
            hasMoved = NO;
}

 if (hasMoved == YES && hasShrunk == NO) {
            _myIcon.transform = translate;
            hasMoved = NO;
    }

Set icon to be at the current touch location
}
}
```

> **Note** In the video, in the second if statement, I write myIcon.transform = translate, and not
> CGAffineTransformMakeTranslation(0,0);. It doesn't make too much difference, but it's better
> to use the latter because this is the new way of programming Xcode (letting Xcode instantiate the make
> translation portion for the compiler). In the code that you download, it's the latter.

The last thing you need to do is set the location of the icon to the exact position that the fingertip is moving it at any moment. This is stock boilerplate code that you will use over and over again to keep track of an object as a fingertip moves it around the screen. You use variable name.center = [touch locationInView:nil], as indicated in the following code:

```
-(void) touchesMoved:(NSSet *)touches withEvent:(UIEvent *)event{
UITouch *touch = [[event allTouches] anyObject];

    if (CGRectContainsPoint([myIcon frame], [touch locationInView:nil]))
    {
        if (hasMoved == YES && hasShrunk == YES) {
            _myIcon.transform = CGAffineTransformTranslate(size, 0, 0);
            hasMoved = NO;
}
```

```
if (hasMoved == YES && hasShrunk == NO) {
        _myIcon.transform = translate;
        hasMoved = NO;
    }

_myIcon.center = [touch locationInView:nil];
    }
}
```

You've now completed writing the touchesMoved method. Compare your code to how mine looks in Figure 5-31.

30. Drag the DemoMonkey file named 04 ViewController.m shrink into the implementation file, as shown in Figure 5-32.

Figure 5-32. Bring in the shrink method code

Coding the Shrink Button

You now want to write the code you'll invoke once the user taps the Shrink button. Remember how, in the header file, you created an outlet that lets you to change the label's text from *Shrink* to *Grow* when the button is tapped? That's because you can't allow the lulu fruit to be shrunk twice in a row or it would virtually disappear! So, you need to change the text. The second thing you need to do is keep track of the possible states of the Shrink and Hide buttons so you can tell the CGAffine to properly transform the lulu fruit icon for you. The code looks something like this:

```
-(IBAction)shrink:(id)sender
{
if it has not been shrunk, keep the text saying Shrink, else change it to Grow
if it has not been shrunk  - do stuff
else - do stuff
}
```

To change the text, you'll use the setTitle and forState:UIControlStateNormal with the following format: your variable namesetTitle:@"your text" forState:UIControlStateNormal. You've called the outlet for your Shrink button, shrinkButton, when you declared it many years ago in the header file. The text you'll use will be *Grow* once it's been changed, and then *Shrink* once it's been changed again; this loop continues forever, as illustrated by the following:

```
-(IBAction)shrink:(id)sender
{
    if (hasShrunk) {
        [_shrinkButton setTitle:@"Shrink" forState:UIControlStateNormal];
    } else {
        [_shrinkButton setTitle:@"Grow" forState:UIControlStateNormal];
    }

if it has not been shrunk  - do stuff
else - do stuff
}
```

You'll set the animation to null, update the animation, center the icon, grow or shrink it depending on whether it's already shrunk or not, and then change the status of shrunk or not to the opposite.

```
- (IBAction)shrink:(id)sender {
    if (hasShrunk) {
        [_shrinkButton setTitle:@"Shrink" forState:UIControlStateNormal];
    } else{
        [_shrinkButton setTitle:@"Grow" forState:UIControlStateNormal];
    }

    if (hasShrunk == NO) {
        [UIView beginAnimations:nil context:NULL];
        [UIView setAnimationDuration:1.0];
        _myIcon.Center = CGPointMake(0,0);
        _myIcon.transform = CGAffineTransformTranslate(sizeShrink,165,0);
        [UIView commitAnimations];
        hasShrunk = YES;
    }

    else {
        [UIView beginAnimations:nil context:NULL];
        [UIView setAnimationDuration:1.0];
        _myIcon.Center = CGPointMake(0,0);
```

```
_myIcon.transform = _myIcon.transform = CGAffineTransformTranslate(sizeGrow,0,0);
[UIView commitAnimations];
hasShrunk = NO;
    }

}
```

31. Make some space between the curly brackets in the hide method. Then drag the DemoMonkey file named 05 ViewController.m hide into that space you created, as shown in Figure 5-33.

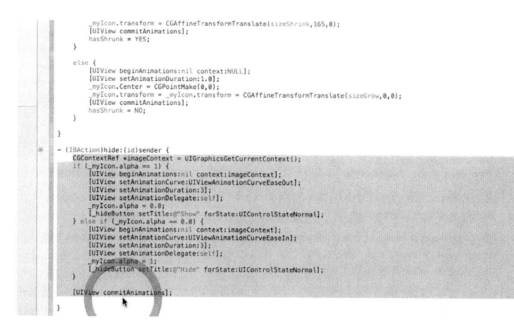

Figure 5-33. *Coding the Hide button that makes the icon fade in and out*

Coding the Hide Button

Causing an object to fade in and out of sight can create some pretty cool effects that come in handy for games and animations. Because you have only one button in this example that does both, you toggle between hiding your icon and showing it. You do this by keying off of the alpha value of your icon. If the alpha value is 1 (100 percent visible to the user), you'll fade it out of view by gradually changing alpha from 1 to 0 (0 percent visible to the user). To get the icon to reappear, gradually change alpha from 0 to 1 over three seconds.

Doing that is rather simple but requires an understanding of how to use animations in Objective-C. First, you must tell the UIView object the context on which to perform drawing or animations. In this case, it's the same context that your ViewController object is under. The imageContext variable will hold this information after you've assigned it the current context:

```
CGContextRef imageContext = UIGraphicsGetCurrentContext();
```

The first part of your function will handle the case where the icon is currently visible; it will fade the icon from the user's sight. Look at this code:

```
if (_myIcon.alpha == 1) {
     [UIView beginAnimations:nil context:imageContext];
     [UIView setAnimationCurve:UIViewAnimationCurveEaseOut];
     [UIView setAnimationDuration:3];
     [UIView setAnimationDelegate:self];
     _myIcon.alpha = 0.0;
    [_hideButton setTitle:@"Show" forState:UIControlStateNormal];
```

That code tells the view to start the animation sequence using your current graphics context. Notice how you pass imageContext into the beginAnimation method; this method tells the UIView object to prepare for animation. The UIView will remember the current state of everything within the current context. Next, set your animation curve. The animation curve indicates how you want your animation to progress over time. In this case, you're using UIViewAnimationCurveEaseOut. An ease-out curve causes an animation to quickly begin and then slow down as it completes. There are other curves as well. Apple describes them as follows:

- UIViewAnimationCurveEaseInOut: An ease-in ease-out curve causes the animation to begin slowly, accelerate through the middle of its duration, and then slow again before completing. This is the default curve for most animations.

- UIViewAnimationCurveEaseIn: An ease-in curve causes the animation to begin slowly and then speed up as it progresses.

- UIViewAnimationCurveLinear: A linear animation curve causes an animation to occur evenly over its duration. You can try using these last two curves on your own to see how they affect your animations.

setAnimationDuration tells the UIView how long the animation sequence will be. In our case, it will be three seconds. It will take three seconds to fade out the icon. Because your UIViewController has the built-in ability to handle the animation details, you tell the UIView that the ViewController will handle any technical details for you by setting setAnimationDelegate to self.

Finally, you set the alpha value of your icon to 0. So, when your last line in the function, [UIView commitAnimations], is invoked, the icon's alpha value will slowly change from 1 to 0 over three seconds. When commitAnimations is invoked, the UIView applies your changes to the icon while transitioning from the starting state (alpha = 1) to the final state (alpha = 0).

The button text is changed to reflect the fact that the icon is no longer visible; the user will have to tap Show to bring it back. To get the icon to come back, simply execute the following code; it's very similar to the preceding code, except now it's fading the icon back into view by changing alpha from 0 to 1 over three seconds:

```
else if (_myIcon.alpha == 0.0) {
     [UIView beginAnimations:nil context:imageContext];
     [UIView setAnimationCurve:UIViewAnimationCurveEaseIn];
     [UIView setAnimationDuration:3];
     [UIView setAnimationDelegate:self];
     _myIcon.alpha = 1;
     [_hideButton setTitle:@"Hide" forState:UIControlStateNormal];
```

It's amazing how astonishing these effects can look in apps with just a little code that describes in simple terms how you want things to unfold!

32. Make some space between the curly brackets in the change method. Then drag the DemoMonkey file named 06 ViewController.m change into that space you created, as shown in Figure 5-34.

Figure 5-34. Code the Change button

Coding the Change Button

The only thing left to do now is to write the code that will change the backgrounds when you tap the Change button.

Essentially, you'll perform five jobs:

1. Increment the current background.

2. Make sure the incrementation keeps the images contained in your array.

3. Initialize the UIView.

4. Create animations for your backgrounds as they get loaded.

5. Commit and change the background.

Your starting roadmap for your change method is as follows:

```
-(IBAction)change:(id)sender
{
Increment background to the next background image
Check to see currentBackground doesn't go off the array
Initialize the UIView
Create animations
Commit and change
}
```

As I've said, each time you tap the Change button, the number of the background image changes. If wallPaper_01 is presently housed in the background, and you tap Change, then you'll increment it—meaning, you'll add 1 and bring on wallPaper_02 as the next background. All this means is that each time the Change button is tapped, before you do anything else, you need to increment the currentBackground as follows:

```
-(IBAction)change:(id)sender
{
currentBackground++;
Check to see currentBackground doesn't go off the array
Initialize the UIView
Create animations
Commit and change
}
```

If you keep incrementing, you'll go beyond the number of images lined up in your array. Therefore, you need to reset the count back to 0 once you reach the number of images in your array, as illustrated by the following:

```
-(IBAction)change:(id)sender
{
currentBackground++;
if(currentBackground >= [bgImages count])
               currentBackground = 0;
Initialize the UIView
Create animations
Commit and change
}
```

To initialize the UIView, you need to do two things, but I've added a third task just to be cool. You have to reset (reboot, set to 0—however you want to say it) the beginAnimations method that those incredibly supercalifragilistic dudes at Apple wrote. Then you need to set how long each animation is going to be. As mentioned when you did the initializing before, I set the initializing in-between changes to 1 second. To be cool, I incorporated a third task: determining how smoothly each animation will start and end using the UIViewAnimationCurveEaseInOut method, as illustrated by the following:

```
-(IBAction)change:(id)sender
{
currentBackground++;
if(currentBackground >= [bgImages count])
```

```
currentBackground = 0;
[UIView beginAnimations:@"changeview" context:nil];
[UIView setAnimationDuration:1];
[UIView setAnimationCurve:UIViewAnimationCurveEaseInOut];
Create animations
Commit and change
}
```

> **Note**   To actually change the backgrounds, be careful how you wrap your head around this concept.
> Read this section carefully and follow along.

The changing of each background is divided into two steps:

- First, ask whether the current background's numerical value, or tag, is the one you're dealing with. If so, perform the code within the curly brackets (shown in the next bullet).

- Second, use the setAnimationTransition method to perform whatever other method you've chosen. There are methods to curl up, curl down, hide in from the left or right, flip this way, do that, or do this. Or you can create your own method . . . when you become an übergeek. Right now, you're just using curls and page flips, so I'll call these *transitions* appropriately.

Looking at things a little more closely, for each animation, use the form as follows:

```
if(currentBackground ==the # we want)
[UIView setAnimationTransition:
↳UIViewAnimationTransition the animation we choose
↳forView:self.view
↳cache:YES];
```

Now repeating this method and using randomly chosen animations for each animation, the code takes on the following form:

```
-(IBAction)change:(id)sender
{
currentBackground++;
if(currentBackground >= [bgImages count])
currentBackground = 0;
[UIView beginAnimations:@"changeview" context:nil];
[UIView setAnimationDuration:1];
[UIView setAnimationCurve:UIViewAnimationCurveEaseInOut];
if(currentBackground == 1)
[UIView setAnimationTransition:
↳UIViewAnimationTransitionFlipFromLeft
↳orView:self.
↳view cache:YES];
```

```
if(currentBackground == 2)
[UIView setAnimationTransition:
↳UIViewAnimationTransitionCurlDown
↳orView:self.
view cache:YES];

if(currentBackground == 3)
[UIView setAnimationTransition:
↳UIViewAnimationTransitionCurlUp
↳orView:self.
↳view cache:YES];

if(currentBackground == 4)
[UIView setAnimationTransition:
↳UIViewAnimationTransitionFlipFromRight
↳orView:self.
↳view cache:YES];

Commit and change

}
```

The last step, as before, simply commit the change and execute the code:

```
-(IBAction)change:(id)sender
{
currentBackground++;
if(currentBackground >= [bgImages count])
currentBackground = 0;
[UIView beginAnimations:@"changeview" context:nil];
[UIView setAnimationDuration:1];
[UIView setAnimationCurve:UIViewAnimationCurveEaseInOut];
if(currentBackground == 1)
[UIView setAnimationTransition:
↳UIViewAnimationTransitionFlipFromLeft
↳orView:self.
↳view cache:YES];

if(currentBackground == 2)
[UIView setAnimationTransition:
↳UIViewAnimationTransitionCurlDown
↳orView:self.
↳view cache:YES];

if(currentBackground == 3)
[UIView setAnimationTransition:
↳UIViewAnimationTransitionCurlUp
↳orView:self.
↳view cache:YES];
```

```
if(currentBackground == 4)
[UIView setAnimationTransition:
↳UIViewAnimationTransitionFlipFromRight
↳orView:self.
↳view cache:YES];

[UIView commitAnimations];
myBackground.image = [bgImages objectAtIndex:currentBackground];
}
```

Check your code against mine, as illustrated in Figure 5-37. You're done. Can you believe that? All you need to do is run it, and your code will work beautifully!

Running the Code

Let me explain something. The odds that it will work are small, and that's okay. Somewhere between 80–90 percent of my students have some error, even while using DemoMonkey. It's all right if your code doesn't work at first. Expecting your code to run beautifully the first time is similar to what my mother told me a couple of years ago. She called from across town at 5 p.m. and said, "Darling I'm just leaving now; I know it's 5 o'clock, but I should be there soon because I hope there won't be too much traffic today!" I couldn't believe what she had just said. I replied, "Mom, rather than expecting to be here in 20 minutes, hoping there won't be traffic, only to be horribly let down, why don't you expect it to take an hour and enjoy that new Deva Premal meditation CD I bought you? Relax and enjoy yourself!"

Likewise, you should expect errors. Debugging our code is a *huge* part of being a computer scientist, and expecting not to see any errors will only let you down. If there were no errors, then you'd be lucky!

33. Once you run it (see Figure 5-35), you can do four things: tap one of the three buttons or hide the icon. This initial view is shown in Figure 5-36.

Figure 5-35. Save it and run it

Figure 5-36. Left to right: Initial screen, moving the icon with finger (touchesMoved), tapping the Shrink button and seeing how it changes the text to Grow and shrinks the icon

Figure 5-37. *Left to right: Touching the Hide button to see icon fading, Hide button turns into Show, Shrink being touched again*

34. Figure 5-38 illustrates the page curling to the fourth background and the lulu fruit icon being Hided by the touches function.

Figure 5-38. *Three changing screens*

Digging the Code

Typically, I spend time digging the code that we flew over. However, this chapter was a huge leap, and I can't justify making you flip back to understand what was going on while you typed the code. As far as going deeper into the code is concerned, there's not much left to dig into—we did a pretty thorough job on it.

In the next chapter, you'll look at Switch Views; you'll "quickly" run the code and then come back to what you really did in the "Digging the Code" section. You'll examine how a team of characters or roles within your code will work together to direct an outcome, or a series of outcomes, that will give the user the sense of seamless flow. You'll learn about delegators, classes and subclasses, and "lazy loads." You'll get into the nitty-gritty of the `.xib` files, examine the concept of memory deallocation, and learn about imbedded code comments. It's getting curiouser and curiouser. . .

Let's close this chapter and give your brain a break.

Onward to the next chapter!

Chapter 6

Switches

After finishing the touches app in Chapter 5, you can say without flinching that you've coded Objective-C apps! You're not alone if, while coding Chapter 5, you felt as though you were struggling to make your way across a tough and rocky road. I say this because all programmers have had to journey over this road. It's absolutely okay to look back on that chapter and not remember what you did. That's normal, and I'm about to prove to you that it's normal. First, I need to explain why you're going to take time out at this point.

In my experience, when teaching students languages such as C, C++, C#, assembly, machine languages, Java, and others, many students drop out even when they seem to be doing fine. In recent years, I began to catch students as they neared this junction, and I would ask them why they were contemplating dropping out. They would all tell me something similar to this: "I can see I did the homework but I'm scared I will fail because it's just not sinking in. I don't grasp it." About four years ago I tried an experiment. When the students walked into the lecture hall they were in shock when I told them to close their textbooks, close their laptops, and put away their books because we were going to take a journey inside their brain and have a class on neurology. In fact, we were going to scientifically illustrate why many felt they were stupid, not getting it, and essentially feeling like a dork. The entire lecture hall collapsed in laughter. At the end of the lecture that I now call "Don't Freak Out! Let's Have a Look at Your Brain!" some students were crying and came up to me after class and thanked me. Not a single student dropped out.

Right now, I bet that you feel that you've not retained anything from Chapter 5 and that you feel a little overwhelmed and insecure in your geek abilities. Well, that's okay—just read on and you'll see why you feel a little uneasy. Even if you do feel confident at this point, you'll probably falter at some point down the road as it gets harder, but I still want you to read on. This is important, so I want you to really understand this.

Don't Freak Out: Let's Look at Your Brain!

One of the best ways to explain this is to ask you something that has nothing to do with Objective-C and computer science. It's about childhood memories.

Do you ever smell something you've not smelled before and without any warning your brain immediately takes you back to a place in your early childhood? This happens to all of us. After smelling this smell, you'll suddenly see everything clearly in your head: the walls, the people—it's all crystal clear. And sometimes it may overwhelm you emotionally. You may feel blown away that you've not thought about those walls or images for many years, and now suddenly they're overwhelming your senses. Let me explain why this happens. I will use my smell of old-fashioned soap to illustrate this, and then show how this is related to the neural connectors you've just created.

Look at Figure 6-1. Under the first title, ILLUSTRATION, you see a very simplified illustration of how, once your brain receives a new input that it's never experienced before, it creates a nucleus housed inside a cell body that retains that event. This is connected to the rest of your brain by threads and axons. As you experience new events that relate to this new event, a tree of synapses and neurons connect to this nucleus. Some of these connections become quite full of what are called *dendrites*.

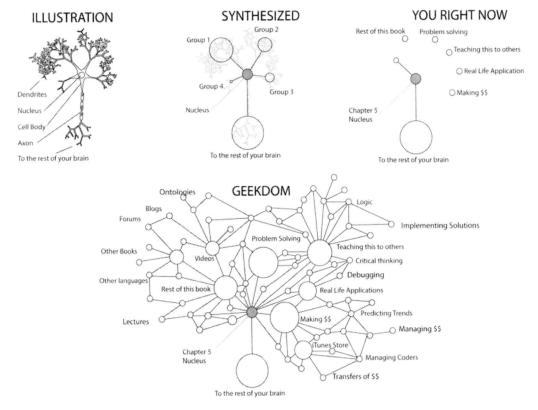

Figure 6-1. Don't freak out: Let's have a look at your brain

When I was a little boy in Durban, South Africa, I went down to where the servants were washing laundry. Back in 1963, most families used old-fashioned ammonia-filled soap that had a very distinct smell. This smell created a new nucleus in my baby brain. It connected with the joyful songs the Zulu servants were singing as they hand-washed the laundry. My brain also connected the imagery of the walls, the paint, and my dog Samson. These connectors of the singing, the walls, the paint and the dog formed four groups of connections to that new smell, as illustrated under SYNTHESIZED in

Figure 6-1. Some groups immediately had more connections, such as songs, because I used to sing many Zulu songs as a small boy. The next biggest group was probably that of my dog. I've labeled the groups from 1 to 4 in order of size.

Many years later, in New York City, probably around 1993, I was rushing to keep an appointment with a law professor who had said he would meet me for lunch at a little restaurant. As I was running across 8th Avenue, I noticed some people cleaning the sidewalk in front of another restaurant. They were using soap and water and scrubbing it with these large straw brushes. Suddenly I smelled it. The smell I hadn't smelled since I was three in that laundry room. I suddenly saw those servants, I could hear their songs and laughter, and I could see my old dog Samson. I became so overwhelmed with that day, the people, and the energy from so long ago that I stopped running and started crying. When I reached the restaurant, the law professor stood resplendent in his tweed suit and said, "Rory, it's okay that you're a couple of minutes late. Oh, my gosh, are you crying?"

So what happened? What happens when you experience similar events? Why does this often happen with smell? Let's first look at events in life, such as the first time you realized that $1 + 1 = 2$. Do you remember the first time you realized $1 + 1 = 2$? Probably not. That's because after you created a nucleus associating $1 + 1 = 2$, trillions of connectors were going to $1 + 1 = 2$. Every time you perform any function that relates to $1 + 1 = 2$, your brain makes a connection to the nucleus housing $1 + 1 = 2$. Even as you flip through this book and it goes from page n to $n + 1$, you make synaptic connectors to dendrites and groups of associations connected to $1 + 1$. Somewhere in those trillions of $1 + 1 = 2$ connectors are the visuals and sound effects of the room where you realized this, but it is lost in the maze of trillions of other connectors.

That rare smell though, that's different. Think about it. I have illustrated four groups associated with that smell from when I was three. Over the next 30 years, following the creation of that nucleus and the four groups linking it, there was never a connection made. It just lay there. However, as I crossed 8th Avenue and smelled that smell, it immediately invoked that same nucleus *and* the contents of the four groups connected to that event. These connectors were *strong* because they were not interconnected with other complex relationships. This made the singing, the feeling I had towards my dog, the laughter, and the other events come hurtling into me.

Now go back to when you read Chapter 5 for a moment. Look at the YOU RIGHT NOW illustration in Figure 6-1. You created a set of nuclei when you made your way through Chapter 5. Let's imagine, for the purposes of illustration, that it was only one event or one thing you learned while reading Chapter 5. The nucleus containing that knowledge is housed in the light grey circle. You may, at the most, have created one semblance of connectivity to some related thought or concept. That's why I connected one small group to the Chapter 5 knowledge nucleus. More importantly, notice that I've created five other groups of potential connectors to Chapter 5: they are "Rest of the book," "Problem solving," "Teaching to others," "Real life application," and "Making $$." Right now it's absolutely natural that these groups have *no connectivity* to the nucleus of Chapter 5's knowledge because you have not had time to create these connections. For example, right now, as you read this chapter, you probably "feel" like you have no connection to the knowledge you gained in Chapter 5. That's because there is no connection to it as you read this. There is also zero connectivity to making $$ from what you learned in Chapter 5, nor to the other groups.

I carefully choose topics, innuendo, and semantics to optimize, as best I can, connectivity between what I teach at the moment to what was taught in the past. By the time you reach the end of this book, create your first app, and sell it, your brain will have begun to create many connectors to Chapter 5. I've illustrated this in Figure 6-1 under GEEKDOM. Something that connects a huge amount of synapses to nuclei containing a difficult-to-understand concept is *teaching others*. It's great to go onto forums, such as mine at `www.rorylewis.com/ipad_forum/`, and help out newbies with their questions (even if you're a newbie yourself) because it creates many connections to that difficult concept, making you smarter. In essence, helping others forces one to answer the same question in thousands of different ways. So, I strongly encourage you to go to the forum, ask questions, and then, as you become wiser, help others.

So, the first good news is that it's okay to feel disconnected to what you coded in Chapter 5. You'll make those connections as you move forward. The second piece of good news is that Chapter 6 will not be as huge a leap as Chapter 5 was. Instead, you're going to take a break from serious code and connect new ideas to the synapses that you connected with code in Chapter 5. In fact, in both Chapters 6 and 7, there will be very little code! Instead, I will connect cool new thoughts to the portion of your brain that's associating code with ideas explored in Chapter 5. Once you've established these connections in your brain, you'll associate more code. In Chapter 6, you'll explore a popular method for navigating through iPhone apps using the platform of a *Tabbed Application*. But for now, just relax and enjoy the chapter.

switches: A Tabbed Application

So far, you've written code that allows the user to poke or prod an iPhone or iPad in certain ways to make it do interesting things. That's now going to change. In this chapter, you'll demonstrate how to create an iPhone app that allows you to do all of these cool functions without overwhelming your user, by dividing the functionality into several easy-to-locate tabs. This model, called the *tabbed model*, is so popular among app developers that Apple has included a basic Tabbed Application project in the New Project options in Xcode. In other words, the people at Apple recognize how much programmers like to use this model, so they created most of the code you need. When you're all done writing this app, you'll have a display with two tabs at the bottom. The content of the first tab will be an image that you set using Interface Builder with a button overlaid on top of it. This button will cause Mobile Safari to open the Apress web site. The content of the second tab will be a different image, but you can set the image name and other attributes in the implementation file.

Obtaining the Resources

You can watch a video of this switches app at `http://bit.ly/SFmG64` and simply follow along with me. You can also download the code to this project at `http://bit.ly/SzvMif` where you can visually compare your code with mine. Most importantly, you'll need to download the 16 images and DemoMonkey file from `http://bit.ly/SFn70d`.

1. Start off by cleaning out your desktop so there's nothing on it except for the `files` folder you downloaded from `http://bit.ly/SFn70d`. This is shown in Figure 6-2.

Figure 6-2. Download the three images onto your squeaky clean desktop

2. This second step is only necessary if you've decided to not use my files and use your own. If you use my files, go to step 3 now. To make your own files:

   ▪ Create eight 512 × 512 pixel icons representing eight of your favorite social media sites.

   ▪ Also create one 740 × 366 Apress splash screen.

   ▪ You'll need two iPhone icons for this app, one retina icon at 114 × 114 pixels and another regular icon at 57 × 57 pixels.

   ▪ You'll also need three splash screens: one Retina "35" at 640 × 640 pixels, another "40" retina splash screen at 640 × 366 pixels, and a regular splash screen at 320 × 480 pixels.

   ▪ You'll need two wallpapers at 638 × 997 pixels for each of the two views.

Creating the App

Now, let's create the app.

3. Start this app just as you've started all the apps so far: use ⌘+⇧+N to start a new project. Select Tabbed Application from the sheet that appears. This template sets up a significant portion of the tab framework for you, so you can focus on filling in the content and not worrying about the gory details of the interaction model. Click Next, as illustrated in Figure 6-3.

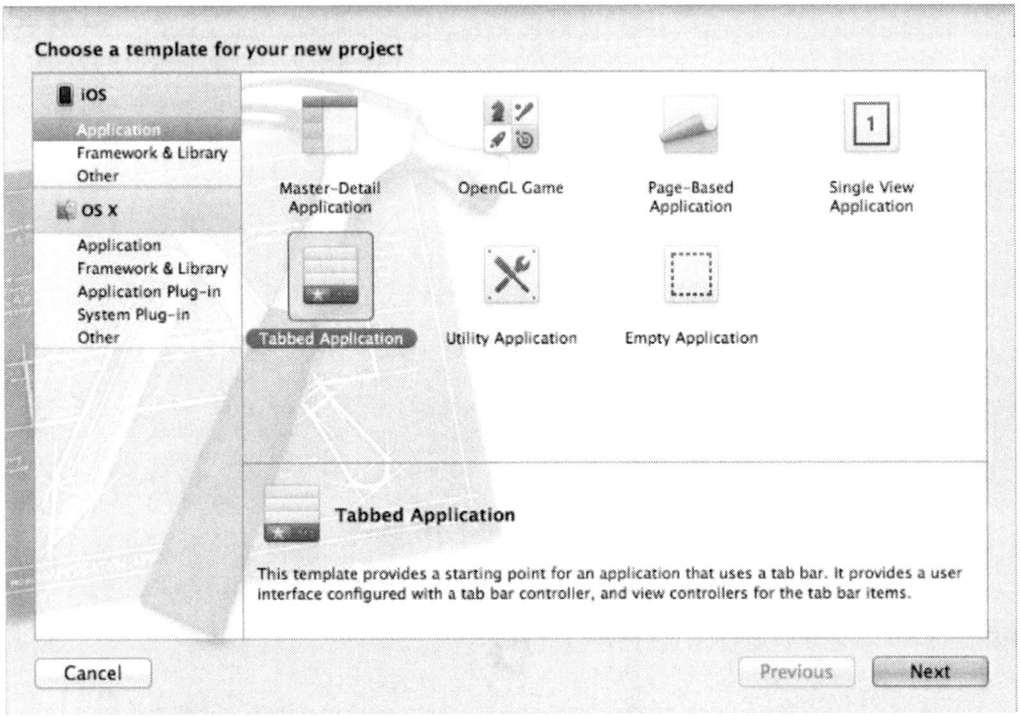

Choose a template for your new project

iOS
Application
Framework & Library
Other

OS X
Application
Framework & Library
Application Plug-in
System Plug-in
Other

Master–Detail
Application

OpenGL Game

Page–Based
Application

Single View
Application

Tabbed Application

Utility Application

Empty Application

Tabbed Application

This template provides a starting point for an application that uses a tab bar. It provides a user interface configured with a tab bar controller, and view controllers for the tab bar items.

Cancel   Previous   Next

Figure 6-3. Start a Tabbed Application

4. As illustrated in Figure 6-4, name your app switches and ensure that both of the checkboxes are unchecked. Use Storyboards drastically changes how a Tabbed Application is set up and is explored in detail in Chapter 7. In this app, you'll specifically target the iPhone because tabs become cumbersome on the iPad.

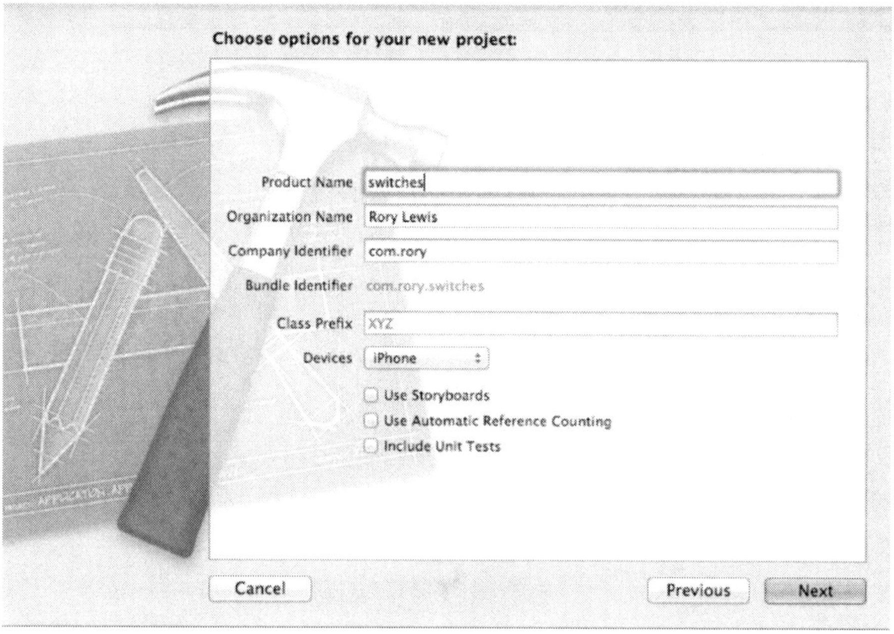

Choose options for your new project:

Product Name: switches

Organization Name: Rory Lewis

Company Identifier: com.rory

Bundle Identifier: com.rory.switches

Class Prefix: XYZ

Devices: iPhone

☐ Use Storyboards
☐ Use Automatic Reference Counting
☐ Include Unit Tests

Cancel   Previous   Next

Figure 6-4. Name the app switches

Note   I have not selected Automatic Reference Counting in this project because there will be no need to use large memory management here. Automatic Reference Counting makes Xcode manage memory on the compiler and manage retain, release, and autorelease.

Adding the Images to the Project

At this stage, it's probably a good idea to drag your imagery to use on the tabs, so you won't have to worry about it later.

5. Drag your images from the desktop into Supporting Files, and in the process develop a very good habit for yourself. Figure 6-5 only shows the first four images being dragged in. I later select them all. After dropping your images into the folder, you'll see the dialog shown in Figure 6-6.

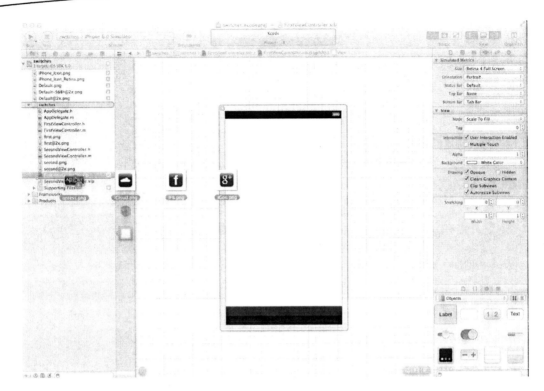

Figure 6-5. Drag in your three images from the desktop

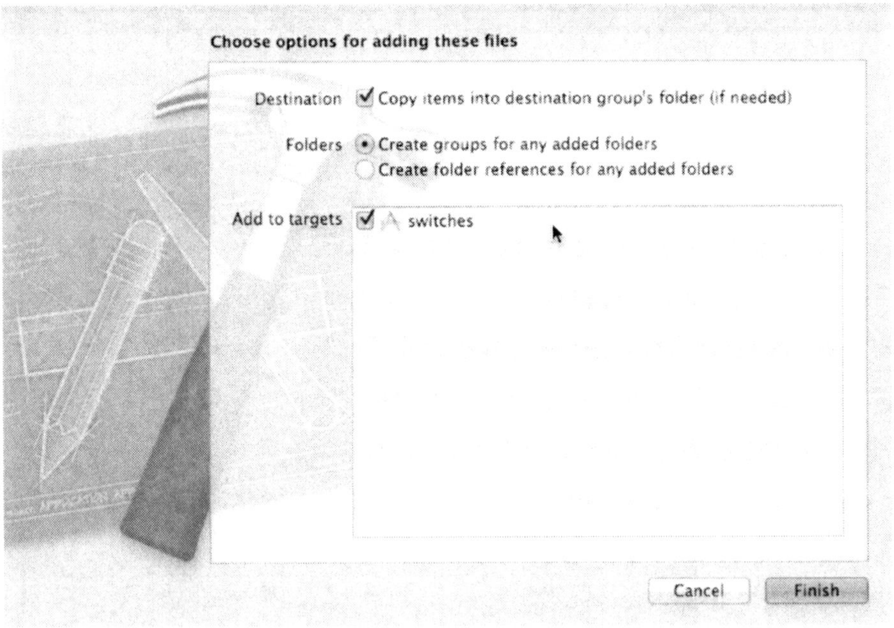

Choose options for adding these files

Destination ☑ Copy items into destination group's folder (if needed)

Folders ⦿ Create groups for any added folders
         ◯ Create folder references for any added folders

Add to targets ☑ A switches

Cancel   Finish

Figure 6-6. Copy the items into the destination page's folder

6. Xcode recognizes that the images are not already part of this project, so it strongly recommends that you let it add them for you. As mentioned before, it's also making sure that it has encapsulated your images inside itself, so if you go to another computer to run it, it will be able to find your images and display them. This dialog also gives you the opportunity to change the actions it's about to perform, but, in general, the assumptions it makes are correct, so accept Xcode's recommendations, as illustrated in Figure 6-6.

7. Drag your icon files to the app's properties. Notice how Xcode takes care of putting it in the right place in your project and setting up all the necessary linkages. This step is not critical if you don't have an appropriately sized .png readily available. You can always change the icon later. Note that it only allows you to drop the correct-sized icon into each specific box. In Figure 6-7, you see the icon being dragged into the app's icon property. Sometimes, as seen in these earlier versions of Xcode 4, the image of the splash screen doesn't show up. This is fine—just look in your root folder on the upper left-hand corner, and if you see it's there, then all is cool. This will most probably be fixed by the time you read this.

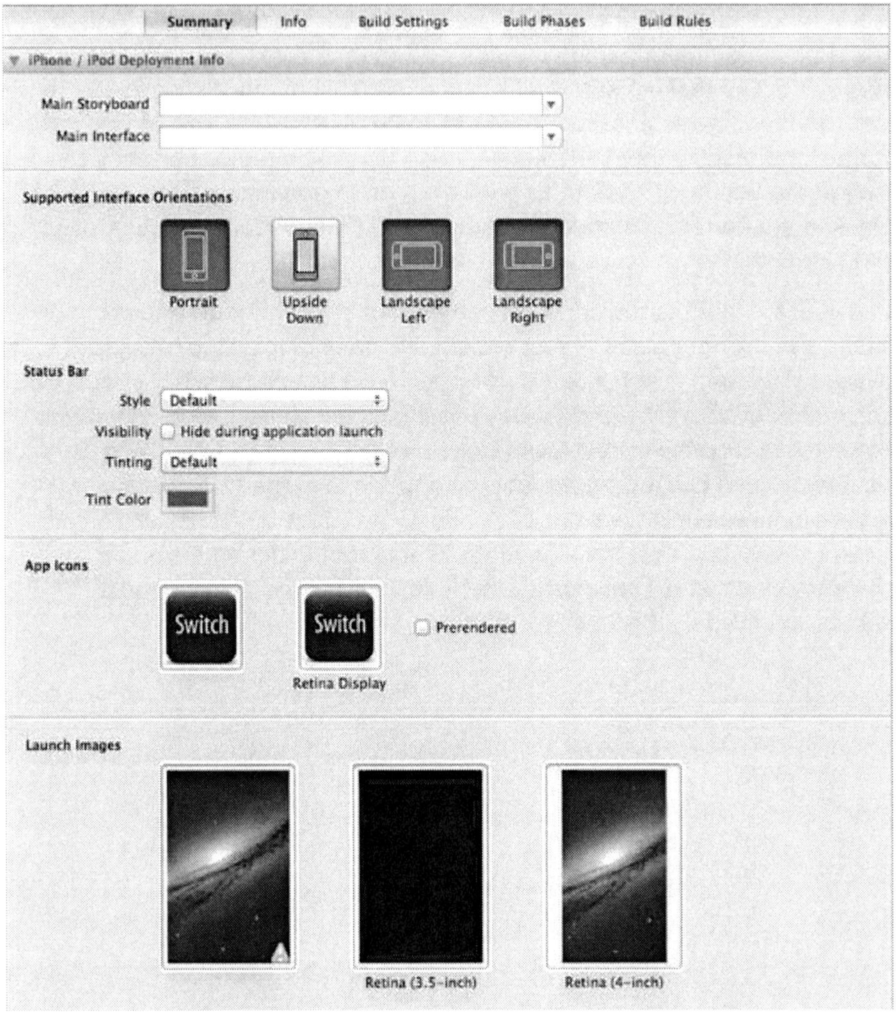

Figure 6-7. Drag your icons to the app's icon property

8. As with previous apps, you need to do some housekeeping. The default placement of the icons you just dragged in is in the root directory. So, move them to your `Supporting Files` folder as shown in Figure 6-8.

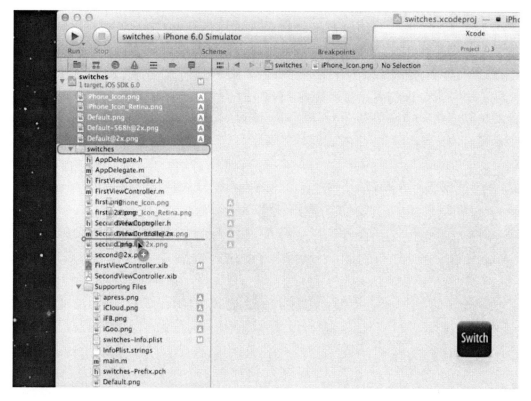

Figure 6-8. *Housekeeping: move icon apps to Supporting Files folder*

Running the App

Some of the readers of previous editions of this book and students from my former classes actually work at Apple, developing iOS code and doing the very special things you're about to see in this in step 9. That's why I love to say, "The clever people at Apple have coded…" because these clever people at Apple include people just like you, who began right here, reading the first version of this book. Right now, you probably just want to see what the clever people have coded for the Tabbed Application.

9. Run the app by clicking the Run button or pressing ⌘+R, as shown in Figure 6-9. If you've followed the instructions faithfully, you'll see a "Build Succeeded" message, and the iOS Simulator will start. Note how now all three of the splash screens are visible!

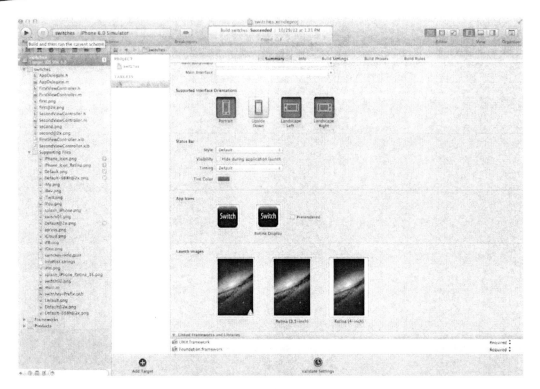

Figure 6-9. Run it so you can see what Apple has already coded for you

10. As shown in Figure 6-10, after you run the app, you'll see how the iOS Simulator pops up a First View. This is quite amazing. Those clever people at Apple have coded so much hardcore stuff and cool things that it leaves very little for you to do. Go ahead and play around with the app; click the tabs to see that there really are, in fact, two different sets of content being shown. Remember that you haven't even touched the .xib files or any of the code! However, this is exactly the point where the magic of the Tabbed Application template ends and your creative input begins.

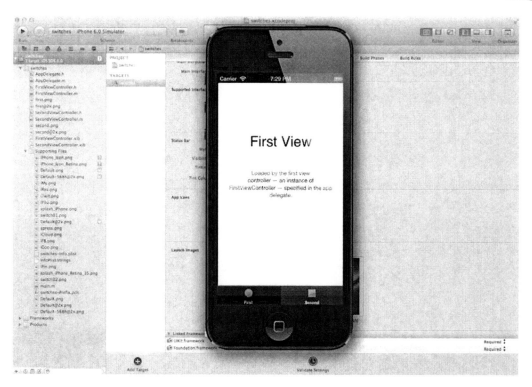

Figure 6-10. The first view to pop up will be the . . . First View

11. When you click the Second tab at the bottom of the screen, you'll see that
Second View pops up. So, the tabs are actually working perfectly.
I'm sure you'll notice that while the Tabbed Application template sets
up quite a bit and has prefilled some content, it's rather drab and
uninteresting. Most importantly, it doesn't reflect anything that you might
want it to do. Let's fix that.

Customizing the Views

That Second View that you see in Figure 6-11 can be replaced, along with the introductory
First View, with code, or the next level of a game, or the details of an address tab or recipe.
For your purposes, simply insert a first image into the First View and a second image into the
Second View.

Figure 6-11. The Second View appears when you select the Second tab

12. Switch back to Xcode and click the Stop button. Select the .xib file called
`FirstViewController.xib`. This shows what you saw in the iOS Simulator,
minus the actual tabs on the Tab Bar. Let's set up your environment to make
it easier for you to edit the nib (.xib). If you don't already have the Utilities
View visible, click the appropriate view button to make it visible at the right
side of the screen. Then select and delete all the text so that it looks like
mine in Figure 6-12.

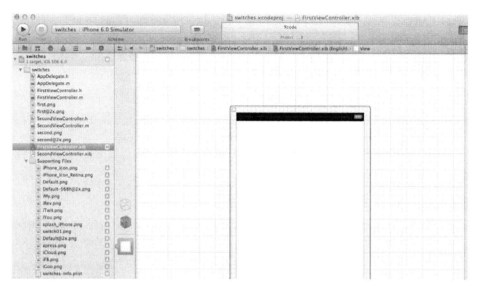

Figure 6-12. Open up the First View nib file

13. From the toolbox at the bottom of the Utilities View, find the Image View
(UIImageView) icon and drag it into the main area. As you do so, it expands to
the same size as the area you can fill (in this case, the whole view). Use the
guides to line up the UIImageView with the borders of the simulated iPhone
window, as shown in Figure 6-13.

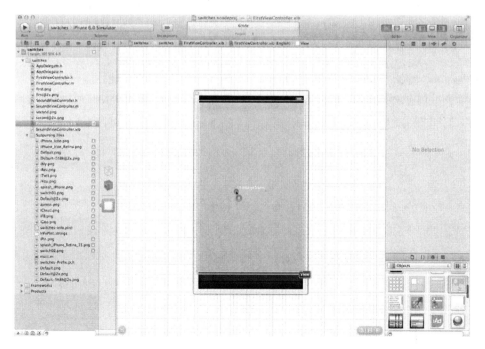

Figure 6-13. Drag a UIImagView onto your view

14. In the Utilities View, go to the Attributes Inspector (%⌘4) and click the Image drop-down, as shown in Figure 6-14. This list is populated with a list of images that Xcode has found in your project: select switch01.png, and Xcode will instantiate it in the UIImageView.

Figure 6-14. Associate your first images with the first UIImageView

15. You now need to repeat the last three steps for the Second View; associate the second background image with the Second View. Select the .xib file called SecondViewController.xib as shown in Figure 6-15. Then select and delete all the text.

Figure 6-15. *Open up the Second View nib file*

16. Go to the Utilities View and drag another `UIImageView` into the main area. Remember to use the guides to line it up with the borders of the simulated iPhone window, as shown in Figure 6-16.

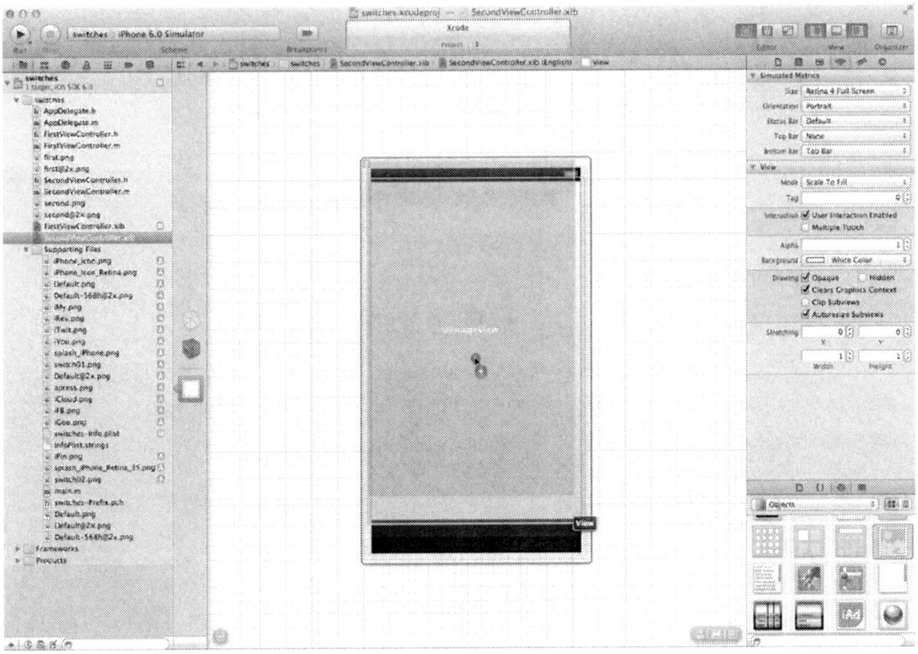

Figure 6-16. *Drag a UIImagView onto your view*

17. Go to the Attributes Inspector (⌥⌘4) and select switch02.png. Xcode will instantiate it in the UIImageView, as shown in Figure 6-17.

Figure 6-17. *Associate your second images with the second UIImageView*

Customizing the Buttons

Okay, you've successfully populated the background of both views with some cool wallpaper. In essence, you've customized the two views to look pretty cool and pretty custom. Now you'll move on to customizing your buttons. Up until now, you've used the default buttons, and you may have thought to yourself how come all the cool apps I see have buttons that look so different and so innovative? Well, just as you customized the views, you're going to learn how to customize your buttons. You'll have a custom button going to the Apress web site on the First View, and then eight custom buttons in the Second View going to various social media sites.

18. You need to first drag the button that will be the customized Apress button onto the canvas of the First View. So, open up the First View (nope, I'm not holding your hand through each step—if you need to refresh your memory, go back and see how you've done it before) and drag a button to the First View, as shown in Figure 6-18.

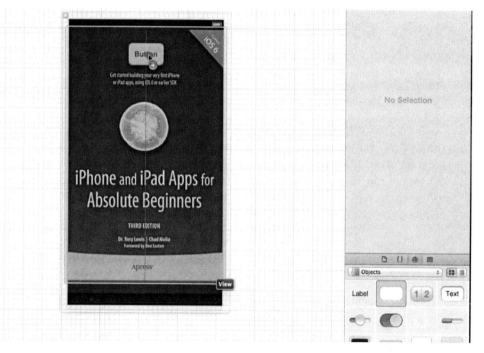

Figure 6-18. Drag a button onto the First View

19. Click once on your button to select it. Now go to the Attributes Inspector and in the Button drop-down menu, change it to a Custom button, as shown in Figure 6-19.

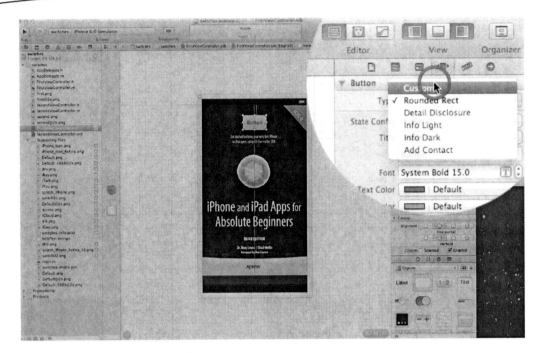

Figure 6-19. *Change the Apress button to a Custom type*

20. You'll be inserting an image inside the button so it will show a beautiful glossy "gel" button surface covering the image of the Apress logo. This means that you don't want any silly text getting in way of the Apress image. So, delete the "Button" text, as shown in Figure 6-20. This is something that will come as naturally as closing the car door before you drive off. When you create a custom button with an image, you always delete the text.

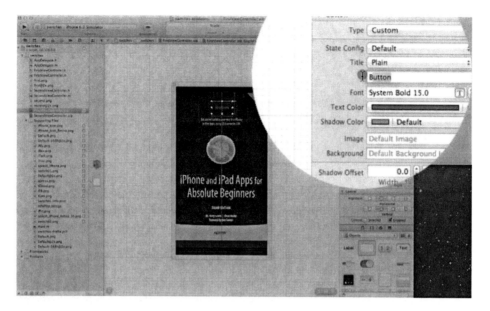

Figure 6-20. Delete the default text from the Apress button

21. Let's see, you've created the custom button and deleted the text that would be in the way. But now, you need to associate apress.png with this button. Go down to the Image slot and select apress.png from the drop-down menu, as shown in Figure 6-21. Immediately, you'll see the Apress logo appear inside the button. Cool, huh!

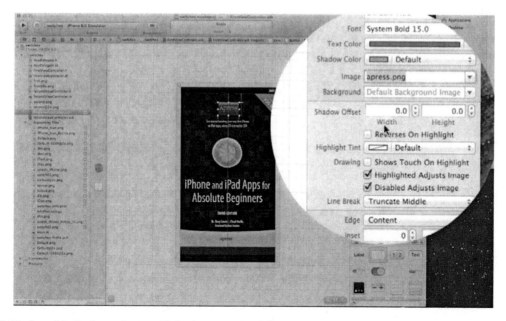

Figure 6-21. Associate the Apress image with the Apress custom button

22. You now need to do something that you'll probably do over and over and over: adjust the size of your custom button to the size of the custom button's image. If your custom button is *x* pixels long and *y* pixels high, you'll go to the size Editor and make your custom button exactly *x* pixels long and *y* pixels high. In this case, I made the Apress image 111 pixels in width and 54 pixels in height. So, go to the size Inspector and make the Apress custom just that: 111 pixels wide and 54 pixels high, as shown in Figure 6-22.

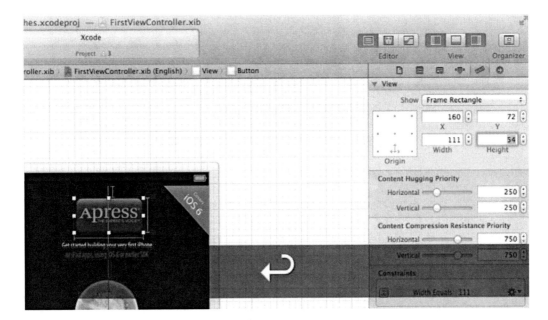

Figure 6-22. Adjust the size of the button

23. Save everything and run it (please don't let me hear you asking how to run it). You'll see that without typing any code, you have two views that work beautifully when you switch from the First View to the Second View and back. You can also see that you have an absolutely beautiful custom Apress button, as shown in Figure 6-23. What do you notice happens when you tap it? It does nothing! That's correct, you haven't associated an action with this button in the header file, and you haven't associated code that the button will implement when you click it. Just a hint: you'll use a method called NSURL to have your button go to the Apress URL.

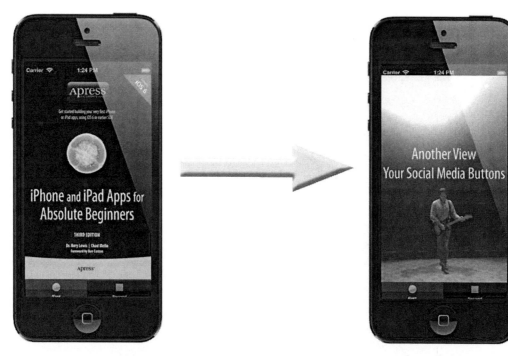

Figure 6-23. Run it: you have two views and a custom button already!

24. You need to start populating buttons onto the Second View. Now, you're not going to repeat the entire process you went through on the Apress button on the First View. Instead, you'll make one social media button in this Second View and then copy and paste it in a specific way to reduce your work. Open your Second View and drag a button to the upper left-hand corner, as shown in Figure 6-24.

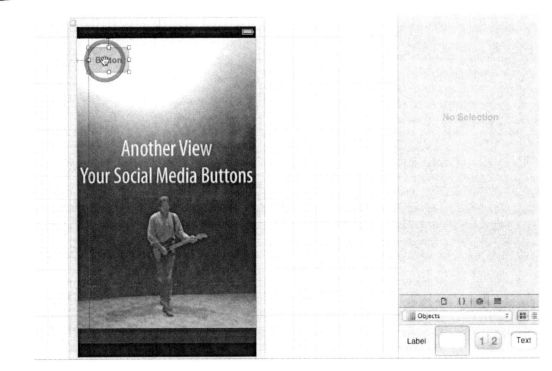

Figure 6-24. Add the first button to your Second View

Creating the Second View

Looking back at what you've done and where you want to go: you've created the Apress button on the First View. You now want to create eight buttons on the Second View that link to various social media sites.

25. As you know, you're going to first create one fully loaded custom button for your social media sites on the Second View. You'll do this in five steps, which you've just done for the First View. Now you'll do them, with less handholding from me, as shown by the five arrows numbered 1–5 in Figure 6-25. Select the social media button you just dragged onto the canvas in Figure 6-24 and, with it selected, in the Attributes Inspector change it to Custom (arrow 1), then delete the text (arrow 2), and then go to the Size Inspector (arrow 3) and change the size of the button to 66 × 66 pixels, as shown by arrow 4. Finally, associate the Facebook image with this icon by going back to the Attributes Inspector and selecting iFB.png from the Image drop-down menu, as shown by arrow 5.

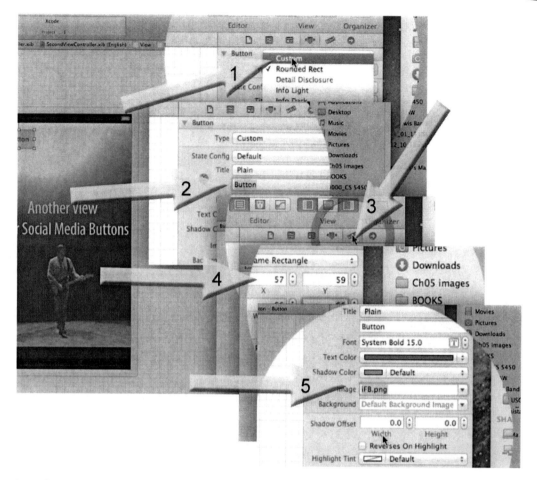

Figure 6-25. Create the first custom button for the Second View

26. Select the first Facebook button you just created and copy, as shown in Figure 6-26.

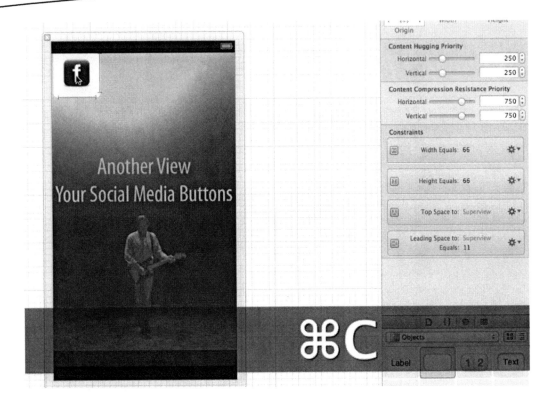

Figure 6-26. Copy the first button

27. Once you've copied the first button, paste the copy alongside the first one, as shown in Figure 6-27. This may seem trivial, but you'll be duplicating these two buttons four more times. In other words, you'll be duplicating the exactness of the distance and alignment between these two buttons four more times. It's important to space them in a way that will look plausible when there are four buttons going across, and to align them perfectly, as shown in Figure 6-28.

Figure 6-27. Paste the copied button alongside first one

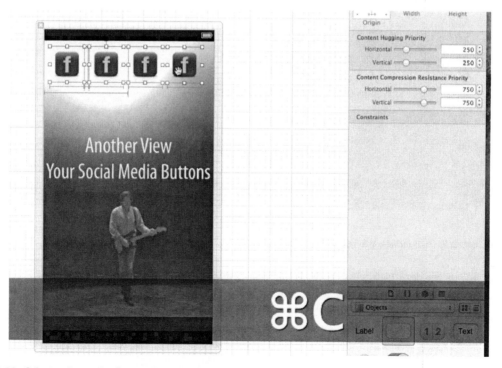

Figure 6-28. Select and copy the first two buttons and paste them

28. Select the first two buttons you've created from Figure 6-27. Copy and paste them alongside those first two buttons, as shown in Figure 6-28. Notice that because you've been very careful to make sure they are properly aligned, the buttons look professionally placed. Once they're placed as shown in Figure 6-27, select all four of them and copy them.

29. Paste the four buttons you copied. Initially, they will paste "over" your initial four buttons, as shown in Figure 6-29. Don't worry about this. They're still all grouped together as one. In the next step, you'll move them appropriately. The reason I'm forced to include the step is because I can't tell you the number of times students have called me over to their desk when they've pasted these four icons and said, "They're all lying on top of the other ones, Dr. Lewis." So again, this is perfectly acceptable; see you at the next step.

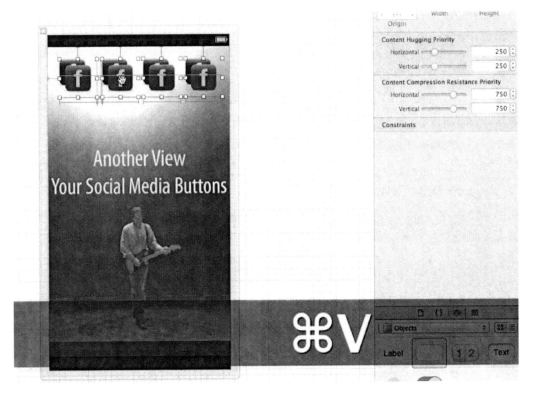

Figure 6-29. *Paste the four buttons you copied*

30. Move the four buttons directly under the original four buttons and drop them there. Now you need to start changing the images in all the buttons. Select the second button from the left and associate it in the Attributes Inspector image drop-down menu with the Twitter image named iTwit.png, as shown in Figure 6-30. You'll continue associating all the buttons this way. The

following table shows the name and .png for each of the eight icons. Note that you have already completed Facebook (iFB.png) and Twitter (iTwit.png) in row 1, so go ahead on your own now and complete associating the remaining six icons, and I'll meet you at the next step.

Figure 6-30. Name the remaining icons

Table 6-1. The Eight Icons

	1st Column	2nd Column	3rd Column	4th Column
Row 1 Name	Facebook	Twitter	Google +	Pinterist
Row 1 PNG	iFB.png (done)	iTwit.png (done)	iGoo.png	iPin.png
Row 2 Name	ReverbNation	SoundCloud	MySpace	YouTube
Row 2 PNG	iRev.png	iCloud.png	iMy.png	iYou.png

Connecting and Coding the Buttons

You now need to code the lone Apress button on the First View and then the eight social media buttons you've just created in your Second View. Because you're here on the Second View with your social media buttons, let's first connect these to the Second View's header file. Once that's done, you'll then go back to the First View and connect your Apress button to the header file.

Once all y our buttons are connected, you'll code the First View's implementation file's NSURL by hand, so you can learn it the old-fashioned way. Last, you'll bring in the eight NSURL instances for the Second View all in one swoop via DemoMonkey to save time and tediousness. I do things this way because there's always a balance between encouraging students to type code the old-fashioned way, doing it by hand, so that the synapses make appropriate connections, and not making them do tedious work that in the real world would be done differently using tools. If you just use tools to bring in code, you never get to learn how to code yourself or what the small nuances of each line of code really mean. On the other hand, if I only make you type in all that code by hand, then you miss out on having hands-on experience using tools used in the workforce, such as DemoMonkey.

Having you code the Apress URL in the First View by hand and then learning DemoMonkey gives you the best of both worlds.

31. As you've done before, you need to set up your canvas so you can start to code. Open up the Assistant and, if you're short of space, close the Utilities panel, as you can see me doing in Figure 6-31.

Figure 6-31. Get your canvas ready for coding

32. Control-drag from the Facebook icon in your nib file over to the Second View's header file, as shown in Figure 6-32.

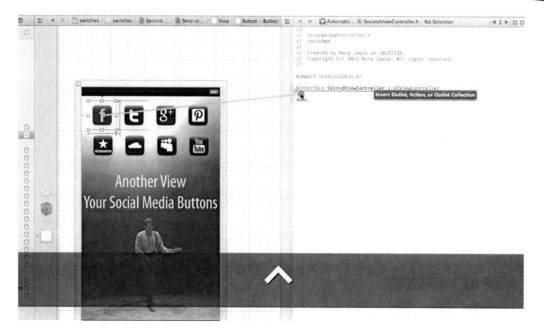

Figure 6-32. Re-inspecting the code

33. The Facebook button, like the other seven social media buttons, will be of type Action, because when the user taps the button it will use the NSURL method to go over to a web site, and that is indeed an action. This is shown in Figure 6-33.

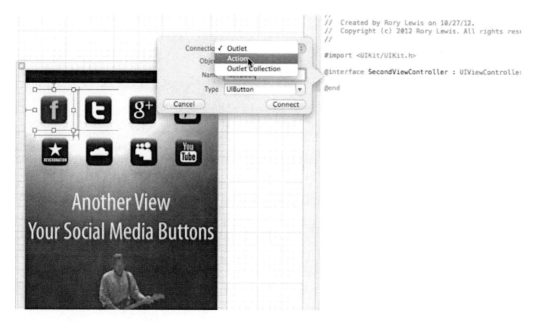

Figure 6-33. Make the connection an Action

34. You want to call the Facebook connection facebook, as shown in Figure 6-34. You may wonder why I'm showing a complete view for such a simple step. The reason is because you'll be doing the remaining seven icons on your own. Figures 6-32 through 6-34 demonstrate these three elementary steps you have done before. For your convenience, I put them here so that you have a reference. I want to encourage you to try and do the remaining seven buttons on your own without making reference to the book at all except for the naming change, as shown in Table 6-2. Of course, you can name them anything you please. But if you want to compare your code to mine and follow along with me, I suggest that you pay careful attention and name your buttons and actions exactly as I have named them, paying careful attention to their cases. There are no capital letters.

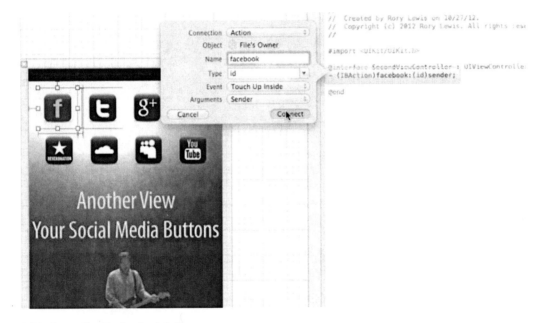

Figure 6-34. *Connecting the Facebook button*

Table 6-2 *Renaming the Buttons*

	1st column	2nd column	3rd column	4th column
Row 1 Name	Facebook	Twitter	Google +	Pinterist
Row 1 *.h Name	facebook (done)	twitter	google	pinterest
Row 2 Name	ReverbNation	SoundCloud	MySpace	YouTube
Row 2 *.h Name	reverbnation	soundcloud	myspace	youtube

35. Complete your eighth button and connect the YouTube button to your Second View's header file, as shown in Figure 6-35. You may note that I misspelled *Pinterest* in the code. You, of course, will spell it correctly; everything will work just fine if you do.

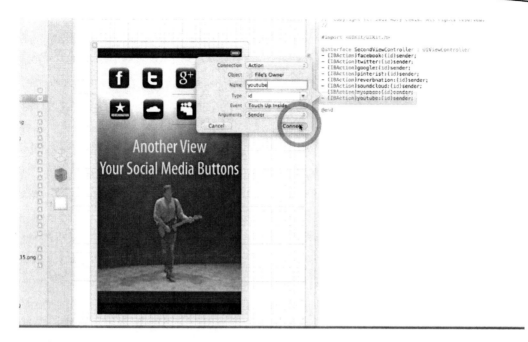

Figure 6-35. *Connecting the last of the social media buttons*

36. As mentioned earlier, if you want to be able to check your code against mine
     in the event things don't quite work out, it's critical that you name your actions
     exactly as I have. Figure 6-36 is a screenshot of my page before I move onto
     the First View. You may want to check that yours is exactly like mine.

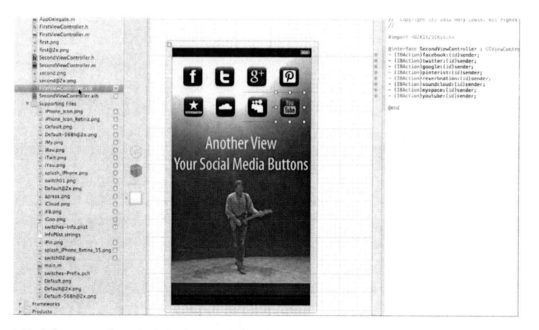

Figure 6-36. *Before you continue, check that your page is like mine*

37. Notice that I haven't held your hand, showing you exactly how to go back and close your Second View's nib file and open your First View's nib file. Once you've opened the First View's nib file, make sure you have the First View's header file on the right-hand pane. Control-drag from the Apress button over to the header file, as shown in Figure 6-37.

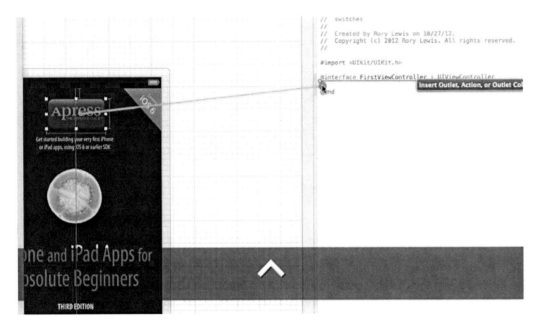

Figure 6-37. Back to the First View

38. Once you've dropped it into the header file, as you have done eight times already today, change it from an Outlet to an Action. In Figure 6-38 you see me selecting the Outlet right before I change it to an Action.

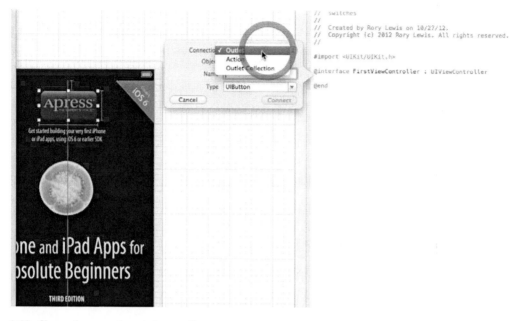

Figure 6-38. *Change from an alternate to an action*

39. As shown in Figure 6-39, name the button apress. Make sure you only use lowercase letters.

Figure 6-39. *Name it apress*

40. Again, before you move on to coding, make sure and check that your buttons are Actions and named like mine, with no capital letters, as shown in Figure 6-40.

Figure 6-40. Make sure your code is like mine

41. You've seen in previous chapters that you typically code in the Standard Editor. This lets you see one screen and stay focused. So, go ahead and click the Standard Editor, as shown in Figure 6-41.

Figure 6-41. Set the stage for coding

42. I had mentioned earlier that you'll code the First View by hand, go through each step slowly and learn as you do it, and then you'll have some practice using DemoMonkey to bring in a chunk of code that you'll be quite familiar with by the time you do it. Start by opening up the First View's implementation file. Click the FirstViewController, as shown in Figure 6-42.

Figure 6-42. Start with the First View

43. You've Control-dragged a connection from your Apress button in your First View's nib file over to the header file. You made it an action and called it apress. This instantiated, for you, without any coding, an apress method for your Apress button. It is in here that you want to tell the compiler what actions to execute when the user taps the Apress button. Therefore, you need to code what happens in this method called apress. Scroll down to the bottom of your implementation file until you see the apress method. You have to create space to code, so place your cursor inside the first open squiggly bracket and press Return, as shown in Figure 6-43.

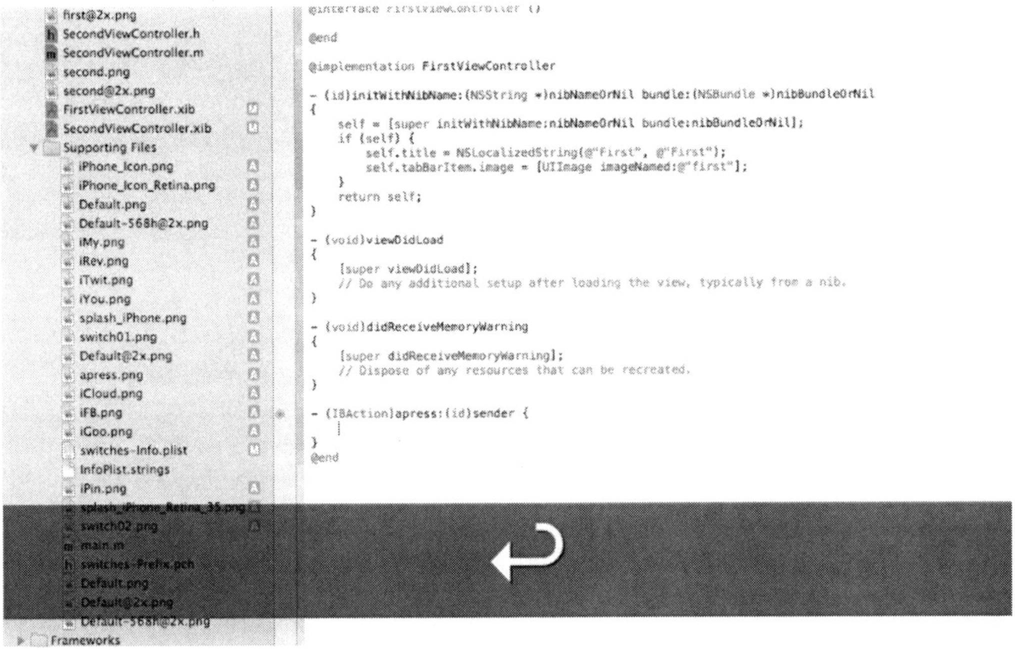

Figure 6-43. Go to the apress method

44. You'll use Apple's Code Sense to help you type code. Some people still call it Code Completion, but that's wrong. As time goes on, you'll learn many shortcuts, but for now, let's assume that you know just one thing in pure Xcode tautology, and that is that whenever you see code inside a set of square brackets, you know that its sending stuff, things, commands, whatever, to either an object or a class. I've touched on this in previous chapters, and not knowing it all now is fine. You'll use two calls to classes, and they'll be nested (stop thinking about classes, just pretend you know what they are for now, this is how I teach). If they're going to be nested, then you need a set of square brackets nested inside an outer set of square brackets. Do it! This is shown in Figure 6-44.

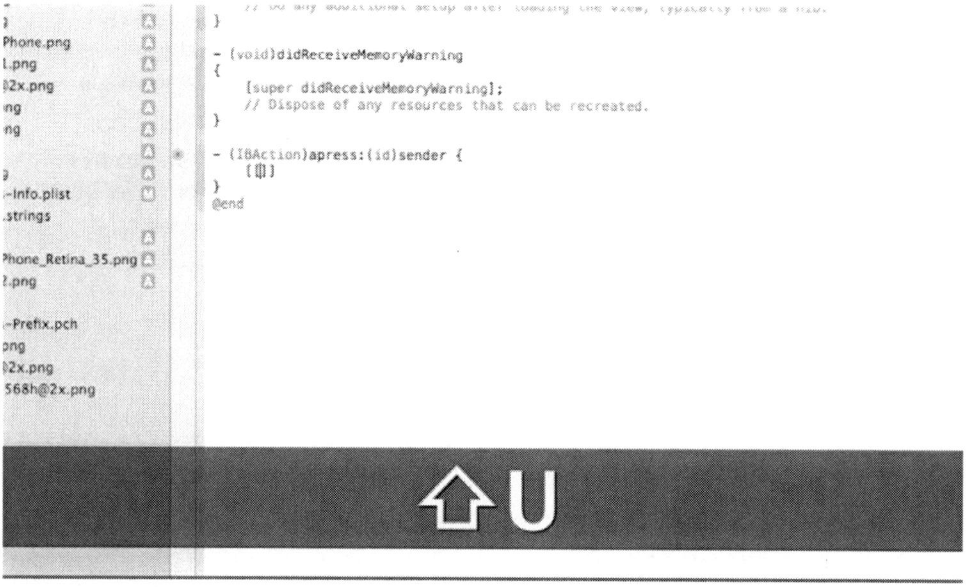

Figure 6-44. *Create two sets of square brackets*

45. You first need to have a UIApplication, so type UIAp and when you see UIApplication show up in Code Sense, scroll down to it and press Enter or tab, as shown in Figure 6-45. This thing called a UIApplication is a *class reference*, which creates an environment that defines and groups a bundle of code such as the stuff you're about to code.

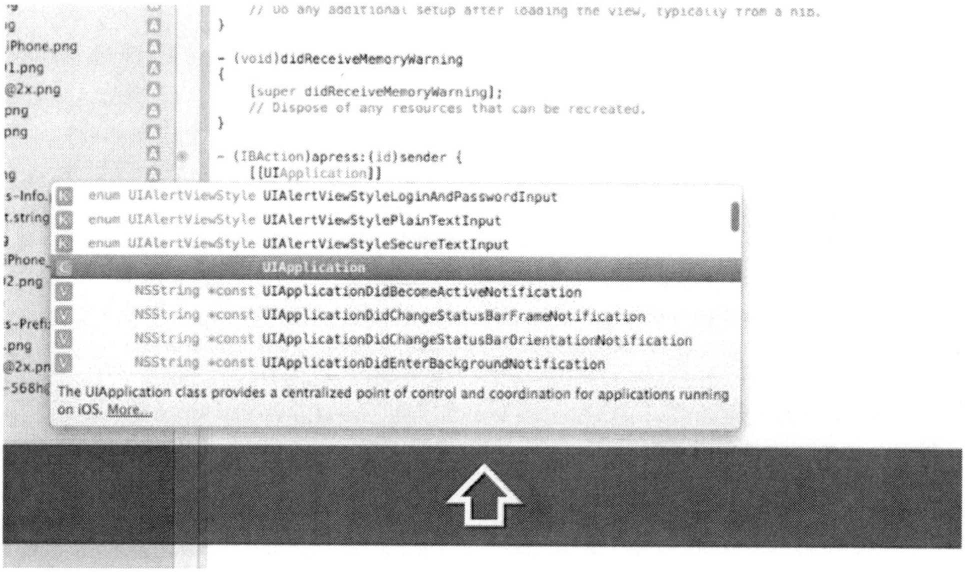

Figure 6-45. *Type UIApplication*

46. You want your UIApplication to call a *handler* to call and start execution code in the background and share the compiler resources while in that thousandth of a second the user sees the button being pressed in. For that, call an instance method called sharedApplication. So enter sha, and Code Sense will know to bring up sharedApplication because as sure as a paint brush will be dipped in paint, a UIApplication will call sharedApplication to return something to you … hmmm … what could that be … oh, yeah! A URL to Apress that you can execute! Awesome! This is shown in Figure 6-46.

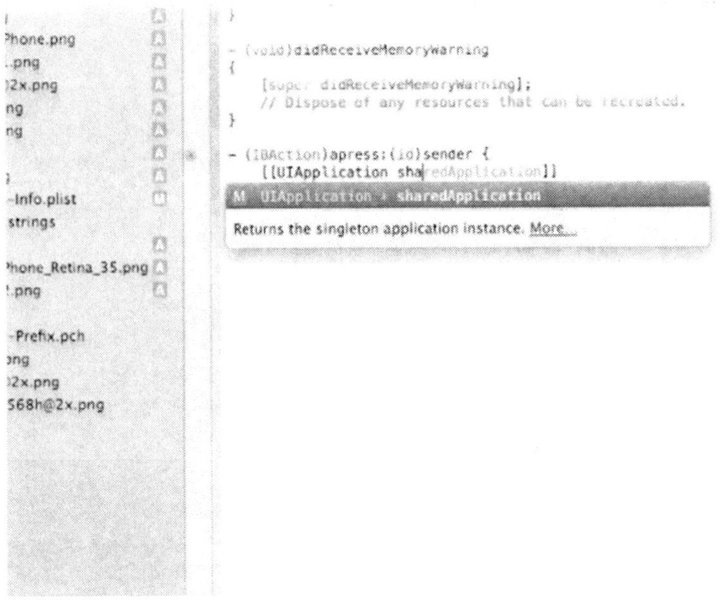

Figure 6-46. Enter sha

47. You know you're calling the compiler to show you something. You've got that down. Now you need to step out of the first inherited call and code what you want UIApplication to bring. This will be the URL, or in Xcode, NSURL. In Xcode you use the NSURL object to call, tweak, store, and manipulate URLs and their contents. This includes of course, just opening up a web site. You want the Apress button to open up the Apress web site so that it fits; this is where you will want to use the NSURL object to do this work for you. Type openURL and Code Sense will know from seeing the UIApplication sharedApplication that you probably want NSURL, as shown in Figure 6-47. Select it by pressing Enter.

```
                                              }

                                              - (void)didReceiveMemoryWarning
                                              {
                                                  [super didReceiveMemoryWarning];
                                                  // Dispose of any resources that can be recreated.
                                              }

                                              - (IBAction)apress:(id)sender {
                                                  [[UIApplication sharedApplication] openURL:(NSURL *)]
                                              }
                                              @end
```

M BOOL openURL:(NSURL *)

Opens the resource at the specified URL. More...

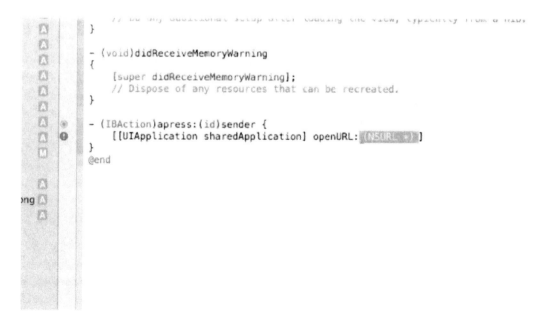

Figure 6-47. *Step out of the first set of squiggly brackets*

48. You want an NSURL with a string of text showing precisely what you want, so you need to delete the grey shaded (NSURL *) shown in Figure 6-48 and enter in its place your specific type of NSURL in the next step.

```
                                              }

                                              - (void)didReceiveMemoryWarning
                                              {

                                                  [super didReceiveMemoryWarning];
                                                  // Dispose of any resources that can be recreated.

                                              }

                                              - (IBAction)apress:(id)sender {
                                                  [[UIApplication sharedApplication] openURL: NSURL * ]
                                              }
                                              @end
```

Figure 6-48. *Delete the NSURL pointer*

49. You want to have a URL that will call a function. This means you'll need another bracket, so type it, retype NS, and select NSURL from Code Sense, as shown in Figure 6-49.

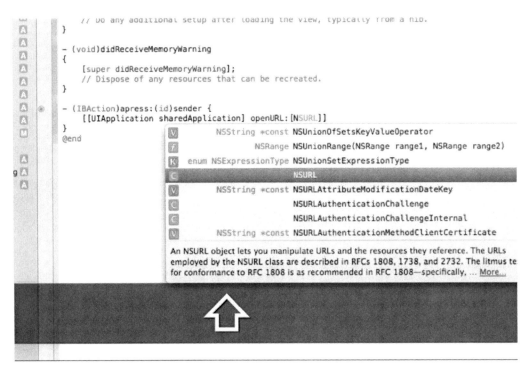

Figure 6-49. Enter [NS for a bracketed NSURL

50. Once NSURL is located inside the new square bracket, Code Sense knows exactly what you want. You only need to enter U, and it produces id URLWithString: (NSString *), which you'll select, as shown in Figure 6-50.

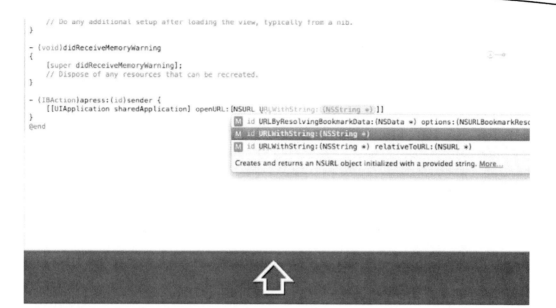

Figure 6-50. *Bring in the URL with string*

51. You want to type text inside the "string" portion that represents a URL, so
    delete the (NSString *) in the grey coded sections, as shown in Figure 6-51.

```
    // Do any additional setup after loading the view, typically from a nib.
}

- (void)didReceiveMemoryWarning
{
    [super didReceiveMemoryWarning];
    // Dispose of any resources that can be recreated.
}

- (IBAction)apress:(id)sender {
    [[UIApplication sharedApplication] openURL:[NSURL URLWithString:(NSString *)]]
}
@end
```

Figure 6-51. *Delete the string section*

52. Enter the Apress URL after the @, as shown in Figure 6-52. You'll soon know
    that UIApplication sharedApplication] openURL:[NSURL URLWithString: is
    what you need to code before you call a URL in Xcode. It sounds complex,
    but really, you don't think about the 20 things your body does as you get
    into a car, sit down, shut the door, put on the safety belt, turn on the ignition,
    wait until the engine is on, put it into gear, look in your rear view mirror, open
    the garage door, and then release the brake to allow yourself to reverse out
    of the garage. No. You barely think of any of this. You probably only wake
    up halfway to work. Such is the case with certain snippets of code. When
    you want to call a URL, you'll enter UIApplication sharedApplication]

openURL:[NSURL URLWithString: before you even realize you need to recheck where the actual address of that web page is. See … you're getting the geek thing into perspective now! Awesome. So enter: @"http://www.apress.com" as shown in Figure 6-52. Yeah!

```
    return self;
}

- (void)viewDidLoad
{
    [super viewDidLoad];
    // Do any additional setup after loading the view, typically from a nib.
}

- (void)didReceiveMemoryWarning
{
    [super didReceiveMemoryWarning];
    // Dispose of any resources that can be recreated.
}

- (IBAction)apress:(id)sender {
    [[UIApplication sharedApplication] openURL:[NSURL URLWithString:@"http://www.apress.com"]];
}
@end
```

Figure 6-52. *Enter the Apress URL*

53. After you run it and click the Apress button, you see the Apress home page appear, as shown in Figure 6-53. When you think about it, it's really amazing that a seemingly complex operation like opening Mobile Safari from within your own app could have been condensed into a single statement by the people at Apple. In iOS, all apps are sandboxed into their own little piece of the system's resources. The topic of sandboxing is so complex that books can and have been written about the subject, so I won't go into detail here. Instead, it's sufficient to understand that iOS isn't going to let your app just do whatever it wants, so you have to use certain APIs that Apple has provided to tell the underlying system to do these things on your behalf. In this case, send a message to the UIApplication class to obtain a reference to sharedApplication—that is, an object representing your application's gateway to the rest of the system. This object has a method called openURL, which does exactly that when passed as an instance of NSURL. To pass openURL an instance of NSURL, send the NSURL class the URLWithString message, which transparently converts the string you provide into an instance of NSURL.

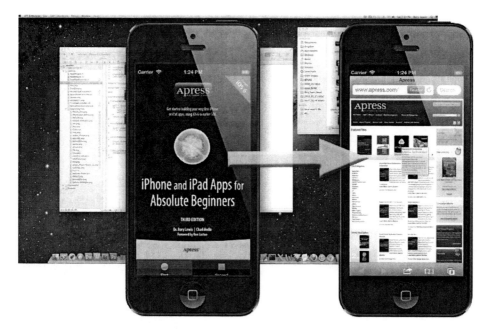

Figure 6-53. *Run it and click the Apress button*

54. You're about to use DemoMonkey to drag in a whole bunch of NSURL instances all in one swoop. Open your SecondViewController implementation file, as shown in Figure 6-54.

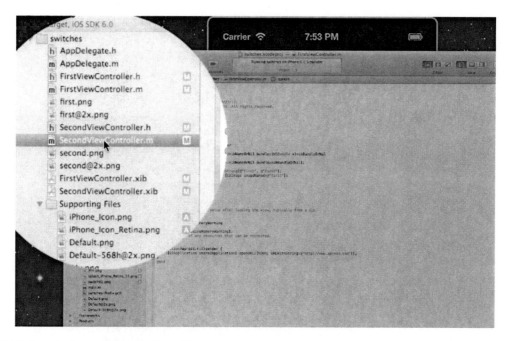

Figure 6-54. *Open the SecondViewController.m file*

55. When you scroll to the bottom of the Second View's implementation file, you see your eight social media methods all empty, just as you first saw an empty apress method before you coded it. You could code each one if you wanted to, but you'll be using DemoMonkey. So, select the eight methods and delete them, as shown in Figure 6-55.

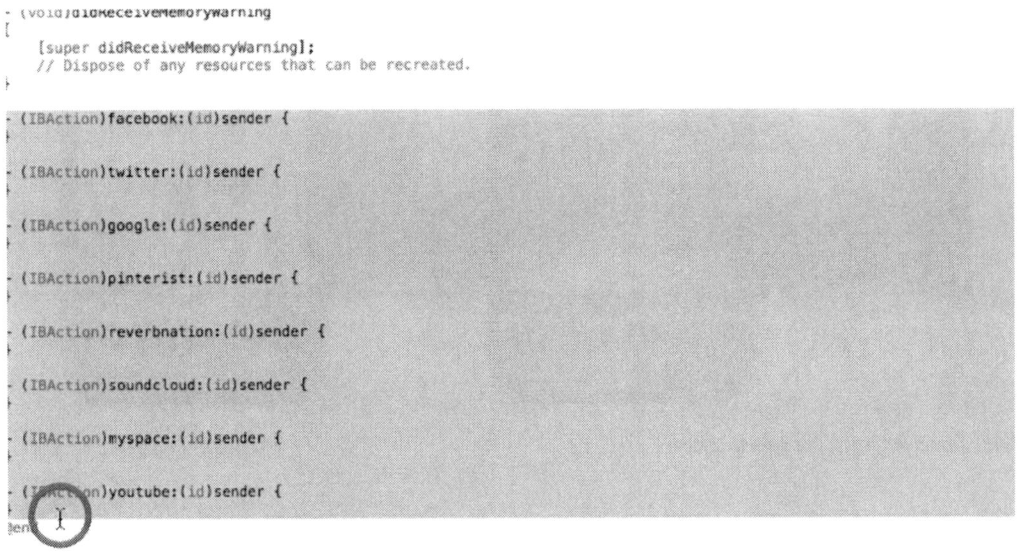

```
- (void)didReceiveMemoryWarning
{
    [super didReceiveMemoryWarning];
    // Dispose of any resources that can be recreated.
}

- (IBAction)facebook:(id)sender {
}

- (IBAction)twitter:(id)sender {
}

- (IBAction)google:(id)sender {
}

- (IBAction)pinterist:(id)sender {
}

- (IBAction)reverbnation:(id)sender {
}

- (IBAction)soundcloud:(id)sender {
}

- (IBAction)myspace:(id)sender {
}

- (IBAction)youtube:(id)sender {
}
```

Figure 6-55. Delete the instantiated empty methods

56. As shown in Figure 6-56, you see a green + sign being dragged over from the DemoMonkey folder on the right. With your DemoMonkey folder open, simply drag the Second View URL's object text from the DemoMonkey file onto your Second View's implementation file. Once you have it located where you just deleted the eight empty methods in step 6-55, let it go, and all the code I typed for you will magically appear.

```
- (id)initWithNibName:(NSString *)nibNameOrNil bundle:(NSBundle *)nibBundleOrNil
{
    self = [super initWithNibName:nibNameOrNil bundle:nibBundleOrNil];
    if (self) {
        self.title = NSLocalizedString(@"Second", @"Second");
        self.tabBarItem.image = [UIImage imageNamed:@"second"];
    }
    return self;
}

- (void)viewDidLoad
{
    [super viewDidLoad];
    // Do any additional setup after loading the view, typically from a nib.
}

- (void)didReceiveMemoryWarning
{
    [super didReceiveMemoryWarning];
    // Dispose of any resources that can be recreated.
}

@end                     second view urls
```

Figure 6-56. *Dragging in our DemoMonkey file*

57. As shown in Figure 6-57, you see all the NSURL instances for the eight social media sites all placed in perfect position. I don't have to explain what each repetitive line of code calling the URLS does because you went through it earlier. The awesome thing is that first you didn't have to code it, and now you have experience with DemoMonkey. Okay, you're done! Run it! :)

Figure 6-57. *The code inside DemoMonkey revealed*

58. When you first run it, you'll see the splash screen. Tapping the home button, you see your beautiful Switches button, as shown in Figure 6-58.

Figure 6-58. Your sixth iPhone app

59. Feel free to enter the URLs of your own social media sites. I've used mine and Apress because it's easy legally. In Figure 6-59, you can see Facebook, SoundCloud, and YouTube.

Figure 6-59. Some of the social media sites

60. Figure 6-60 shows that the app also goes perfectly well to ReverbNation, Google+, Myspace, and Twitter.

Figure 6-60. Four more views

Digging the Code

In this chapter, you spent some time digging the code already. One issue you may want to look at is compiling, how the computer looks at your code and implements what you wrote. Sometimes students get mixed up between *compile-time* and *runtime*. If you feel fresh and want to read this, go ahead. Otherwise, I'll see you in Chapter 7. Good job!

Compile-time and Runtime

Compile-time indicates that something happens when your project is compiled, or built, prior to being run on the Simulator or on a real iOS device. These are things like the definition of classes in .h and .m files, the organization and layout of UIView instances in your nib files, and the configuration you do in Xcode's various inspectors. Everything that is set at compile-time defines exactly the state your app will be in when it's started.

Runtime, on the other hand, describes the segment of time after your app has started running. This is when all the code you've written is actually executed, effecting changes in the state of the app from the way it was set up at compile-time. In this chapter, you specified the image for the second tab through a message in your implementation file. Thus, the image to show was unspecified at compile-time, but at runtime a series of instructions was executed to display the desired image in the UIImageView you provided. In essence, both load at compile time but while the code behind the second image is not executed by the user, it will remain compiled but unspecified. The instant the user executes the code for the unspecified image, the runtime associates the image to the secondViewController and the image is now specified.

Why is this difference significant? You proved, during the course of writing this app, that you can do the exact same thing at runtime as you could at compile-time. However, executing instructions to do what you wanted required several extra clicks and drags and a few more lines of code. If you already know how you're going to configure something at compile-time, the advantages of writing code to do the same thing will diminish. However, if you want to dynamically change the properties of an object during the execution of the app (last chapter's touches app is a great example of this), it's obviously impossible to set all aspects of the state at compile-time.

In short, compile-time defines the starting state of your app, whereas runtime describes the actions that occur once your app begins running.

In Chapter 7, you'll move into the next level of complexity: storyboarding. Storyboarding is the new way Apple lets you lay out how a user moves through an app, in much the same way that a movie producer sets up a storyboard to show how a movie will go from one scene to the next. Storyboarding has *segues* (pronounced "segways") that connect each view in your app with another. It is tempting to just go straight to storyboarding, but it's best to first learn a little about the code behind these buttons and images, as you have done. So take a break, and then let's move on to the land of storyboarding.

Chapter 7

Storyboards

This chapter introduces a new way to create an app quickly and visually. First, you'll lay out some views and you'll see how they can be connected without writing code—plus you'll get some neat transition animations for free. This new technique was first brought to the public's attention when Apple announced that it would be introducing a never-before-seen feature called Storyboards, which would be built in to Xcode. Storyboards would allow the easy layout of workflow apps that use navigation and tab bars to transition between views.

Apple went on to say that the new Storyboards would manage the View Controllers for you, while visually creating an easy-to-manage geospatial view of your project. It would specify the transitions and segues that are used when switching between views, without having to code them by hand! Everyone waited with anticipation for the beta to come out and, when it did, everyone was blown away. It changed the entire coding landscape.

Storytelling

When you tell a story, you communicate with others. Whether young or old, everyone loves a story. When you communicate with a user, you're telling them how to travel a path you've created that will bring them to a place where they will get what they want, be it a map, a song, a recipe, the weather, where they parked their car, a phone number, a movie, or something else. So why wasn't this thought of before? Why was the creation of apps seen as geeks programming code, whereas storytellers were seen as doing something different? I'm not sure of the answer, but as I began to think about it, I realized that this was an incredible concept. Think of it. When Walt Disney began to think of the most efficient means to organize and structure cartoons, back in the early 1920s, he came up with the concept of storyboards. He would gather his artists together, and they would mount a series of boards with key scenes from a story, and then they would organize these boards into a beautiful story. This technique became a huge success; it took over the movie industry, and it is the blueprint for planning every modern film. You can see a great movie that illustrates how Disney's storyboarding took over the industry at http://bit.ly/oWg5mc.

The Storyboard feature, introduced in iOS 5, works on a similar principle, except you're not necessarily looking at pictures; you're looking at a geospatial representation of your app that allows you to organize it beautifully. Before iOS 5 came out, nib files were used to define the user interface (UI). There was no choice but to do that one View Controller at a time. If you had 16 View Controllers, you would have to define the UI 16 times. Not only was this boring, but it became complex and confusing. Conversely, as you'll soon see, a Storyboard file captures all your UIs in one geospatial view and gives you the ability to easily create and edit all your individual View Controllers and the transitions between them. You can move your View Controllers around like cards in a deck, just like the guys at the Disney studios. Storyboards make it easy to realize and edit the flow of the overall UI and experience in your app.

Roadmap Recap

You now know enough of what happens behind the scenes to install a new way of doing things. It's as if you've spent enough time tinkering around with lawnmower engines and basic car engines that you can appreciate installing a brand new engine in your old car. As you install this new engine, you know that inside this engine are pistons, spark plugs, carburetors, and so on. You don't have to yank the engine open to know these items exist; you can just install it and connect it to the chassis, the drive train, and the electronics. In Storyboarding, you're going to use a whole new method for designing your app; you simply connect it to your outlets, View Controllers, and the other elements of your app. You don't have to open up Storyboard and look inside, because you know it works; you simply have to know how to connect things. So let's do it!

This app has been divided into three phases. The most important is Phase I; it's common for most of the potential uses for Storyboarding. Because Phase I is the lowest common denominator for so many of the future Storyboards you'll find yourself doing, you'll focus on it quite a bit, and I encourage you to perform exercises that will enable you to quickly become efficient at Storyboarding. Phase I sets up the root of what will be done over and over again. Phases II and III are specific to this particular app:

- Phase I sets up the core of most potential Storyboarding configurations.

- Phase II starts at Figure 7-20 and is comprised of setting up the View Controllers and establishing their content.

- Phase III starts at Figure 7-32 and is comprised of closure and coding.

Evolve: A View-Based Storyboard Application

Once again, you'll work with images that let you know where in the story you are. In more technical terms, you'll use images rather than code to represent a state in your app. I encourage my students to use images because, if it doesn't work, then you know it's a bug in the high-level code that directs the user from state to state—not a bug in the code for a particular state.

In this app, you'll see a funny set of states that show the state of a male, female, and third kind of human being—a geek. The app shows that when men or women evolve into a higher state of consciousness, they become geeks. Then, to add another state, for fun and to illustrate the purpose, when geeks evolve they become übergeeks! As funny as this is, it simply gives us a nice set of diverse states that in Storyboarding is easy, but that in the old one-at-a-time nib manipulation would have been substantially harder and more complex.

First, download the images from `http://bit.ly/TXN9HM`, where you can also download the code or view the video. Once you've downloaded the zip file containing the images, unzip the folder and store the images on your desktop.

Phase I: Creating Core Storyboarding Configurations

Let's get going with Phase I, where you'll build a core configuration.

1. Start a new project in Xcode by using your keyboard shortcut, ⌘+⇧+N and selecting the Single View Application project type As shown in Figure 7-1. The Single View Application is the starting place for this and many more of this book's applications, and likely many of your own.

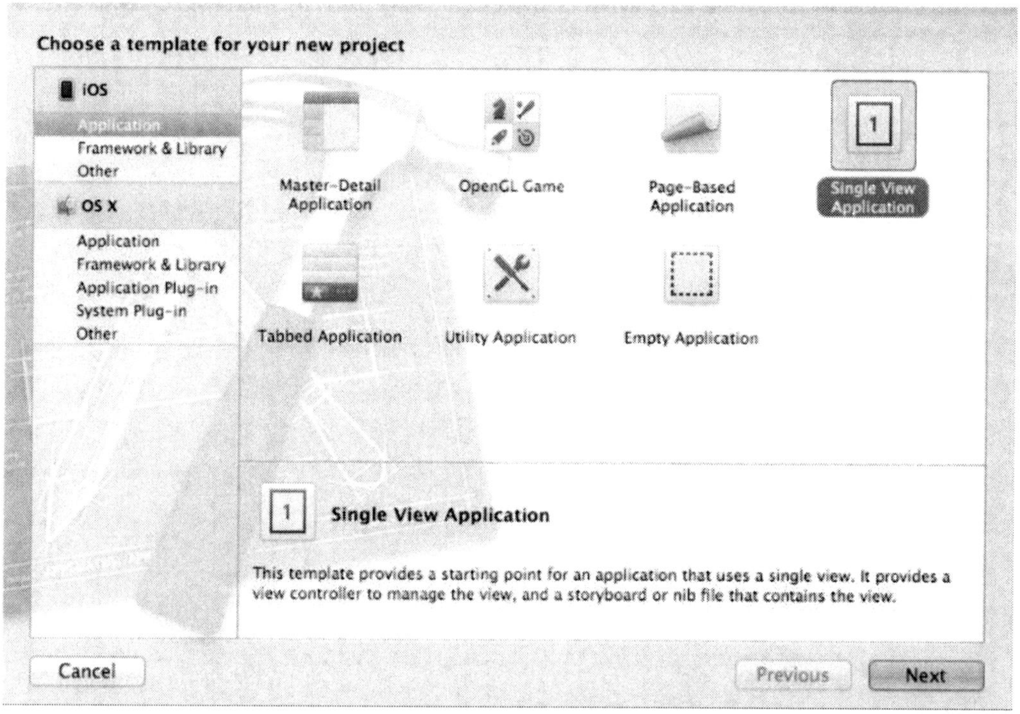

Figure 7-1. Start by choosing a Single View Application skeleton. More views will be added later

2. Let's name this application myStory. The Company Identifier isn't relevant
    right now, so feel free to put something creative there. For simplicity, just
    target the iPhone device family at this time. Check the Use Storyboard option
    This is shown in Figure 7-2. Doing so presents you with a slightly different
    project layout once you've saved the project. Go ahead and save your
    project by clicking Next.

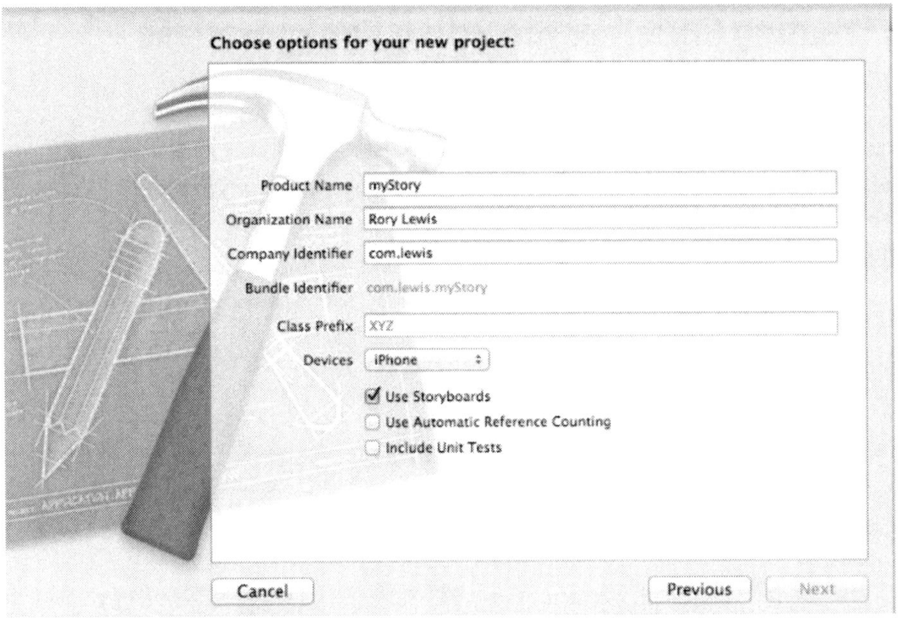

Figure 7-2. *Start with just an iPhone version of the app and the new Storyboard feature selected to let you jump directly into design and layout. I named it myStory*

3. The next step is to drag in your two icons from your images all laid out on
    your desktop. I've already dragged the 114 × 114 Retina Display icon into its
    slot, and I'm dragging the regular icon into its slot in Figure 7-3.

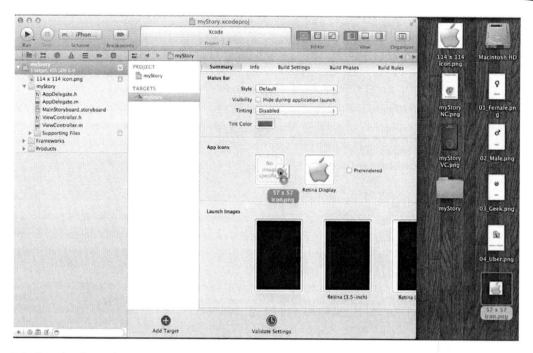

Figure 7-3. Dragging the two icons into the App Icon slots

4. Drag the remaining six items from your desktop into your project's
    Supporting Files directory in Xcode. These six items include the two
    Controller Views which are the Navigation Controller, called myStory NC.png,
    and the View Controller, called myStory VC.png. The four remaining images
    are your views for Female (01_Female.png), Male (02_Male.png), Geek
    (03_Geek.png), and ÜberGeek (04_Uber.png). Figure 7-4 shows the grouped
    files being dropped into my project's Supporting Files directory in Xcode.

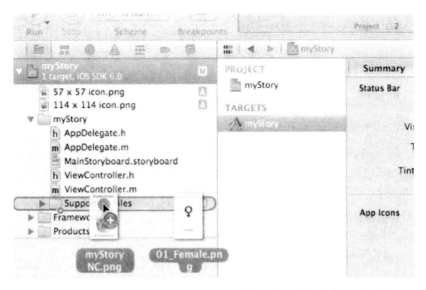

Figure 7-4. *Drag the images that you downloaded earlier to the project's Supporting Files directory in Xcode*

5. Remember that the `Supporting Files` directory you just dropped your images into is just a logical directory, and the files can actually go almost anywhere in the `MyStory` directory. Be sure that these files are copied accordingly, so go ahead and click "Copy items into destination group's folder (if needed)," as shown in Figure 7-5.

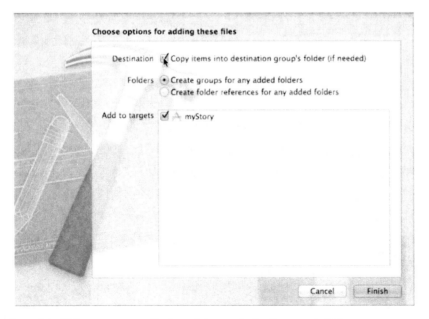

Figure 7-5. *Make sure you copy the items into your destination group's folder*

6. As you've begun to see from previous chapters, the last step in the setting-up-the-images routine is to drag the icons you want into the `Supporting Files` folder. Xcode always inserts them into the target directory, sometimes called the root directory. But we like to keep things organized; you should keep all supporting files you bring into the project in your...erh...`Supporting Files` folder. So, go ahead and drag those two icons into your `Supporting Files` folder, as shown in Figure 7-6.

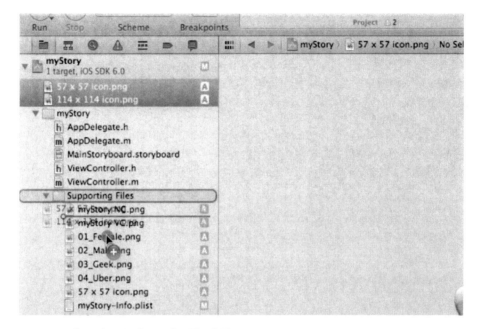

Figure 7-6. Drag your two icons into the Supporting Files folder

7. One reason I'm recording this app on MacBook Pro's the smaller screen is that I've had many e-mails asking me how one manipulates and controls the Storyboard canvas on a small laptop screen. So, in Figure 7-7 you see three arrows. Briefly, arrow 1 opens up Storyboarding, arrow 2 maximizes the canvas, and arrow 3 zooms out the canvas so you can see everything. Note that you just double-click an item to zoom in. Now, select the `MainStoryboard.storyboard` file in Xcode's project file browser, as shown by arrow 1. This shows you something familiar: a `UIView`. But this isn't just a `UIView`—it also has an associated controller that's automatically created and linked to the view. Once you've opened the Storyboard canvas, you want to maximize the real estate of the canvas, as shown by arrow 2. Once you've maximized the canvas, practice zooming in and out (arrow 3) so you become familiar with a tool you'll be using quite often in storyboarding.

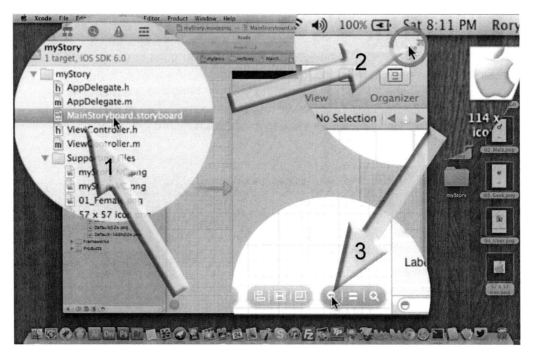

Figure 7-7. Select the MainStoryboard.storyboard file, and you'll be presented with your only default view

Note   You *must* be in *normal viewing mode* to add visual elements to the views. Clicking the center equals sign button returns you to *normal viewing mode*. The two buttons on either side allow you to zoom in and out.

8.   Bring up the Utilities panel. Once you've opened the Utilities panel, locate the Navigation Controller (UINavigationController), as shown by arrow 1 in Figure 7-8. Select it and start dragging the Navigation Controller onto your Storyboard, as shown by arrow 2 in Figure 7-8. Placement doesn't matter at this point; just make sure that when you drop it, it's bounded in the Storyboard canvas. If it's not, it will zoom back into your Library. As you drag the Navigation Controller onto the Storyboard, you'll see that instead of just a Single View, you get a connected pair of controllers depicted as views. Drop it anyplace—move it around as much as you need. This is, in fact, the case for almost everything that you'll do in Storyboards. You're not dealing just with views; you're actually seeing Apple instantiate each UI element into a set of views and controllers that allow you to build transitions. These transitions in Xcode are called *segues*, as shown in Figure 7-8.

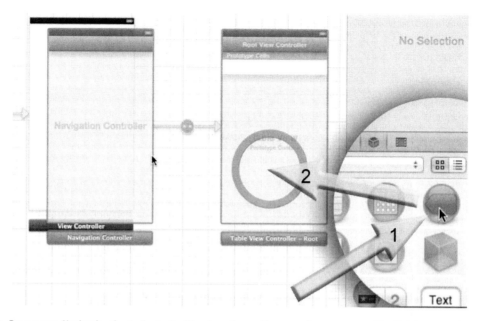

Figure 7-8. Drag a new Navigation Controller to the Storyboard area. Two new views appear, with a link between them

9. When Xcode instantiates the UINavigationController, it defaults its
   accompanying View Controller with a Table View, as shown In Figure 7-9.
   You don't want a Table View; you want a blank View Controller *into which*
   you can insert your images. So, click the Table View once and delete it so you
   can replace it with a clean View Controller.

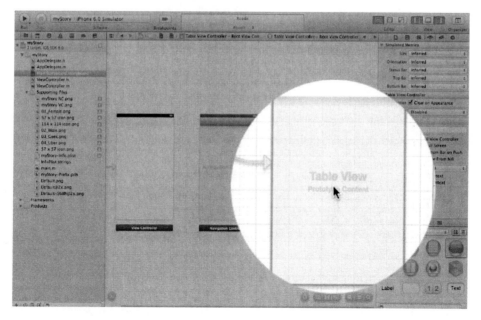

Figure 7-9. Delete the Table View

10. Replace the deleted Table View with a View Controller (`UIViewController`).
     Select it (arrow 1 in Figure 7-10) and drag it to the right side of the Navigation
     Controller (arrow 2).

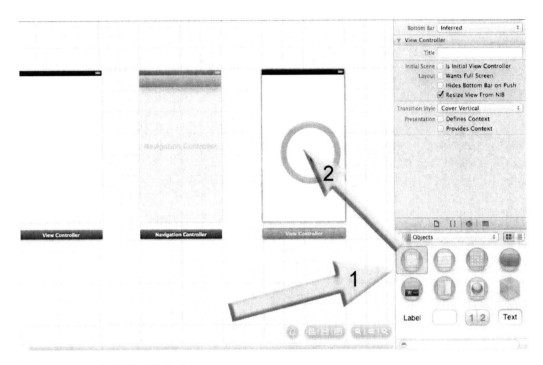

Figure 7-10. Drag on a simple View Controller

11. Control-drag from your Root View Controller to the new View Controller and
     select the "root view controller" option from the dialog box, as shown in
     Figure 7-11.

Note If you're curious why you need to link the Root View Controller to the Navigation Controller, well, unfortunately that's beyond the scope of this book. For this book, you simply say that when you replace a View Controller, you connect it as a Root View Controller. But if you want a quick explanation: deep in Xcode, the Navigation Controllers array needs to be linked with the Root View Controller. You can't do that with a push, modal, or custom segue. It has to be a Relationship Segue Root View Controller.

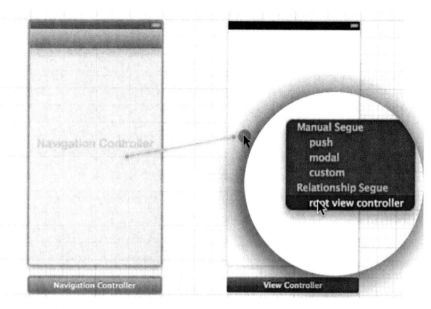

Figure 7-11. Link your new Root View Controller to the Navigation Controller

12. You need to drag Image Views onto the left View Controller and the Navigation Controller so you can place the greeting screens for each of them respectively. Figure 7-12 shows the UIImageView being dragged onto the left View Controller.

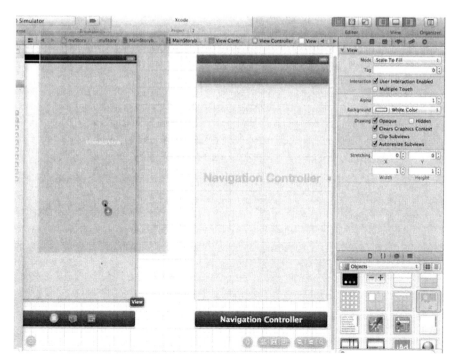

Figure 7-12. Drag a UIImageView onto your View Controller

13. Now drag the second `UIImageView` Controller, this time onto the Navigation Controller's View Controller, as shown in Figure 7-13.

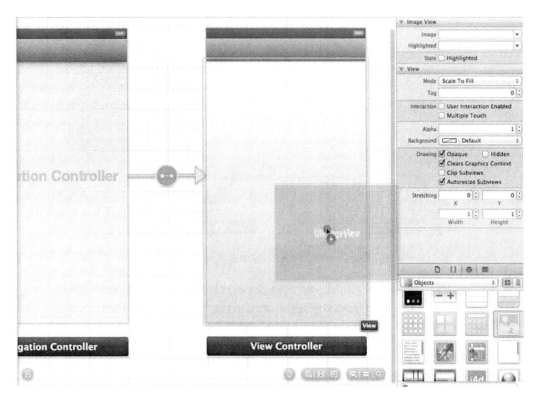

Figure 7-13. Drag a UIImageView onto your Navigation Controller's View Controller

14. Click on the Navigation Controller's `UIImageView` you placed in step 7–13 and select `myStory NC.png` from the Image drop-down menu, as shown in Figure 7-14. Click the View Controller's `UIImageView` you placed in step 12 and select `myStory VC.png` from the Image drop-down menu.

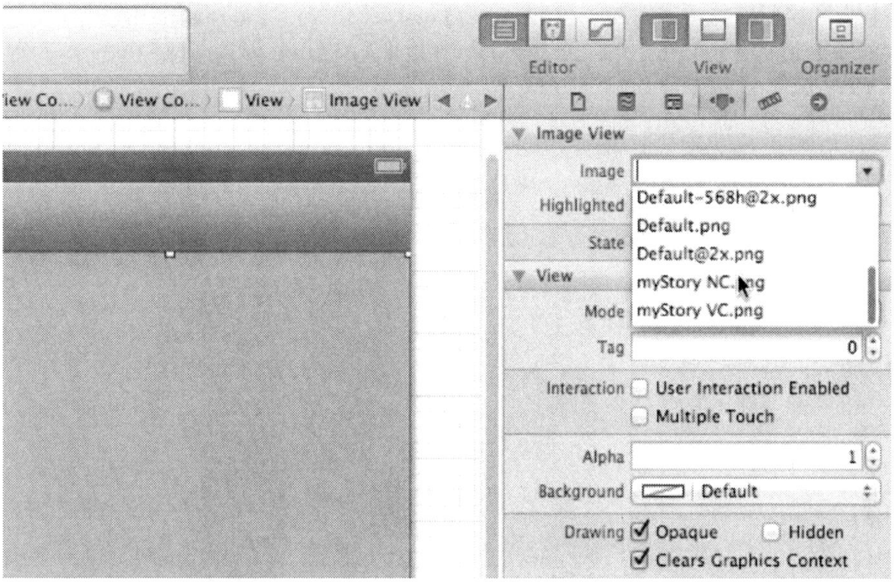

Figure 7-14. *Associate the images for the Navigation and View Controllers*

15. As shown in Figure 7-15, you need to have a button on your Main View Controller, so drag a Round Rect button (UIButtonView) onto it, so that you can have an actionable item to tap, which will push the next View Controller to the stack.

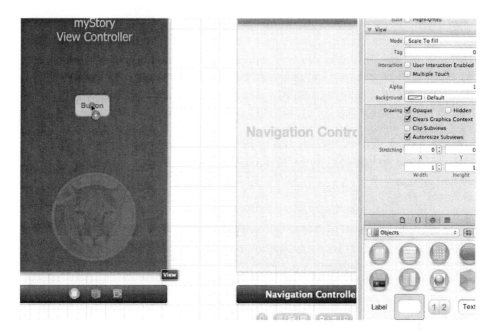

Figure 7-15. *Drag a UIButtonView out to the Main View Controller so that you can have an actionable item in order to push the next View Controller to the stack*

16. When the user taps this first button, you want it to take the user to the Navigation Controller. Let's tell the user this will happen if they tap this button. This is illustrated in Figure 7-16.

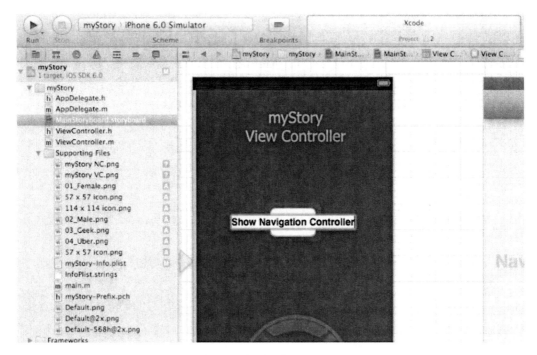

Figure 7-16. *Insert text into your button. I used "Show Navigation Controller"*

17. This step is really the heart of Storyboarding. Let's think about this. You want users to be directed to the Navigation Controller when they tap the Show Navigation Controller button. Rather than writing code, just link the button to the Navigation Controller. Position your mouse pointer over the button, Control-drag, and release over the Navigation Controller to create a transitional link; make sure to select modal from the list too. This is the magic—no code is written to make this transition with animation, as shown in Figure 7-17. It's just free! A gift from the remarkably clever people at Apple, who include—if you don't mind me reminding you again—students and readers of the previous editions of this very book. So hang in there. Don't worry if you don't understand the following bullets—just read them and let the information start brewing in your brain; as you program more Storyboards, it will all become natural:

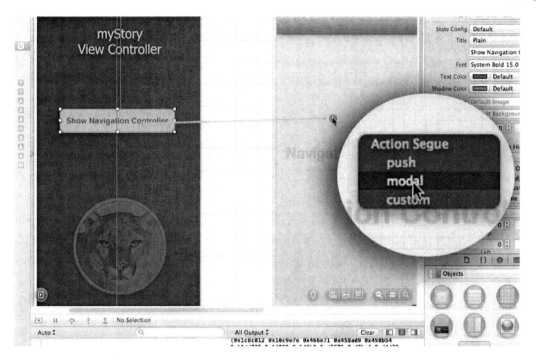

Figure 7-17. Start the actual linking

    a.   *Push* means that a Navigation Controller pushes a new View Controller onto the navigation *stack*. Note that when you use a push segue, you need a Navigation Controller for your View Controller. Conversely, if you don't have a Navigation Controller, you need to use the modal or custom options to manage the swapping of your View Controllers.

    b.   *Modal* is used to present a View Controller modally. Apple explains modal segues best: When you present a Modal View Controller, the system creates a relationship between the View Controller that did the presenting and the View Controller that was presented.

    c.   *Custom* allows you to code your own animation and transitions. That topic is beyond the scope of this book, but it's important to know that you can completely code your own transition and View Controller management.

18. Transitions are the animation types available for each style of segue. Again, just stick with the default. I chose the Flip Horizontal style for no particular reason other than it suits me. You can choose another style if you want. Feel free to experiment here, but keep usability in mind. It's very easy to get too flashy with the animations. I often find that the popular apps, and smarter students, tend to have less flash and more utility and efficiency.

As shown in Figure 7-18, first select the segue connecting the View Controller to the Navigation Controller and then select a transition of your choice from the drop-down menu. At this point, running the app will show you how little you actually had to do to get a working app with some direction. So, click that Run button and see what you have.

Figure 7-18. Select the transition of your choice

Note   You should emulate what I make my students do at this point. I make them erase everything they have done so far, except for the five icons on their desktop. Then I make them repeat these steps over and over again until they can get all the way through step 17, run the app, and have it appear in the Simulator within 50 seconds, without using the book. I *strongly* encourage you to do this. Just as a golfer needs to practice his swing to create muscle memory, you need to be able to get to this point without even thinking. First, do it at your own pace with the book, and then go faster and faster until you get below 50 seconds! Yeah!

19. After clicking Run, the Simulator opens and voila—it works! You've hardly done anything and used no code. You just shifted, dragged, and connected a few items, and you now have a running app. Clicking the button flips the view and shows a blank view, with a navigation bar at the top named Root, as depicted in Figure 7-19. Beautiful!

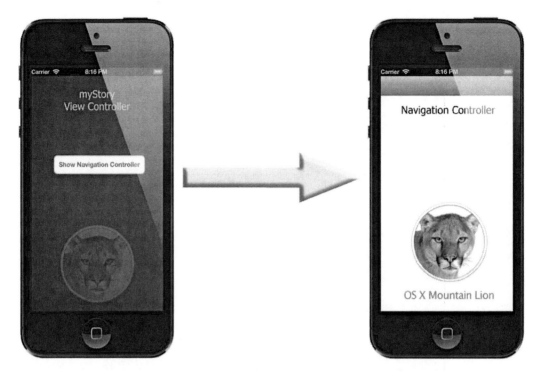

Figure 7-19. And, sure enough, clicking the button flips the view and shows the Navigation Controller

Phase II: Setting Up and Establishing the Content of the View Controllers

Of course, you want to make this app do something more interesting than what you now have. Remember, in this evolving app you have three types of human—men, women, and geeks—and they can all potentially evolve into übergeeks. This means that you need to have three views connected directly to your Navigation Controller. So, before you begin to drag three View Controllers onto the Storyboard, make sure of the following:

- That you can see everything—enough for three horizontally placed UIViewController instances.

- That your alignment on the grid can be kept so that your connection lines don't get silly looking later on, and therefore harder to follow.

20. Let's drop three more View Controllers into the Storyboard, to the right of the Root View Controller. This is a personal preference, but it sure makes you look like a supercalifragilistic geek if you can do it. You can watch me do this in the video at http://bit.ly/Tlh0eU. Try to get your screen looking like the one in Figure 7-20, which shows the first of the three UIViewController instances being dragged onto the Storyboard. Remember, if you're having trouble with the zoom, just click the equal button in the zoom control area so that you can add other stuff to the individual controllers.

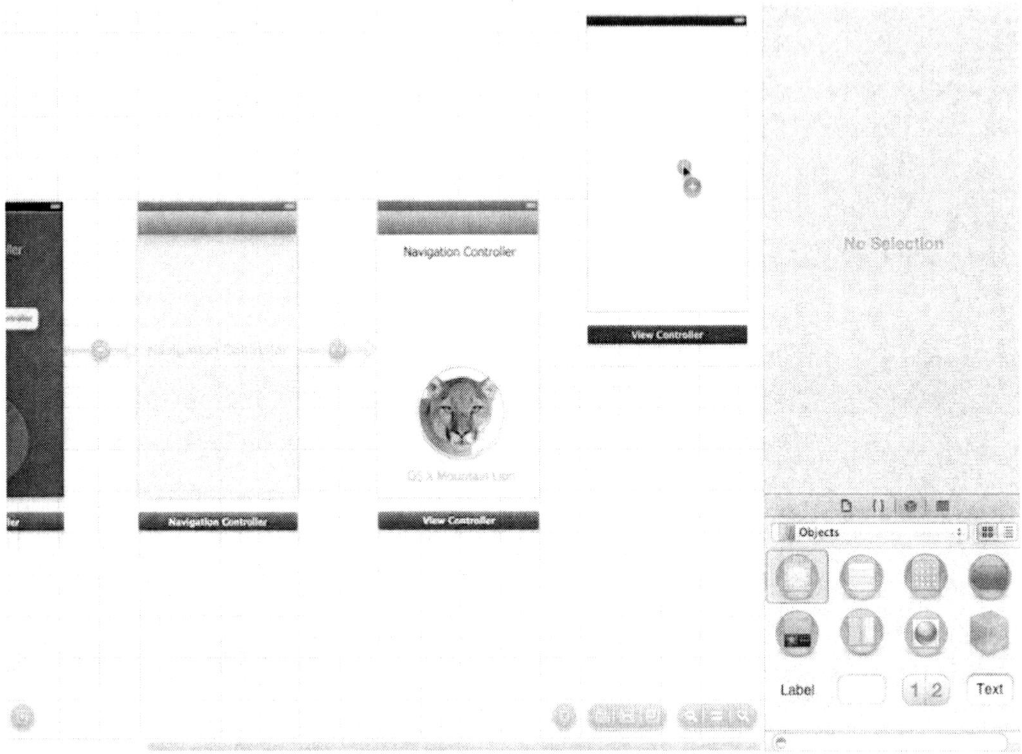

Figure 7-20. *Zoom out and drag a new View Controller onto the Storyboard*

21. Figure 7-21 shows how your screen should look after you've dragged all
three View Controllers onto your Storyboard. Note that they're aligned,
spaced equally apart, and locked into the grid.

Note Objects not sticking? It will get frustrating if you continually try to drag objects to a view, and
they never stick, so be sure you return to the normal zoom level.

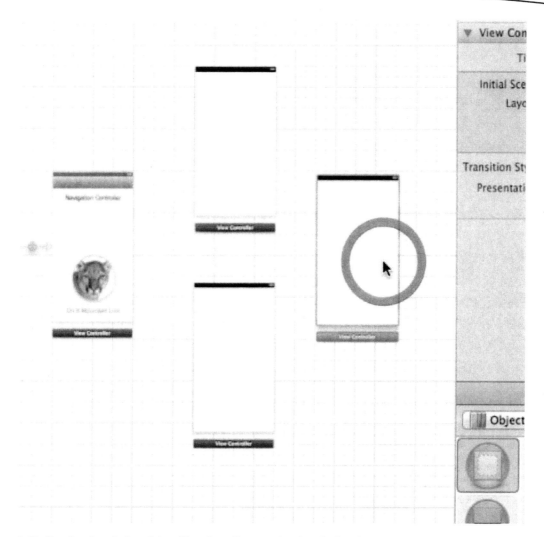

Figure 7-21. *Your Storyboard after all three View Controllers are placed on the Storyboard*

22. As shown in Figure 7-22, add a new `UIButtonView` to the view. Use each
     button's activation to move to another view. You can either drag three buttons
     by repeating the process three times or practice using the Option-drag
     technique: So, Option-drag from the first button you've placed and duplicate
     it twice, because you need three. These will now only need relabeling. Name
     the buttons Female, Male, and Geek in descending order and resize them as
     you see fit.

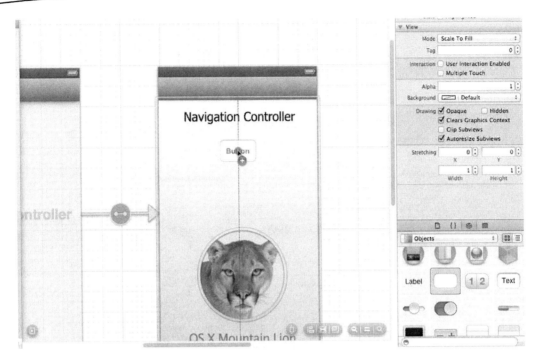

Figure 7-22. Drag a UIButtonView to the Navigation Controller and duplicate it

23. You need to create segues from each of your three buttons to their associated
    View Controllers. So, as before, Control-drag from each button to another
    View Controller to create a segue link for each button. These will all be of type
    Push. I connected Female to the top, Geek to the bottom, and Male to the
    center, as shown in Figure 7-23, because it makes the link lines look nice and
    organized. Connect all three View Controllers to their appropriate buttons,
    remembering to make them of type Push.

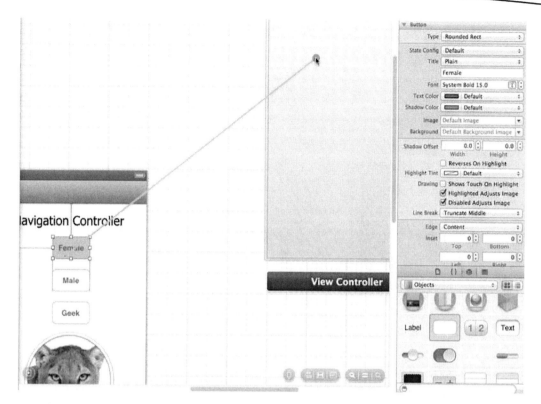

Figure 7-23. *Create more segues from each button to the three View Controllers*

24. Naming the Controller Bar titles in Storyboarding actually instantiates connectivity under the hood, and this eliminates the need to code some of these segues if at some point you advance to the point where you'll code. Right now for this app you're doing no coding; however, it's a good habit to name the Controller Bars in the same manner that you may name a view's corresponding pointers and classes too. Just double-click toward the center of the Controller Bar and start typing. Do these with your Male, Female, and Geek Controller Bar titles. In Figure 7-24, you can see that the default value of the Female controller has already been changed from "_" to "Female." I'm renaming Geek's Controller Bar in Figure 7-24. Go ahead and name the Male Controller Bar too.

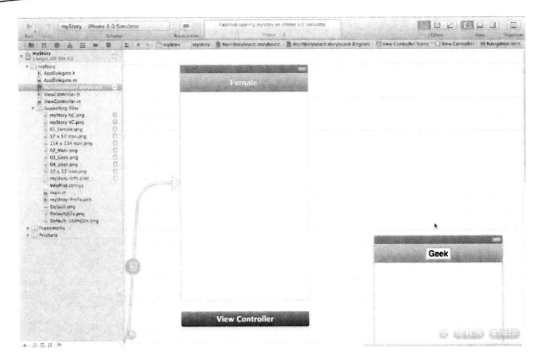

Figure 7-24. *Name the Controller Bar titles*

25. Your next step will be to add images to your Male, Female, and Geek View Controllers. Let's start at the top and drag an Image View onto the Male view, as shown in Figure 7-25. Go ahead and drag Image Views onto the Geek and Female View Controllers too.

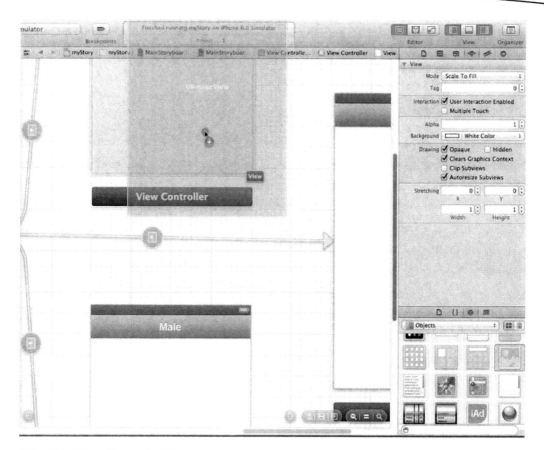

Figure 7-25. Add a UIImageView to the Male view

26. Associate the 01_Female.png image with the Female controller by selecting it from the Attributes panel, as shown in Figure 7-26. Go ahead and associate the 02_Male.png image with the Male controller and the 03_Geek.png image with the Geek controller. Then run it, and let's see what we have.

Figure 7-26. *Select the image to use for Female from the Attribute panel*

27.   It works! Figure 7-27 illustrates how the app, without any coding, is working beautifully. All the images show not one state but the transition between two states, connected by the segue. The figure also illustrates the flow of the Storyboard from the View Controller to the Navigation Controller's three buttons that segue to three views of Female, Male, and Geek. Almost done—let's do the last step now.

Note   Because you didn't change the segue type, you have the push effect for each of the three segue transitions created.

Figure 7-27. Workflow is working already

28. You're now getting to the fun portion of this app that makes students laugh out loud in class. In your app, you're going to show the world that evolution is still happening. You're going to show the world that both males and females can still evolve to a higher level of consciousness—and that, of course, is the state of being known as … yes, you got it … geek! You need to add a segue going from your Male and Female state to Geek. How should you do this? How about adding a Button Bar icon to both the Male and Female Views' Navigation Bars and giving them the title *Evolve*? After that, you can segue from these Evolve buttons to Geek. Start off by dragging a Bar Button icon onto the Female, as shown in Figure 7-28. Once you've dropped your second Bar Button item onto the Female, double-click it and type the word *Evolve*. Repeat the same process for the Male.

Note   Button Bar icons act just like regular `UIButtonView` instances, but they look different and are designed to go in only one place: a Navigation Bar. There's something important I want you to remember about Button Bar icons.

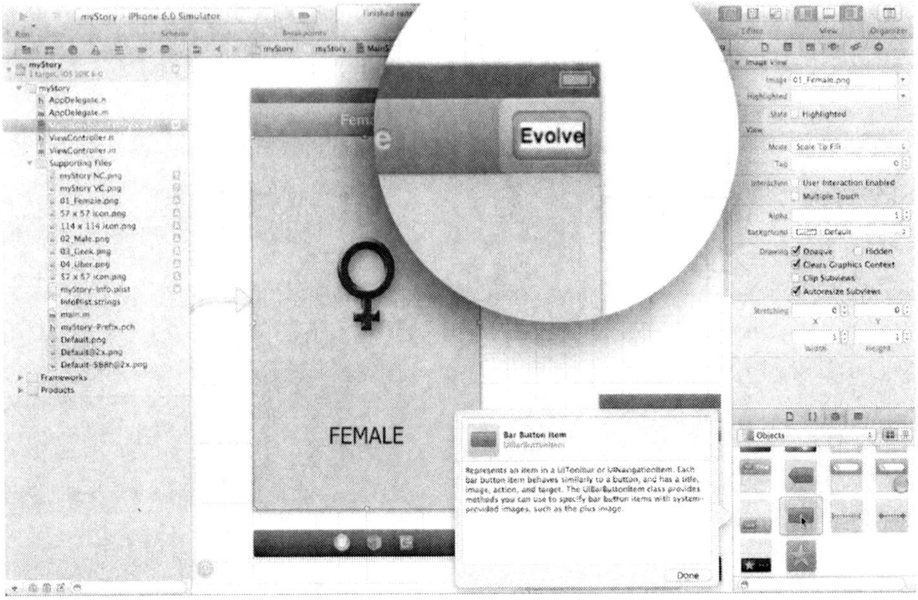

Figure 7-28. Now let's "evolve"

29. Control-drag from the Male's Evolve button to the Geek View Controller and make it of type Push, as shown in Figure 7-29. You want to segue from the Evolve button to Geek. Note that I kept the transitions linear for simplicity. They can have loops or be entirely circular. Repeat the same process from the Female's Evolve button, also making it of type Push.

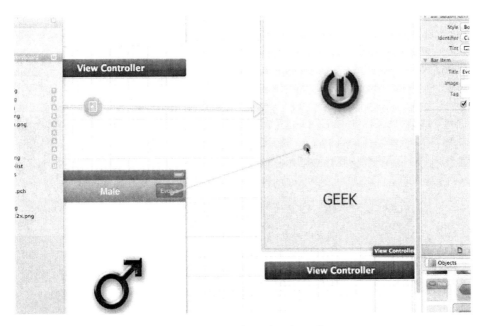

Figure 7-29. Control-drag from the Male's Evolve button to the Geek View Controller

30. Now that you've been living in the geek world for a few chapters, you've probably caught on to the fact that geeks know something normal people are completely unaware of. Yup! There's an even higher state of humankind than a geek. Übergeeks are very rare and can only be recognized by geeks. But this will be illustrated in your app. You need to add another state of human evolution beyond that of geek, which can only be seen by geeks. Add one last `UIViewController`, which will demonstrate how to gain programmatic access to the Controller and its data, as illustrated in Figure 7-30.

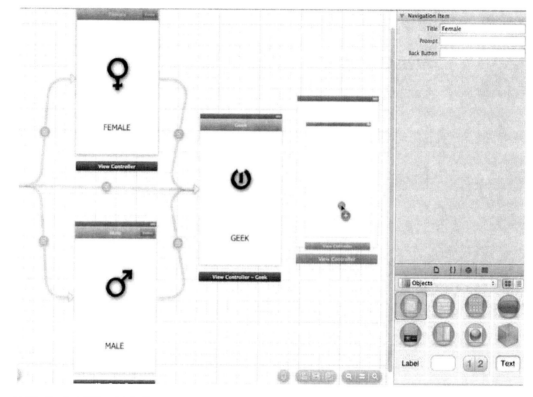

Figure 7-30. One last UIViewController

31. The next state up, ÜberGeek, is invisible. So you need to make an invisible button so that only Geeks will know segues to the higher ÜberGeek state of consciousness. As shown in Figure 7-31, drag a seemingly innocent, benign round rectangular button onto your Geek object.

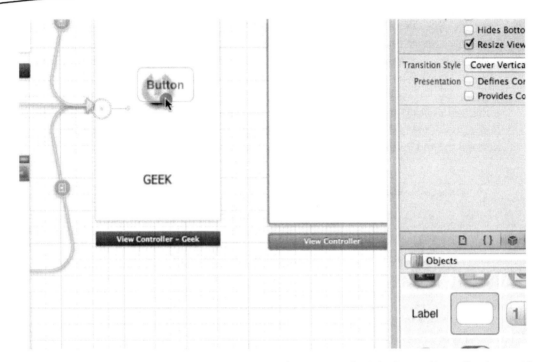

Figure 7-31. *You can use an invisible button over your background imagery as a simple hack to avoid spending time working on a fancy button*

Phase III: Working on Closure and Coding

You're in the final phase now, so let's finish the app.

32. As shown in Figure 7-32, once your button is placed on the Geek object, expand it so it covers the entire Geek symbol.

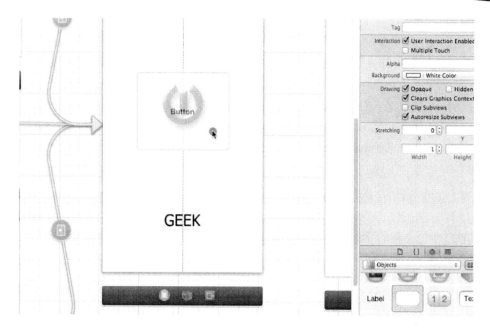

Figure 7-32. Cover the entire Geek symbol, for starters

33. You want to make it invisible, so set the button type to Custom, as shown by arrow 1
     in Figure 7-33. The GUI will immediately default to making the button invisible,
     though still clickable for Geeks ... almost! You can see that the text "Button" is still
     there though. No problem. Simply delete the button text, as indicated by arrow 2.

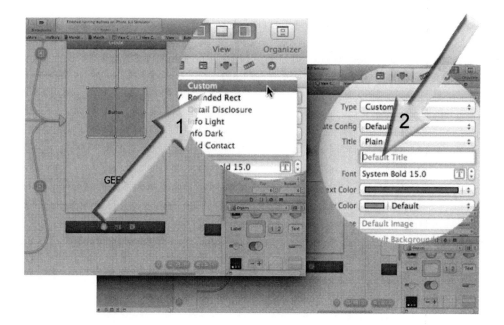

Figure 7-33. Make that button vanish into thin air

34. Now that you've made your invisible button, you need to make a segue to the next transition and make it of type Push. Click where you know your invisible button is and then Control-drag over to the new View Controller, as illustrated in Figure 7-34.

Figure 7-34. Control-drag from the invisible button to the next View Controller

35. Almost done! You need to add an image onto the new view. Drag a UIImageView onto the view, as shown in Figure 7-35.

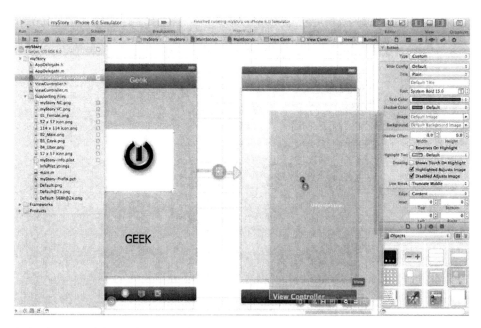

Figure 7-35. Let's add another UIImageView to the view

36. Figure 7-36 shows the association of the 04_Uber.png with the ÜberGeek's View Controller.

Figure 7-36. Associate the 04_Uber.png image with the UIImageView

37. Similarly to how you named the title bars previously we will name this title bar ÜberGeek. To get the umlaut (two dots), press Option+U. Once the two dots appear, press Shift+U to capitalize it, as shown In Figure 7-37.

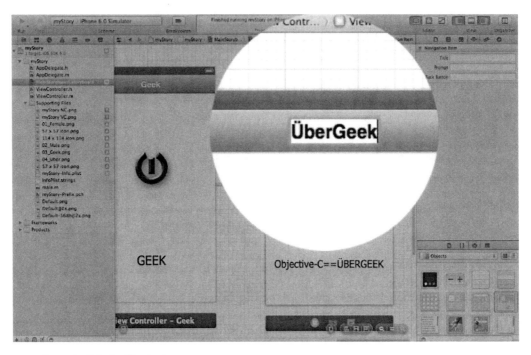

Figure 7-37. Name the Title Bar ÜberGeek

38. Initially, I didn't think I would have to spend much time arranging the objects/views on the Storyboard. But after having some difficulty myself, and then seeing the wonderful spaghetti messes that some of my students came up with, I've decided to spend a little time coming up with some basic principles, which, if adhered to, will prevent a chaotic and tangled mess. Zoom out, as I have, and then move your objects around accordingly as you follow the three protocols I've developed:

    a. *Mutual exclusivity*: Keep the order of your buttons mutually exclusive from the order of your views. The buttons on the Navigation Controller go Male, Female, and then Geek. Maintaining that order on the Storyboard would create problems, because it would violate other principles I'm about to mention.

    b. *Maintain initial momentum*: If, for example, on the Female View, at the bottom of Figure 7-38, you have a fan of 10 segues to 10 views that were all void of segues to the Geek branch, then keep those Female-based segues going downward.

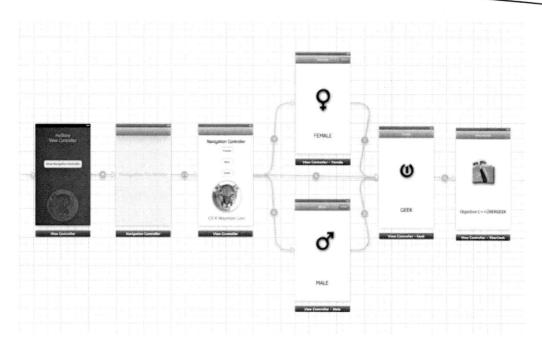

Figure 7-38. Zoom out and arrange/neaten up the views

Looking at Figure 7-39, one can see a perfect example of how *not* to maintain initial momentum. Not only are the segue connections hidden, they also overlap and disrupt the ability to follow where the segues start and end.

c. *Minimize segue connection angles*: This is easier explained when you first see it: look at the Male and Female segue connections from the Navigation Controller in Figure 7-38. Notice how they first slope back and then slope forward, as compared to the less angular connections from the Navigation Controller to the same two Male and Female Views depicted in Figure 7-39 and onward. An easy way to adhere to this protocol is this: once the segue is connected, move the object it's connected to horizontally and vertically until the segue connection is almost perfectly horizontal or vertical.

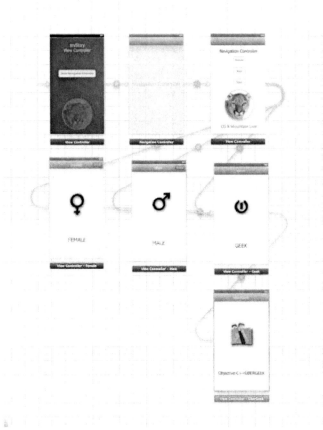

Figure 7-39. *Oops! Violation of the "maintaining initial momentum" protocol*

39.   You really need to be careful how you place your objects because the GUI can make things look very odd, as shown in Figure 7-39, which demonstrates a violation of the protocol of maintaining initial momentum. But note that because you moved the Male and Female to the top and bottom respectively in Figure 7-38, you can see that you've adhered to the protocol of minimizing segue connection angles.

40. Run it! As you go from screen to screen it will flow similarly to the sequence shown in Figure 7-40. It's amazing how you did all that without a single word of code. You may want to know that in the first edition of this book, this app took three chapters of complex code. :)

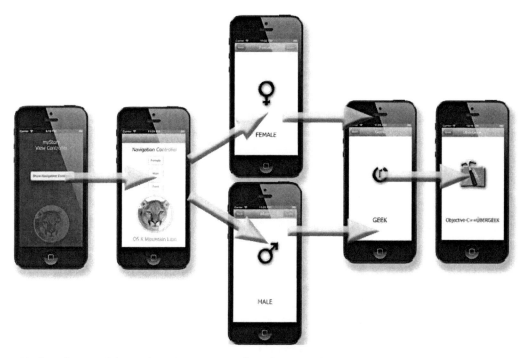

Figure 7-40. Try to keep track in your head. It can get complicated, but you did not type one word of code. Amazing!

Finally, if your Storyboard isn't connected to your Destination View Controller, you can create it programmatically; but the author hasn't explored this in depth on the Apple Dev site. I have no idea why you would want to do this, but it is in the *View Controller Programming Guide for iOS* on the Apple web site. If you want to understand Storyboarding, remember two things:

▨ First, it inherits from, and conforms to, NSObject.

▨ Second, its framework is from /System/Library/Frameworks/UIKit.framework.

The important issue I want you to understand is that, right now, you can program endlessly using what you already know about Storyboarding. Keep in mind the basics, and really understand these basics. Forget about programming Storyboards programmatically. Use them as they are, and understand the basics.

Storyboards all need to begin with an initial View Controller that represents the starting point of your app and connects to your UI. This is the first screen your user sees. In your case, it was My Story's View Controller. If you have a bug, you may want to check your transitions to the initial View

Controller in a different Storyboard file. That's the Storyboard file specified in the application's `Info.plist` file using the `UIMainStoryboardFile` key, which is the initial View Controller that's loaded and presented automatically when your program begins.

In Chapter 8, I introduce you to the world of MapKits. This is very exciting because everybody loves MapKit apps. Chapter 8 is the introduction, and Chapter 9 really digs down into MapKits to make an awesome app.

Onward to the maps that await us in the next chapter!

Introducing MapKit

In this chapter, you'll get started using MapKit, one of the most successful frameworks for iOS. You'll also explore some cool apps that are currently based on the MapKit framework. Of course, in addition, you'll create your first MapKit app. This app will run on both the iPhone and iPad and allow you to scroll through Apple's world map, zoom in, and zoom out—all with no code from you whatsoever! This is the simplest way to dip your big toe into the waters of MapKit-based apps.

Although MapKit, as a toolbox, is a challenging set of utilities and devices, you'll soon see just how easily you can put together a basic app using MapKit. Before going any farther, however, I want to talk about *frameworks*. After that, we'll dig deeper to see what other programmers have done using MapKit and glean what we can from them. Then you'll see what MapKit can already do without your having to program anything at all.

The objective here is to get you to a place where you can say, "I've programmed a basic MapKit app and I understand how to move forward with confidence into the more advanced goal of utilizing MapKit to create more advanced map applications."

A Little About Frameworks

When Steve Jobs was fired from Apple, he formed a computer company called NeXT. In the early 90s, his company produced beautiful, black, streamlined computers that made me drool with envy. A few of my professors owned NeXT computers, and I was aware of their capabilities. The most profound aspect of this outfit was not that they cranked out these black, streamlined boxes, but rather that they used a language called Objective-C. Jobs had found that, even though programming in this complex language was difficult, the code it produced was able to "talk to" the microprocessor quite elegantly. So, what does this have to do with MapKit?

What NeXT did was create *frameworks* of complex Objective-C code, which you can think of as the tools that a carpenter might have in his toolbox. When you use MapKit, you're bringing into your own code a framework of map-related tools—just as a carpenter may have one set of tools for cabinetry and another specially made set specifically for making intricate furniture. Such specialized tools differ significantly from the type of tools that a roofing carpenter might use.

To this end, you'll bring the MapKit framework into Xcode. It will be almost as if you'd been learning techniques as a flooring and cabinetry carpenter in Chapters 1–7, but now you're going to the hardware store to get outfitted for your next gig, which will be audio–video installations in walls and ceilings. Therefore, before you continue on to the next program, you're going to have to go buy a brand new tool. In this case, the tool is MapKit, and it lets you interact with maps in a number of different of ways. You'll use MapKit in both this project and the next. In both chapters, it's the centerpiece of our discussion.

With the iPhone and iPad, Apple helped to bring maturity to the modern interfaces we now use to interact with our mobile devices. Before the advent of these slick devices, 99 percent of all interactions with computers were based on the mouse and keyboard. In the examples you've already programmed, you've used unique methods and classes to jump between screens and sense when a user is pinching, tapping, or scrolling on the screen. These tools are also built in to MapKit. For a user to have basic interaction with the map, you don't have to supply any code, as you did in previous chapters. The map reacts to the user's touches without intervention because it incorporates some of the very same techniques you've already learned.

MapKit Showcase: Preinstalled Apps

Since the first version of the iPhone, Apple has been steadily building out its map technologies to provide readily available geo information on the go. For those who carry an iPhone or iPad everywhere, it's rare to be truly lost, no matter where you travel. Today, you can move about the world with confidence and freedom, thanks to your friends at Apple, who continually work to improve the technologies that affect our daily lives. Keep in mind that Apple's MapKit, coupled with its other technologies like CoreLocation, serve to inspire very smart and innovative people who provide us with beautifully ingenious apps every day. This is illustrated in Figure 8-1 where one can see the new vector-based Apple maps that keep crisp no matter how much you zoom in or out.

Figure 8-1. Apple's latest Maps application—vector-based maps that keep text crisp, graphics clear, and panning and zooming smooth and responsive

To take maximum advantage of the new ideas presented in this chapter, and to be prepared to stretch and expand into a new level of creativity, you'll first take a tour of the existing apps that are preinstalled on the iPad and iPhone. You want to become familiar with these so that you can gain ideas for adding your own bells and whistles to your creations.

Turn-by-Turn Navigation

iPhone owners no longer need to carry around separate GPS devices to help with travel directions. You can now travel lighter by ridding yourself of other gadgets and replacing them with the iPhone 5. Find your way to your destination using turn-by-turn spoken directions, a 3D view, and real-time traffic information. This is illustrated in Figure 8-2.

Figure 8-2. Navigation—a powerful turn-by-turn navigation tool included on iPhone/iPad

As you approach a turn, Maps speaks directions so you can keep your eyes on the road. In addition, the screen turns into 3D perspective view of the road ahead. Large signs and arrows superimposed over the images show you which way to go and how long it's going to take to get there—even if your screen is locked. When you start a turn, the camera angle changes dynamically to show you where to go. If you miss a turn, don't worry. Maps automatically reroutes you and updates your ETA.

Traffic: A Smarter Way to Cope

With Maps, you get real-time traffic information to calculate your ETA. Maps gives you detailed information on what's causing a backup so you can tell whether there's a major accident or it's just a temporary slowdown. This is illustrated in Figure 8-3. If traffic's a mess, Maps offers alternative routes to save you time.

Figure 8-3. Traffic—get real-time traffic information and re-route around heavy traffic situations

Local Search

Bicycle broke down? Okay, so Apple's iPhone can't fix that flat tire for you, but it can help you find someone who can. Where's the nearest repair shop that's open for service? iPhone with the MapKit framework has the answer, because you can now do a direct search in Apple Maps rather than first searching for a repair shop in your browser and then copying/pasting the address into the app. Essentially, Maps is a one-stop search/find/receive directions app. Accordingly, in this hypothetical, you'd simply type *cycle repair* in Maps' search field or ask Siri, and suddenly nearby cycle repair shops appear, along with their customer ratings on the map, all represented by pins.

Searching works with specific addresses and business names, too. Tap a pin from your search result to see a card full of useful information about that location. View photos, tap to dial phone numbers, get addresses, find web sites, and peruse Yelp ratings and reviews—even find deals to save money. Tap the Quick Route button, and Maps instantly gives you turn-by-turn directions to any search result. This is illustrated in Figure 8-4.

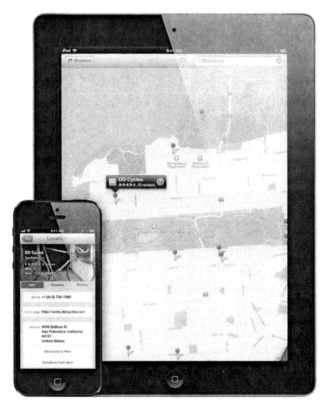

Figure 8-4. *Local Search—use this function to find what you're looking for closest to where you are*

See More, Do More

Apple's new Maps on iPhone 5 looks amazingly crisp and detailed on the high-resolution Retina display. You can switch between map view, satellite view, and hybrid view. You can even see a street-level view or use the new Flyover of a particular address to see realistic, interactive 3D views. As shown in Figure 8-5, You can double-tap or pinch to zoom in and out of a map. Explore in high resolution, pan, tilt, and rotate around cities and their landmarks.

Figure 8-5. From the Ground Up—Apple's new Maps gives you turn-by-turn spoken directions, interactive 3D views, and stunning Flyover feature

Innovative and Popular MapKit Apps Inspire Us

A funny thing happened along the way to teaching MapKit and Storyboarding to my students: most thought they knew what MapKit was but actually had no idea how awesome the MapKit framework really was.

> **Note**   One of my former students began working at Apple on iOS 5. She did exceptionally well in MapKits, and, of all the departments within iOS 5 that she could have worked in, they placed her in the MapKit framework. One of the first things she told me was how huge this division is and how even though she loved MapKits, she'd had no idea that so many teams with so many incredibly intelligent people were all working on one thing: MapKits!

I've found that it really helps my students when, after showing them the prebuilt apps, we spend some time reviewing some super–cool third–party MapKit apps—to inspire them and get their brains storming. So, imagine you're sitting with us and taking this brief tour as well. The following are 11 MapKit apps that have caught my eye, some of which I use regularly. Feel free to look these apps up and even download some of them onto your own devices to see how they work.

- *FlightTrack*: This MapKit app lets you manage every aspect of domestic and international flights with real-time updates and beautiful, zoomable maps. You can receive updates on gates, delays, and cancellations so you can book an alternate flight. The app covers more than 5,000 airports and 1,400 airlines.

- *Metro Paris Subway*: Never get lost in the City of Light. Metro Paris Subway is a comprehensive guide to traveling through Paris, including official metro, RER, and bus maps and schedules. Complete with an interactive map and route planner, Metro Paris Subway has you navigating like a real Parisian in no time.

- *MapMyRide*: I use this MapKit app all the time. I simply turn it on and start riding around on my bike. It tracks my speed, time, and mileage, as well as the incline. It takes into account my age, gender, and body weight and then tells me how many calories I burned. (On a good day, I can burn off two doughnuts!) The point is, this application calculates all these things while I'm just riding along huffing and puffing! When I get home, I can see the route on my computer, iPad, or iPhone. It does most of its work by using and manipulating preinstalled MapKit apps.

- *Plane Finder HD*: This amazing little app provides near real-time "virtual radar" air-traffic radar maps. It shows where a commercial flight, or any plane equipped with GPS-reporting technology, is in the air. Share sightings, see flight paths, filter by airline or aircraft type, get flight information, and see beautifully detailed aircraft illustrations and technical information.

- *Blipstar*: This app converts Internet business URL addresses to the corresponding addresses of their brick-and-mortar stores and presents it all on a cool map.

- *Twitter Spy*: This app lets people see where the person who is tweeting them is currently located. Yep—wacky and crazy, but true.

- *Coverage?*: Overlays and compares phone carrier coverage maps. Perfect for travelers who want to do research about their phone service coverage before they actually travel. The level of coverage details in this app is astonishing!

- *Map Tunneling Tool*: This one is just clever fun. Where would you come out if you began digging a hole straight down from wherever you are? Hint: the answer isn't always China.

- *Tall Eye*: This app shows you where you will go if you walk directly, in a straight line, around the earth, starting at one point and staying on a specific bearing all the way around.

- *Geo Measure*: A simple-to-use app that lets you measure the distance and area of just about any place on the map. Measure the circumference of your yard or the area of your favorite lake. A very cool app.

- *Phone Tracker for iPhones*: A tool that lets you track the location and follow movements of other people. Track multiple people simultaneously. Track your friends and family members, find your friends near you, see where your kids have been that day, and even track your spouse as he or she travels. Kind of Big Brother-ish, but a really nice app with lots of potential.

MyMapKit_01: A Universal Single View Application

It's time to dive into your first MapKit project. This exercise demonstrates the initial ease with which you can incorporate MapKit in your applications and how easy it can be to create an app that works in both the iPad and iPhone—a *universal* app, as it's known. You're going to begin with some simple splash screens and icons that suit your basic requirements. Then you're going to create two very simple View Controllers—one for the iPad and another for the iPod and iPhone. You'll tour some of the same building blocks and files that you've seen throughout this book; yet this app will be one of the simplest you've seen. The next chapter will challenge you as you go beyond the basic MapKit View Controller and into some more advanced code.

This is a good place for a reminder of the title of this book: *iPhone and iPad Apps for Absolute Beginners*. This exercise won't tax your thinking too much, but it will help ease you into the right frame of mind for the challenge of Chapter 9.

Preliminaries

As in previous chapters, please download and extract images and boilerplate code for this chapter. Navigate to `http://www.rorylewis.com/xCode/iPhone%205%20for%20absolute%20beginners%20 source%20code%20Xcode%20ios6%20/08_myMapkit_01.zip` and download its contents. The images in the zip file include four icon files and five splash screens, which I explain later. Right now, though, just download it to your beautifully clean desktop. Then you'll extract the files there as well.

Sample code that was programmed on the video is available for download at `http://www.rorylewis.com/xCode/iPhone%205%20for%20absolute%20beginners%20source%20code%20 Xcode%20ios6%20/08_myMapkit_01.zip`. After extracting all the files, remember to delete the `08_MyMapKit_01.zip` and `08_MyMapKit_01_files.zip` folders to avoid overwriting files and/or potential conflicts with the exercise code. To view the screencast of this chapter's exercise, go to `http://www.youtube.com/user/iphoneandipadapps`.

A New Single View Template

Let's get started. Choose the template.

1. Open Xcode, press ⌘+⇧+N, and click the Single View Application template, as shown in Figure 8-6. Call it MyMapKit_01 and save it to your desktop by clicking Next. A folder bearing that name appears on the desktop.

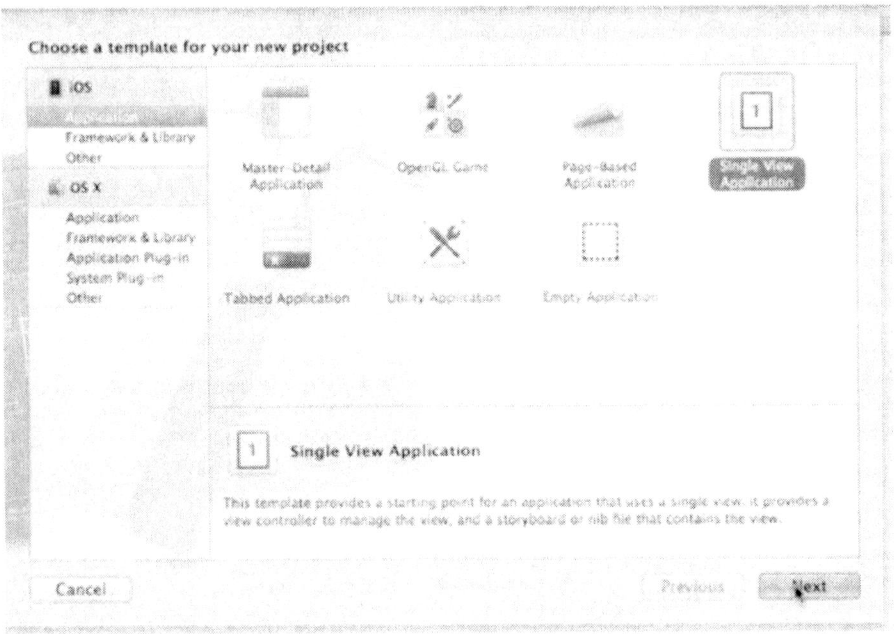

Figure 8-6. Select the Single View Application icon and then press Return or click Next

2. Follow along as closely as possible, because it will get a little more complex
    later. Name your project MyMapKit_01. To do so, select Universal in the
    Devices field, leave the Class Prefix, Use Storyboards, and Include Unit
    Tests options alone, as shown in Figure 8-7. Check that the Automatic
    Referencing option is on. Click Next. The next dialog to come up gives you
    a chance to change the directory or create a new directory where your initial
    project files will be created (see Figure 8-8). Here you won't change anything.
    Instead, click Create to have initial project files created on the desktop in
    the MyMapKit_01 folder. Make sure you don't select the "Create local git
    repository for this project" option at the bottom of the dialog.

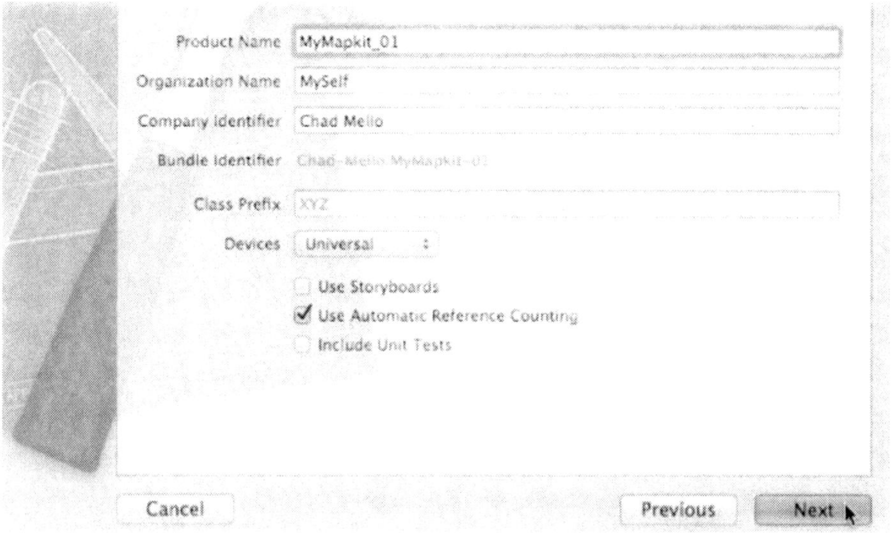

Figure 8-7. Name your app MyMapKit_01, making sure you selected Universal in the Devices field and that Automatic Reference Counting is on

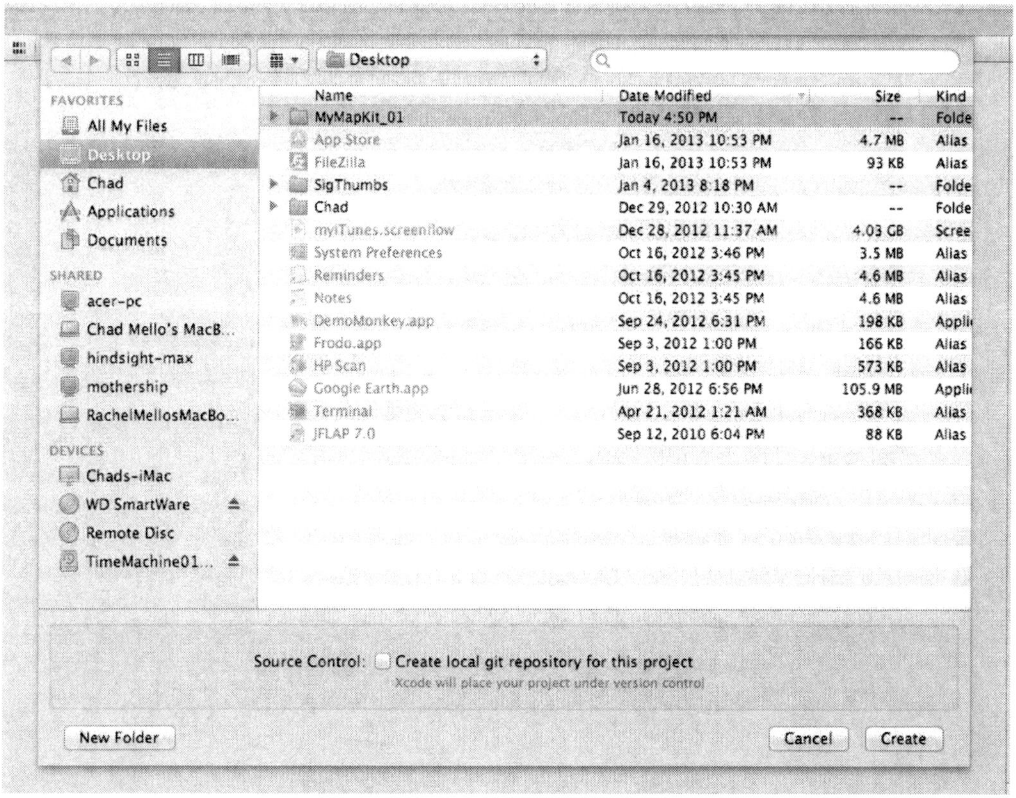

Figure 8-8. You won't be creating a local git repository—just click Create, and Xcode creates your initial project files on the desktop

Preliminaries: Adding the MapKit Framework

3. You need to add the MapKit framework to your project before you can show a map in your app. For a newbie, I'd say, "A framework is a set of super code that is used for specialized stuff. It's too big to be carried around all the time, but if you write an app that needs a framework—then you drag this framework into your code." Yeah, but you're not a newbie anymore—you're heading at a fast and furious pace to becoming a bona fide coder, respected by others who have been left in the swamps of technology. So, let's look at this. Yes, it's specialized code. You'll put it in a hierarchical directory that encapsulates dynamic shared libraries such as nib files, image files, localized strings, header files, and reference documentation in a single package. When you bring MapKit into your app, the system loads it into memory as needed and shares the one copy of the resource among all applications whenever possible. So, go to your root directory, select MyMapkit_01, and click the Targets tab, as shown in Figure 8-9. Click the Link Frameworks and Libraries bar and then click +.

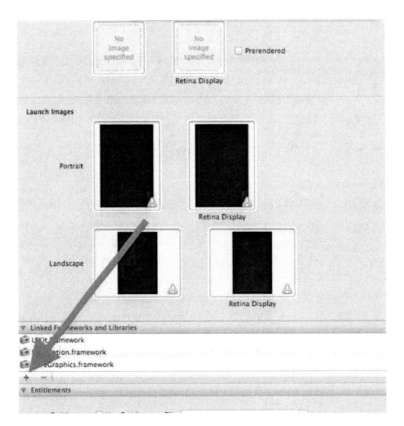

Figure 8-9. *Click the Linked Frameworks and Libraries bar and then click +*

4. You'll either scroll through all your options or enter *map* in the search bar and select the MapKit.framework framework. Click Add or press Enter/Return, as shown in Figure 8-10.

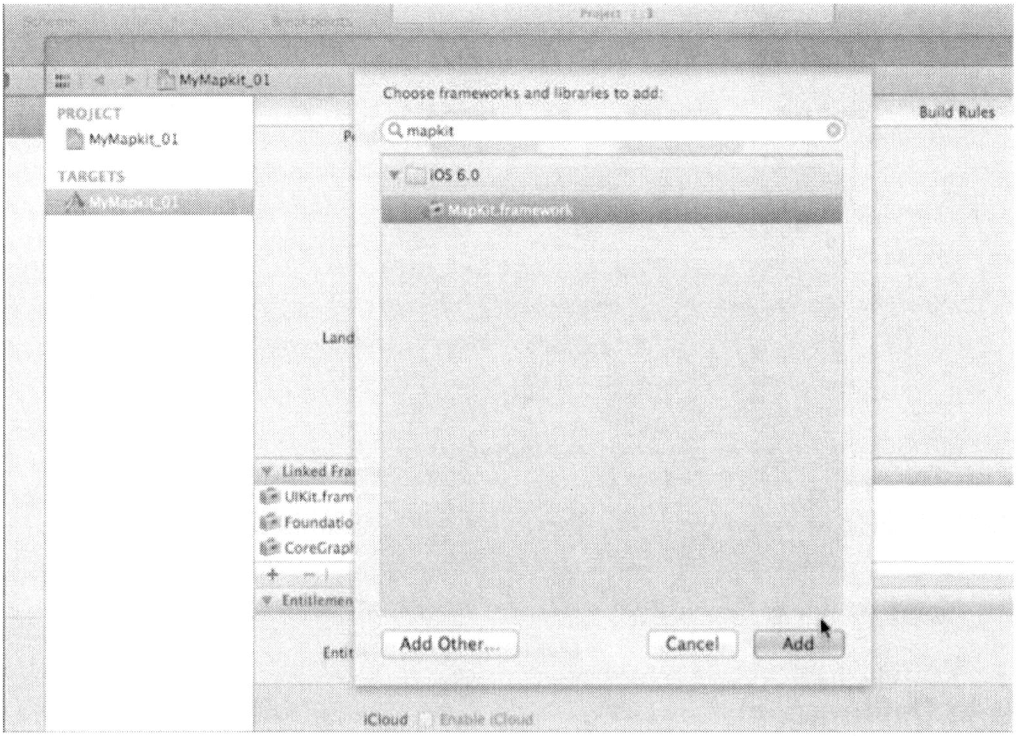

Figure 8-10. Select the MapKit framework

5. As shown in Figure 8-11, grab the newly imported MapKit framework that is by default stored in the root directory. Drag and drop it into your Frameworks folder. It's important to create good habits and store all your frameworks in the correct folder.

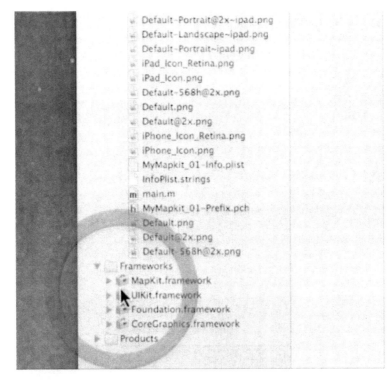

Figure 8-11. Move the imported MapKit framework to the Frameworks folder

Bring in the Images!

You want to have nine essential images for every app you make. For convenience, these are included in the package available for download from my web site at www.rorylewis.com/xCode/iPhone%205%20for%20absolute%20beginners%20source%20code%20Xcode%20ios6%20/08_myMapkit_01.zip. They include the essential icons and splash screens. These include the 57 × 57 px ("px" stands for pixels) for the iPhone classic, the 72 × 72 px for the iPad classic, the 114 × 114 px for the iPhone Retina display, and the 144 × 144 for the iPad Retina display. I've also designed five splash screen images that are available for your use. Splash screens usually only appear for less than a second, but they give the user something cool to look at while the app is loading—and they set the tone for it. You'll need five splash screens because you have to accommodate the various iPad and iPhone configurations that the user using your app might have. The iPad with standard resolution requires a 768 × 1004 px splash screen, whereas the iPad Retina requires a 1536 × 2008 graphic. The 4-inch iPhone Retinas need 640 × 1136, the 3.5-inch Retinas need 640 × 960, and 320 × 480 px is required for the classic iPhone. After you've downloaded them, you can always use them as a template for your future apps.

Note   This app is a universal app. With a universal app, a single app bundle can run as both an iPhone app and an iPad app. Universal apps usually require different versions of the Main View Controllers that are tuned to the respective resolutions of the iPad and iPhone.

6. Staying in the root directory after importing the frameworks, drag the icon images into the icon boxes. Figure 8-12 shows the standard resolution box (on the left). The icons and splash screens are named so that their functions are obvious. Simply drag these files and drop them into their respective spots. Figure 8-12 shows the five spots where you need to drop your files: two for the icons and three for the various splash screens. Be sure to match these up properly when dropping the graphics in place.

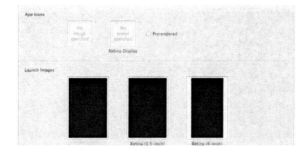

Figure 8-12. Drag in the icons

7. Similar to step 6, after importing the icons, you now need to import your splash screen images into their boxes. Figure 8-13 shows the iPhone Retina 640 × 960 px classic splash screen already in place and the classic iPhone 320 × 480 px splash screen being dragged in. Once you're finished dragging these images in, you're ready to tidy up your project a bit.

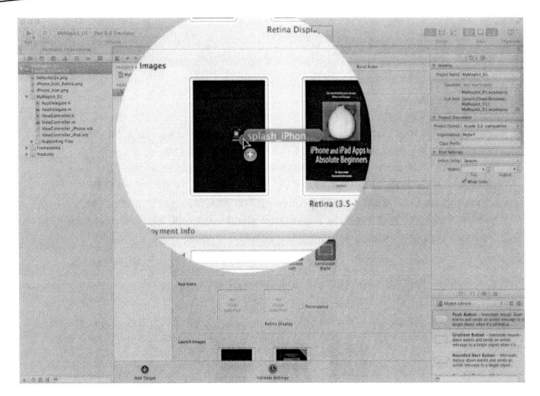

Figure 8-13. Drag in the splash screens

8. Before you start to mess with your project, you need to make sure that all
    the files are in the correct folders. At this point, you know that Xcode will
    recognize the correct icons and splash screens—but look where they are!
    They're in the root directory again. Grab them, as shown in Figure 8-14, and
    move them into the Supporting Files folder.

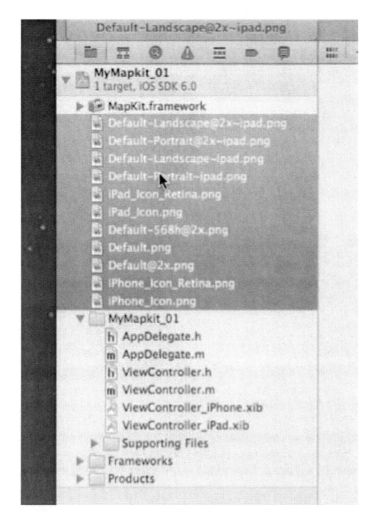

Figure 8-14. Drag in your icons so you can take them to the correct folder

9. The Supporting Files folder is probably not open. That's okay. As you drag
    the icons, slow down as you hover over the Supporting Files folder so it
    opens up. Once it does, drop the files into the folder, as shown in Figure 8-15.

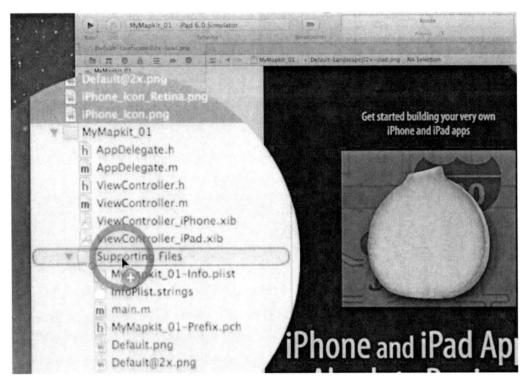

Figure 8-15. *Drop the project icons into the Supporting Files folder*

10. Before moving on, check your project against the example shown in Figure 8-16. You need to make sure that your icons, splash screens, and MapKit framework are placed like those in the example. Once they are, you can move on.

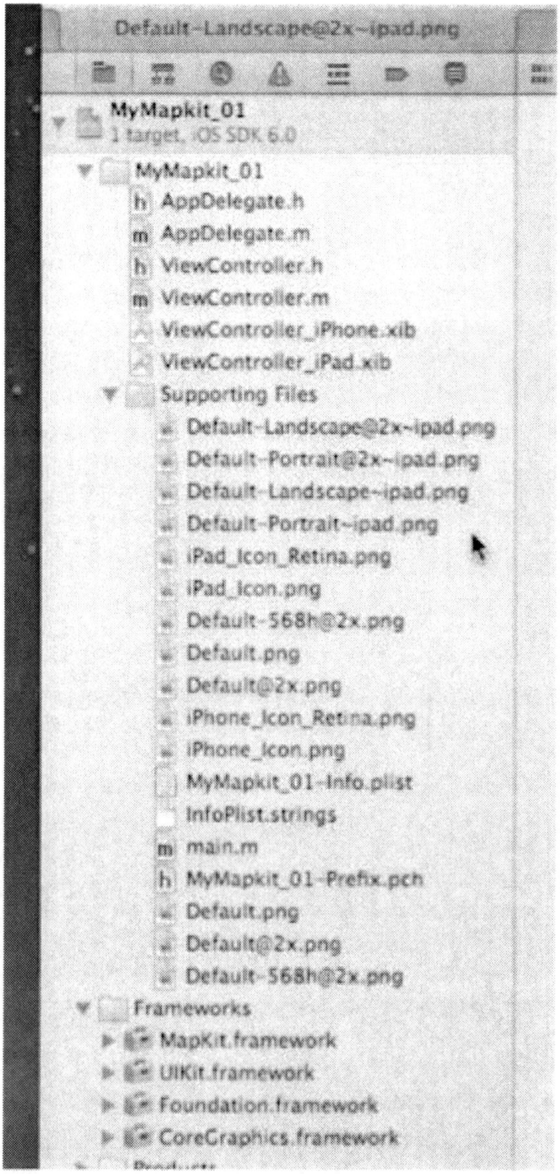

Figure 8-16. Check your directories and files against mine

11. Take a good look at Figure 8-17. You're now ready to finish your app. You need to get used to wanting to see your coding canvas laid out before you ever start working with the app's construction. This is very much like a painter who first buys a canvas, paint, turpentine, brushes, rags, and a model of what will be painted before the first dab is ever painted. That's what you've just done. Get used to first setting everything up before writing your code.

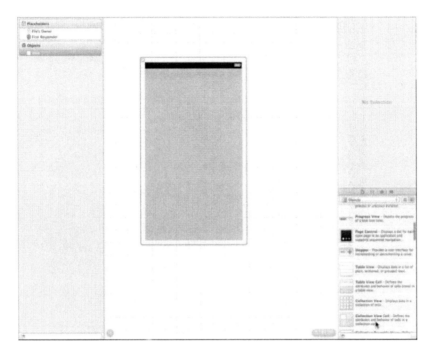

Figure 8-17. Ready to paint ... erh ... create your app

Finishing the View Controllers

This app is a universal app, remember, which means that as a single application it can run as both an iPhone app and an iPad app. As mentioned earlier, universal apps usually require different versions of the main View Controllers that are tuned to the respective resolutions of the iPad and iPhone. Here, Xcode automatically created two versions of your map's View Controller for you. In this case, the only difference is the size of the visual area; however, if this app had other View Controllers, such as informational dialogs or Table Views, the navigation between them would most likely differ. The iPhone has less visible area to work with. That forces you to think about how your app may differ in appearance between the smaller iPhone and the larger iPad. You'll see some of this in the next MapKit project in Chapter 9.

12. Select `ViewController_iPhone.xib` from the Project Navigator on the left. In Figure 8-17, you see the familiar empty canvas of the main iPhone View Controller.

13. You need to get access to the Object Library—the list of objects that you can choose various objects from. Ensure that the Object Library is visible by clicking the cube in the lower right of your screen, as indicated by the arrow in Figure 8-18.

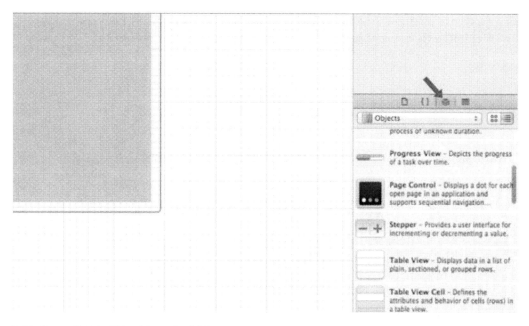

Figure 8-18. *Ensure that the Object Library is visible*

14.   Locate the Map View object from the Object Library, as shown in Figure 8-19.

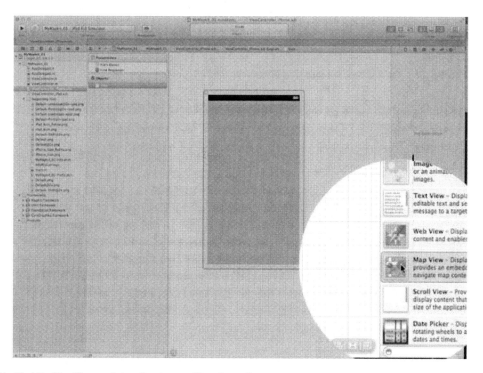

Figure 8-19. *Find the Map View and drag it onto your View Controller canvas*

15. As demonstrated in Figure 8-20, drag the Map View object over the View Controller. Before dropping the object onto the canvas, make sure it's centered and fills the entire viewable area.

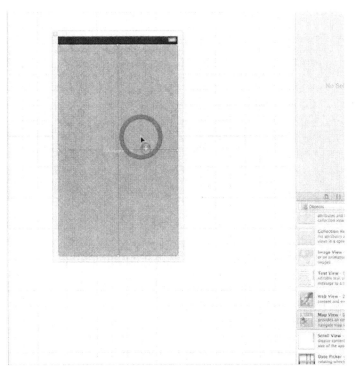

Figure 8-20. *Drag and drop the Map View object onto the View Controller canvas*

16. Do the same for the iPad View Controller. Select `ViewController_iPad.xib` from the Project Navigator and repeat steps 14 and 15 for the iPad View Controller. The only difference here is that the iPad area is much larger that the iPhone.

17. *Do not forget to save your project at this point!* You want to get into the habit of always saving your work before attempting to compile or run your application. Because this app was a quick solution to put together, saving at the end of your work is fine; however, while working with more sophisticated apps, you should save periodically, perhaps every five minutes or so. This way, in the event of a system failure, you're less likely to lose any significant work. A quick way to save is with this simple key combination: ⌘+S.

Making It Go: Running Your First MapKit App

You've finally come to the fun part; the anticipated event is here! Are you ready to see the results of your not-so-hard work? What you're about to see is a fully functioning app that allows users to peruse a map of the world. You're going to run this application in both iPad and iPhone environments.

18. Click the Run button at the top left of your screen. This will run the application in the iPad Simulator (see Figure 8-21).

Figure 8-21. Running your new MapKit app

19. The full-screen splash screen appears, as shown in Figure 8-22.

Figure 8-22. Running your new MapKit app—the initial splash screen

20.   As you can see in Figure 8-23, when the map appears, the user can freely manipulate it by scrolling, pinching to zoom in and out, and rotating the device between landscape and portrait modes. These features are made possible in your app without typing one line of code in this project. Wow!

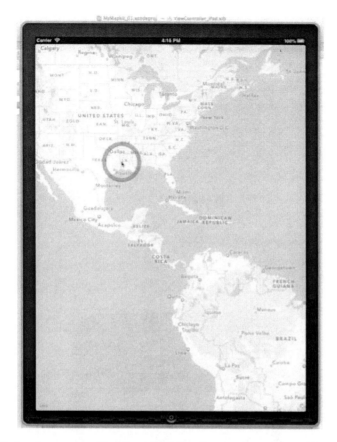

Figure 8-23. Running your new MapKit app: the interactive map. A user can scroll, zoom in, and zoom out of a world map. Not bad for absolutely no coding on your part!

21. You can also run your app in the iPhone Simulator. Simply select the iPhone Simulator option in the upper left-hand part of your screen (Figure 8-24) and run your app the same way you did for the iPad. The results will look like Figure 8-25.

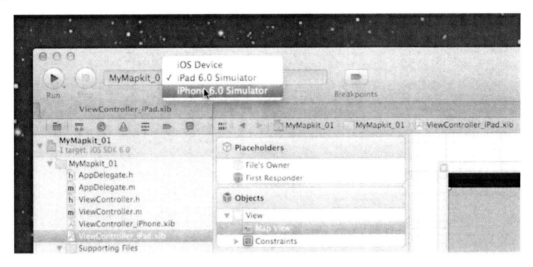

Figure 8-24. *Running your app in the iPhone Simulator*

Figure 8-25. *Running your app in the iPhone simulator*

Time to Show Off!

Wow! Within a few minutes' time, you were able to pull off a pretty good show. Just think: a few short years ago this type of application was all but impossible to create on any device. Now, you can throw together an app with very sophisticated map functions in no time. If that isn't being a geek, then I don't know what is. Time to show this app off while bragging to your friends about how quickly you put it all together.

Okay, this was a cool introduction to MapKit. The next chapter introduces you to some more challenging but very cool concepts. You'll also insert code into your MapKit app for the first time. By the time you finish Chapter 9, you'll have had the introductory experience of this chapter plus a taste of inserting pure Objective-C into MapKits. Awesome! See you in the next chapter.

MapKit with a Little More Effort

In Chapter 8, you were able to create a nice MapKit app with no coding on your part; Xcode did it all for you. That app allowed you to scroll around the world map, zoom in to view more details, and zoom out as well. For all the wonderful technology packed into it, though, your simple app was not very useful beyond perusing the map. In this chapter, you're going to create something that has a bit more usefulness and functionality to it. You're going to consider a variety of components that you'll use to build in to your app.

For this project, programmers like you need to spend a minute recalling some basic earth science and geography so that your code will be as effective as possible. After you've gained sufficient understanding about the geo coordinate system built into MapKit, you can create wonderfully imaginative, fun, and useful map-based applications for the masses.

The central piece of any MapKit-based app is the `MKMapView` class. This complex class provides the core map functionality required so that you, the programmer, can provide users of your app the ability to visualize an abstract view of their world. A Map View contains a flattened representation of a spherical object—Earth in this case.

You need to understand a couple basic ideas about how to specify coordinates in a Map View and how these coordinates ultimately translate to points on the surface of the Earth. This understanding is especially vital if you plan to place custom content on the top of the Map View.

The good news is that you're not required to know more than a few basic concepts, along with some elementary math, to get started. MapKit provides most, if not all, of the functionality you will need to compute geo points and locations related to the Map View.

Understanding Map Geometry and Coordinate Systems

For this app, one of the things you'll do is direct the iPad to animate a pin dropping down onto the map. Your annotation is dropped onto a specific location, giving *longitude* and *latitude*, but before we proceed, you need to know what these terms really mean. Figure 9-1 shows lines of latitude and longitude.

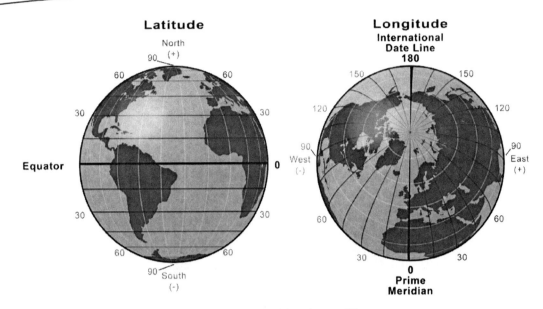

Figure 9-1. Latitude versus longitude, along with the equator and the prime meridian

Lines of latitude, often called parallels, are the imaginary lines that circle the globe horizontally, running east and west. These invisible lines are measured in degrees, minutes, and seconds, north or south of the equator. The *equator* is the elliptical locus of points on the Earth's surface midway between the poles, which physically are *real* points, defined by the Earth's rotation on its axis. The north pole is 90 degrees north latitude; the south pole is 90 degrees south latitude.

Lines of longitude, often called meridians, are imaginary vertical lines (ellipses) that cross through the north and south poles. They're also measured in degrees, minutes, and seconds, east or west of the prime meridian, an arbitrary standard that runs through Greenwich, England. Unlike the equator, which goes all the way around the world—360 degrees—the prime meridian (0 degrees longitude) is a semicircle (semi-ellipse), extending from the north pole to the south pole; the other half of the arc is called the international date line, defined as 180 degrees east and/or 180 degrees west longitude.

To understand the coordinate systems used in MapKit, it helps to understand how the three-dimensional surface of the Earth is translated into a two-dimensional map. Figure 9-2 demonstrates how a projection of the Earth's three-dimensional surface can be flattened into a two-dimensional surface.

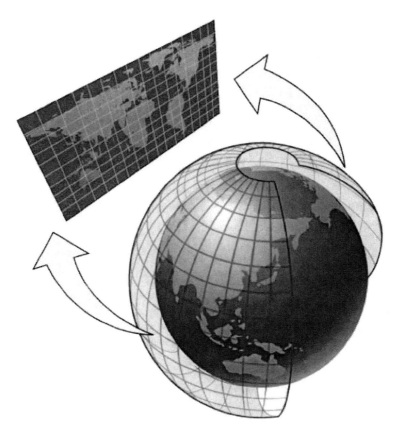

Figure 9-2. Mapping spherical data to a flat surface

MapKit uses what's known as a Mercator map projection system, a specific type of cylindrical map projection, as shown in Figure 9-2. In a cylindrical map projection, the coordinates of a sphere are mapped onto the surface of a cylinder (think of a paper towel role), which is then unwrapped to provide a flat map. An interesting point to note when flattening a sphere in this way is what happens to the lines of longitude.

Looking at Figure 9-2, notice how the longitude lines that normally converge at the poles become parallel, causing land masses to become distorted the farther away from the equator you happen to be. Although this type of view misrepresents reality, the advantage of the Mercator system is that a straight line drawn between two points yields a course heading that can be used in actual navigation on the surface of the Earth. The projection used by MapKit uses the prime meridian as its central meridian. You can see in Figure 9-1 above that the Prime Meridian is the Earth's "zero" of longitude, and it passes right through Greenwich, England.

MapKit supports three basic coordinate systems for specifying map data points:

- A *map coordinate* is a latitude and longitude on a spherical representation of the Earth. Map coordinates are the primary way of specifying locations on the globe. You specify individual map coordinate values using the CLLocationCoordinate2D structure. In conjunction, you can specify areas using the MKCoordinateSpan and MKCoordinateRegion structures. You'll be using both MKCoordinateRegion and CLLocationCoordinate2D in this exercise.

- A *map point* is an x and y value on the Mercator map projection. Map points are used for many map-related calculations instead of map coordinates because they simplify the math involved in the calculations. You'd use map points primarily when specifying the shape and position of custom overlays—something you'll not be doing in this chapter.

- A *point* is a graphical unit associated with the coordinate system of the UIView object. Map points and map coordinates are ultimately translated into a point so that they can be drawn on a view while using the UIView's coordinate system. Most of the time, MapKit does this work for you, and you'll not be doing any of this stuff in this exercise.

In most cases, the coordinate system you use is predetermined by the MapKit interfaces you're using. When the time comes for you to create your own app, and you need to store its data, map coordinates are precise, portable, and the best option for storing location data.

Important Things to Know

In Chapter 8, you put together a fairly simple application with little effort; you were able to create a map app with little to no understanding of MapKit. In this chapter, you can't get away with as much. Before you begin creating this app, you should know a few things about the technical foundation of map-related applications for the iPad and iPhone. The upcoming exercise in this chapter relies on five important tools: MapKit, CoreLocation, the MKAnnotationView class reference, actions, and outlets. You're not going to involve yourself with how these sophisticated tools work so much as you're going to practice the art of deciding *when* to reach for *which* tool in your newly expanded toolbox.

Among other things, these tools let you display maps in your applications, use annotations, work with geocoding (which works with longitude and latitude), and interact with your location (via CoreLocation).

When interacting with Apple's maps, you use the Apple-provided MapKit framework. To obtain your location or do cool things using GPS satellite technology, you use the CoreLocation framework. To put it all together and seamlessly integrate with the user—you take all the aforementioned technology and combine their use in code. Finally, to place pins on a map, create references, draw chevron marks, or insert an image of your dog showing where he is on a map—you call these *annotations* and, thus, use MKAnnotationView. Keep all this in mind while doing this exercise.

myMapkit_02: A Single View iPad Application

This exercise begins with some boilerplate code, splash screens, and icons that suit your basic requirements. You'll modify it from there. You'll pick up from where you left off in Chapter 8, and you'll be challenged to see what areas of the code are pretty much the same as what you've already encountered and what areas are different, given the nature of this application.

The ability to recognize patterns and see structures just under the surface is a powerful aptitude that everyone has, but programmers cultivate theirs to a heightened degree. You'll play a little game to see if you can anticipate some of the moves you'll have to take.

Possible Prepping for the App

For this app, the example used to demonstrate the pin drop on location is our Computer Science offices at the University of Colorado at Colorado Springs. You, of course, can use any location you choose. You may want to use your own address or a well–known landmark. To do that, you must get the latitude and longitude values of that location, most likely from Google Maps or a direct GPS reading. Many sites on the Internet offer these coordinates. Figure 9-3 shows one of them: `http://itouchmap.com/latlong.html`.

Latitude and Longitude of a Point

Figure 9-3. `itouchmap.com` *is one of many sites where you can enter an address and get its longitudinal and latitudinal coordinates*

Here's a thought—let's start at the end of the process and think backwards for a minute. Go ahead and jump forward in this chapter for a sneak peek at what the app will look like—the results it will return if all goes well. In Figure 9-3 you see a picture of a hybrid map showing a red pin sitting next to the entrance of a building. That's the Engineering and Applied Science building at the University of Colorado at Colorado Springs. The picture also has an *annotation*, which is the text. "Chad Mello" is the title, and "UCCS Engineering & Applied Science" is the subtitle.

Later in the tutorial, you'll see that you need to be careful about the title and the subtitle. You can also control the color of the pin and decide on the style of animation—how the pin drops onto the map image.

This is a good place for a reminder of the title of this book: *iPhone and iPad Apps for Absolute Beginners*. My humble goal is not fluency, but reasonable familiarity and a sense of what lies ahead.

If that sounds right, let's get on with it.

Preliminaries

You want to set up the initial project and organize it so that you can put your app together in an organized and systematic way. We developers need to approach application development in a consistent, logical manner so that we make fewer mistakes while coding.

As in previous chapters, please download and extract images and boilerplate code for this chapter. Navigate to my web site and download Chapter 9 contents: `http://rorylewis.com/xCode/ iPhone%205%20for%20absolute%20beginners%20source%20code%20Xcode%20ios6%20/09_myMapkit_ 02_files.zip`. The images include two icon files, four splash screens, and one DemoMonkey file (`Chapter09MapKit.demoMonkey`) for boilerplate code. If you've not gotten DemoMonkey from the site, you may want to do so before starting on the code; download it from `http://rorylewis.com/xCode/ StoryBoarding%20in%20Xcode/Chapter01_Demonmonkey.zip`. Later, I explain what these icons, splash screens, and boilerplates mean. Right now though, just download it to your desktop and extract the files there.

Sample code that I programmed on the video is available as well. In fact, watching the video before proceeding with this chapter may help you. The video shows just how quickly this application can be put together and perhaps could put your mind at ease. Try to view the screencast of this chapter's exercise before starting: `www.youtube.com/user/iphoneandipadapps`.

A New Single View Template

Let's get started and choose the template.

1. Open Xcode and press ⌘+⇧+N. Then click the IOS Single View Application template, as shown in Figure 9-4.

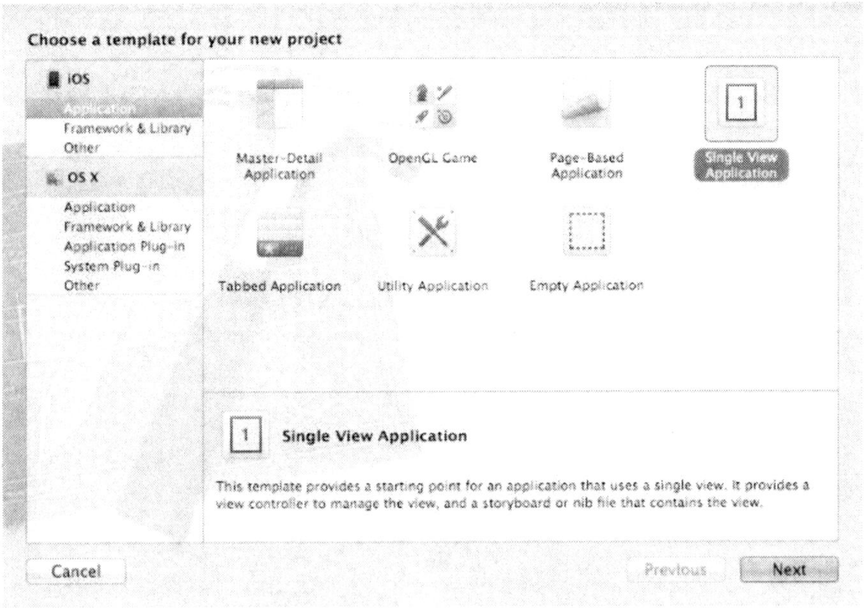

Figure 9-4. Select the Single View Application icon and press Return or click Next

2. In order that you can follow along as closely as possible, because things will get complex later, name your project myMapkit_02. Also, select iPad in the Devices field, not iPhone or Universal. You'll not be using the Unit Tests option or the Storyboards option; however, you do want to use Automatic Referencing Counting. The final settings are shown in Figure 9-5.

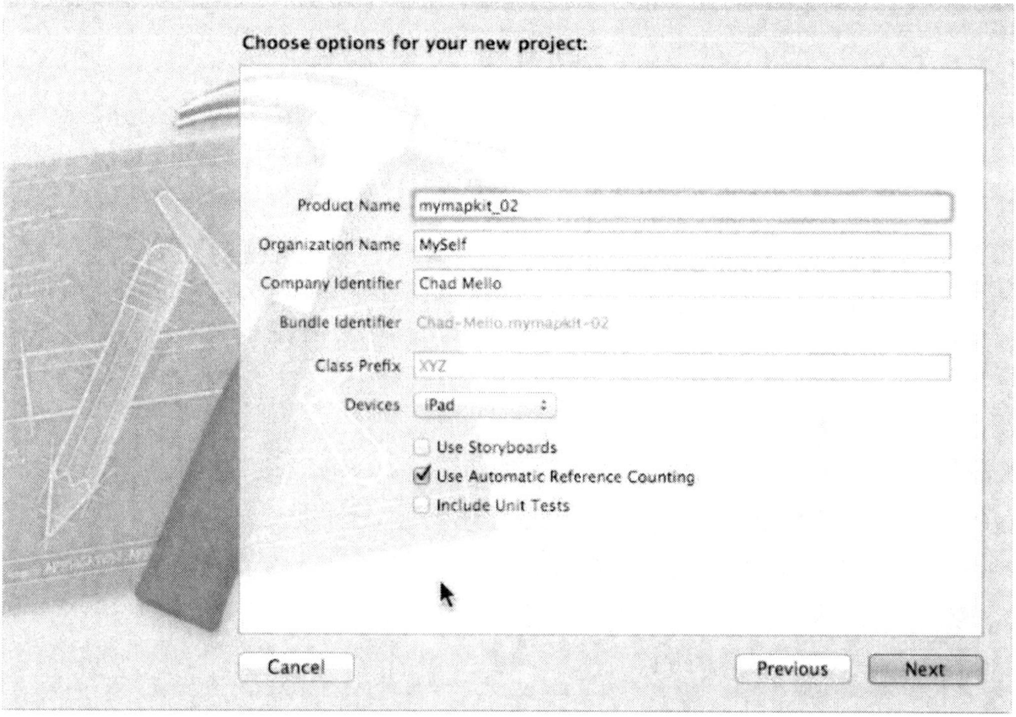

Figure 9-5. Name your app myMapkit_02

3. Open the Supporting Files folder you downloaded from the web site. The folder is called 09_myMapkit_02_files.

4. Open the file named Chapter09MapKit.demoMonkey. You must have DemoMonkey installed to use this file.

5. Your desktop should look something like Figure 9-6, with the DemoMonkey window in the upper-right corner.

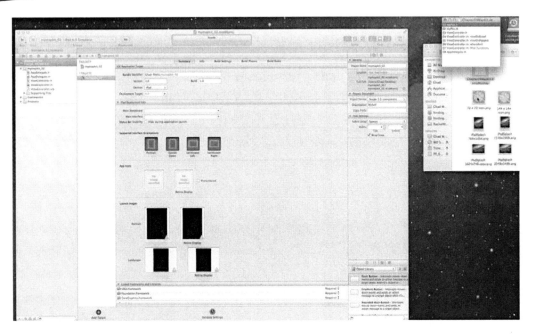

Figure 9-6. Arrange your desktop and prepare to follow along

Preliminaries: Bringing in the Images

For convenience, images are included in the package available for download from the web site. They include the essential icons and splash screens. These include the 72 × 72 px for the iPad standard resolution, and the 144 × 144 px for the iPad Retina Display. I've also designed four splash screen images that are available for your use. You'll need four splash screens because you have to accommodate the various iPad resolutions (standard and Retina) as well landscape or portrait display mode. Included are the 768 × 1004 px splash screen for the iPad's standard portrait resolution and the 1024 × 768 px for its standard landscape resolution. The Retina versions are also in the package. After you've downloaded them, you can always use them as templates for your own cool future apps.

> **Note**   In this application, you're only using the iPad. Keep in mind that you would need other icons and splash graphics sized for the iPhone if you wanted to extend this application (or one of your own apps) into a universal app that supported both iPhone and iPad platforms.

6. Drag the icon images into the icon boxes from the 09_myMapkit_02_files folder. Figure 9-7 shows the 72 × 72 px standard iPad icon being dragged over to its appropriate box.

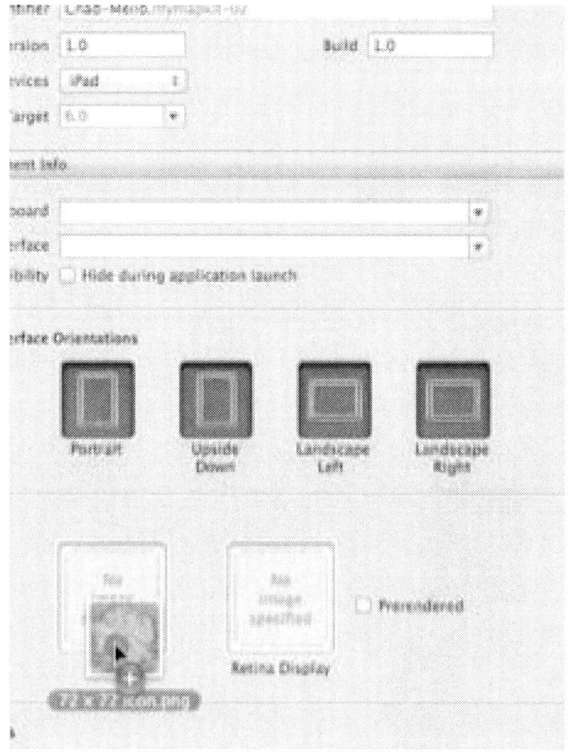

Figure 9-7. Drag in the icons

7. Similar to step 6, after importing the icons, you need to import your splash
    screen images into their boxes. Figure 9-8 shows all the iPad splash screens
    in place while the Retina 2048 × 1496 px is being dragged in. Once you're
    finished dragging these images in, you're ready to start the other half of
    the preliminary work: framework references, the main application view, and
    the addition of a new class file into the project. Note that the Prerendered
    checkbox is checked—that tells the IOS not to put the standard sheen onto
    your icon when it's installed on the device.

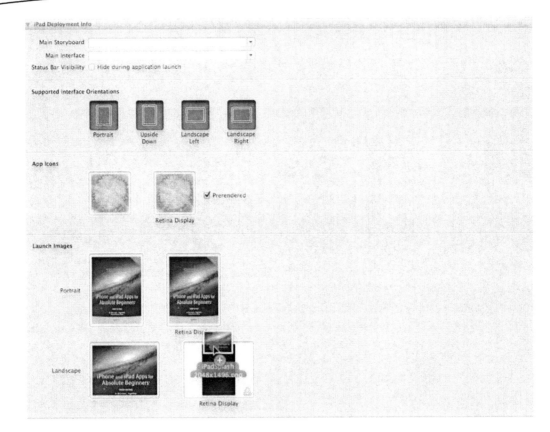

Figure 9-8. Drag in the splash screens

Preliminaries: Adding MapKit and Arranging the Project

It's time to add the MapKit framework. Because you know all about frameworks from the previous chapter, you're no longer a newbie—yep, you're heading at a fast and furious pace to becoming a bona fide geek, respected by others left in the swamps of technology. So, let's look at this. Yes, MapKit is a specialized, shared library of code. You'll put it in a hierarchical list that references dynamic shared libraries such as nib files, image files, localized strings, header files, and reference documentation in a single package.

8. As shown in Figure 9-9, click the + (plus sign).

Figure 9-9. *Click + to bring a framework into our project*

9. Either scroll through your options until you find it or enter *map* in the search
    bar and select MapKit.framework. Then click Add or press Enter/Return, as
    shown in Figure 9-10.

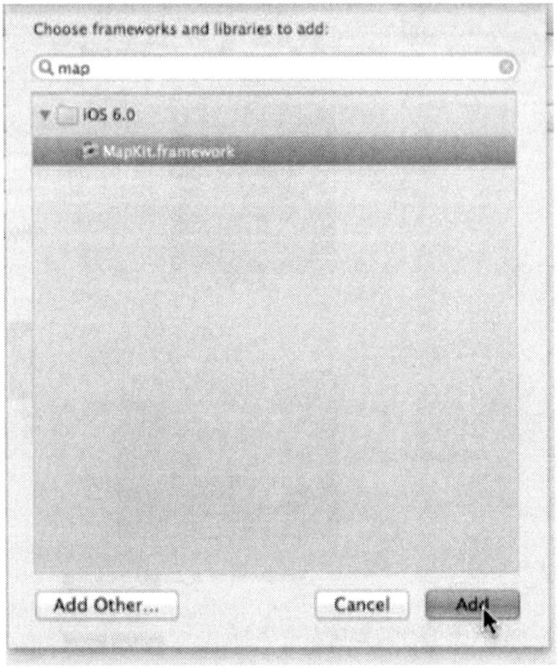

Figure 9-10. Search for and select MapKit.framework

10. Arrange your project files: as shown in Figure 9-11, you'll grab the image files
    we added earlier and drop them in the Supporting Files folder. You'll then
    move MapKit.framework to your Frameworks folder. It is important that you
    develop good habits and store all your files in an organized way and in the
    correct folders.

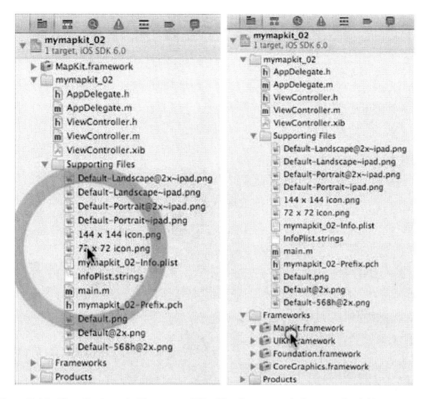

Figure 9-11. *Move the imported images and MapKit reference to their respective folders*

Preliminaries: Adding the Annotation Class

While you're here setting up your project, you need to create an annotation class. For this application, you need a means to control your annotation. The annotation class functions to mark a spot on the map—in this case, the front entrance of the UCCS Engineering & Applied Science building. For that, you'll create an Objective-C class that controls all the characteristics you want to display on this annotation.

11. Right-click the myMapkit_02 main project folder and select New File, as shown in Figure 9-12. Be sure to select "Objective-C class," as shown in Figure 9-13.

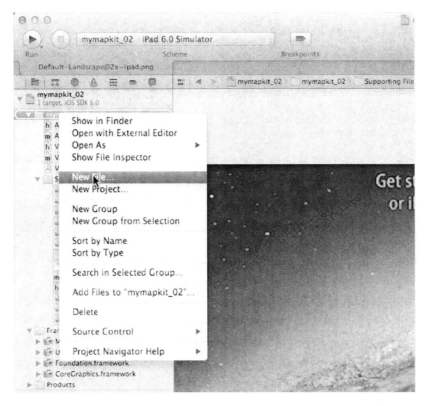

Figure 9-12. Adding a new file to your project

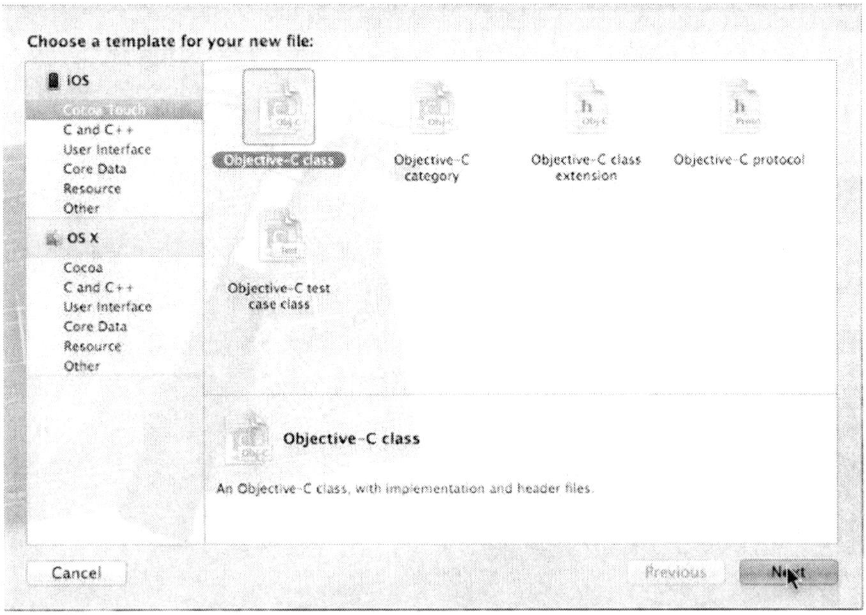

Figure 9-13. Adding a new file to your project: select Objective-C class

12. Because this controller will be in charge of controlling annotations for your position, name it something that correlates to *my position;* how about myPos. Make sure it's a subclass of NSObject and not UIView or any other subclass. This is shown in Figure 9-14.

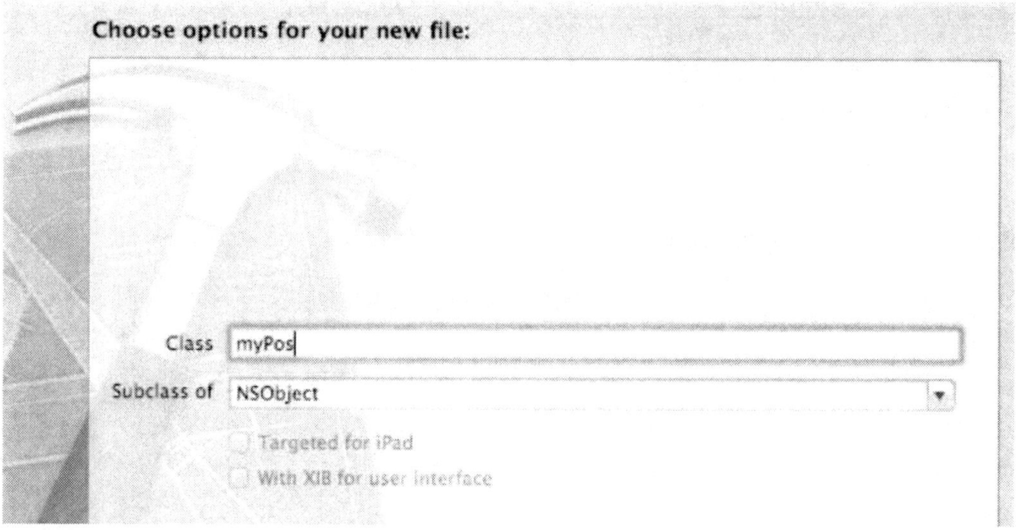

Choose options for your new file:

Class   myPos

Subclass of   NSObject

◯ Targeted for iPad

◯ With XIB for user interface

Figure 9-14. Name your new class myPos and be sure it's a subclass of NSObject

13. As shown in Figure 9-15, save your new file into your project's subfolder, myMapkit_02. This folder comes up by default, so just click Create.

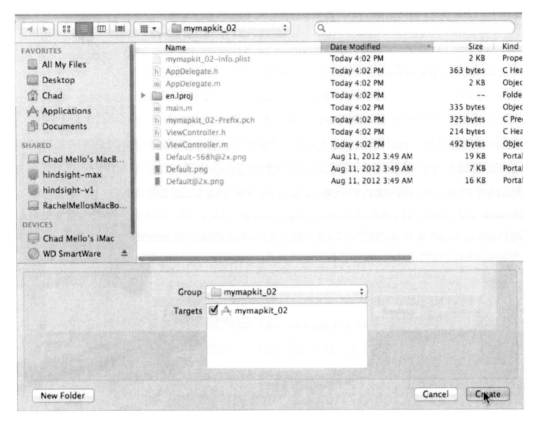

Figure 9-15. Save your new file into the same folder as your project, myMapkit_02

14. Your two newly created NSObject files named myPos.h and myPos.m are
    located in your myMapkit_02 folder, but ordered after the Supporting Files
    folder. You want to move them to the correct place above the Supporting
    Files folder, as shown in Figure 9-16.

Figure 9-16. *Move the newly created files into the correct order under your myMapkit_02 folder*

15. Before moving on, you need to make sure that you check your project against the example shown in Figure 9-17. Make sure the following are all true:

   a. The NSObject files, myPos.h and myPos.m, are in the myMapkit_02 directory.

   b. Your icons and splash screens are in the Supporting Files folder.

   c. Your reference to MapKit.framework is in the Frameworks folder.

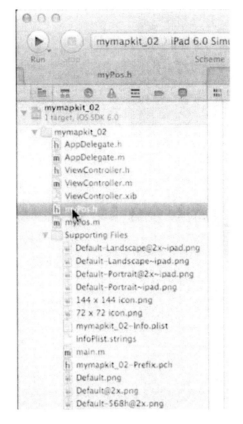

Figure 9-17. Check your directories and files against mine

16. You're now ready to code. Get used to wanting to see your coding canvas laid out before you ever start writing code. As I've mentioned, this is very much like a painter who first obtains a canvas, paint, turpentine, brushes, rags, and a model of what will be painted before the first dab is ever painted. This is what you've just done.

Note I can't understand why some students invariably dive into the code immediately upon receiving an in-class assignment. I stop them right away and make them prep, as you've done here and throughout this book. When I bring in all my files and create whatever new frameworks and NSObject files that I need, I allow my mind to go into a semi-meditative state and quietly plan out how I will write the code.

Coding the myPos Annotation Class

Remember that myMapkit_01 from the previous chapter is a lead-in or segue into myMapkit_02, which is where the real action is. You got away without having to program anything for that app. Now you're going to do some coding, albeit lightweight coding. For starters, you're going to learn how to put together a simple class that will produce the annotated pin you'll be sticking on UCCS's doorstep.

In fact, many MapKit apps need a separate NSObject to keep track of many positions. In this small app, you don't necessarily have to program the myPos.h and myPos.m files at all. But you need to get used to always creating an NSObject myPos to keep track of your position or an array of positions to feed into the annotations and MapKit framework.

17. Click the myPos.h file located in your myMapkit_02 folder inside the root folder. Upon opening it, as shown in Figure 9-18, you see the following:

```
#import <Foundation/Foundation.h>
@interface myPos : NSObject
@end
```

Figure 9-18. *The initial myPos.h source*

There isn't much there to start off with, and you're not going to be adding much more than that. The steps you'll now take are as follows:

d. Add a MapKit framework for your annotations by entering #import <MapKit/MkAnnotation.h> to the @interface myPos : NSObject directive.

e. Add <MKAnnotation>, which is a *protocol*. I explain protocols in the "Digging the Code" section at the end of this chapter, but for now, a protocol means you'll have to write your own annotation object that implements this protocol. Just remember that an object that adopts this protocol must implement a property called the coordinate property. Which, of course, you'll do.

f.   Set your `CLLocation` class reference to incorporate the geographical coordinates and altitude of the device with a variable that you'll name `coordinate`, as shown in Figure 9-19. You do that with this line:

```
CLLocationCoordinate2D coordinate;
```

```
//
//   myPos.h
//   mymapkit_02
//
//   Created by Chad Mello on 10/21/12.
//   Copyright (c) 2012 MySelf. All rights reserved.
//


#import <Foundation/Foundation.h>
#import <Mapkit/MKAnnotation.h>

@interface myPos : NSObject<MKAnnotation>
{
    CLLocationCoordinate2D coordinate;
    NSString *title;
    NSString *subtitle;

}

@property (nonatomic, assign) CLLocationCoordinate2D coordinate;
@property (nonatomic, copy) NSString *title;
@property (nonatomic, copy) NSString *subtitle;

@end
```

Figure 9-19. The finished myPos.h incorporates the geographical coordinates of your annotation class

g.   You need two `NSString` variables to hold your titles and subtitles, which you'll call `*title` and `*subtitle`, as follows:

```
NSString *title;
NSString *subtitle;
```

h.   Finally, create `@property` statements for the coordinate, title, and subtitle, as shown in the code that follows. Once you've made these additions, save our work. Figure 9-19 shows how this file should look after you've made your changes and saved your work.

```
#import <Foundation/Foundation.h>
#import <MapKit/MkAnnotation.h>

@interface myPos : NSObject <MKAnnotation>
{
    CLLocationCoordinate2D coordinate;
```

```
        NSString *title;
        NSString *subtitle;
}

@property (nonatomic, assign) CLLocationCoordinate2D coordinate;
@property (nonatomic, copy)  NSString *title;
@property (nonatomic, copy) NSString *subtitle;

@end
```

18. You're now ready to code the myPos implementation file. Click the `myPos.m` file located in your myMapkit_02 folder inside the root folder. Figure 9-20 shows how the `myPos.m` file looks when you open it. Here you synthesize your coordinate, title, and subtitle with an `@synthesize` statement, which includes `coordinate`, `title`, and `subtitle`. To do this, make a space under the mypos.h `@implementation` and type the following:

```
@synthesize coordinate, title, subtitle;
```

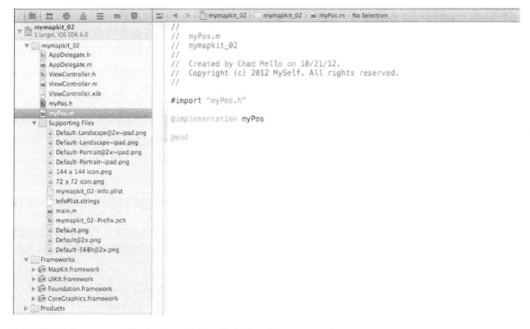

Figure 9-20. This is how your myPos implementation file looks when we open it

Your file should look similar to Figure 9-21. Save your work.

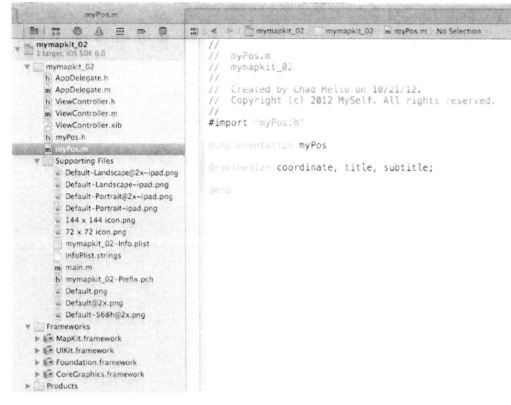

Figure 9-21. This is how the myPos implementation file looks after the synthesis

The User Interface

The mechanism whereby the user interacts with your app is called the *user interface*, abbreviated UI. This is where you lay out the visual design in your View Controller. Fortunately, this UI is fairly simple, and it won't take you very long to define it. You'll leave most of the hard work for MapKit to handle. All the finger gestures for zooming and scrolling around the map will be handled directly by the MapKit framework, saving you many hours and hundreds of lines of coding effort.

19. Click ViewController.xib from the Project Navigator window. Xcode automatically brings you into Interface Builder. At this point, the View Controller's canvas has nothing on it. Find the Map View (MKMapView) control in the Object Library list at the lower right of the window and drag it onto your iPad View Controller. See Figure 9-22.

Figure 9-22. Looking at the Interface Builder. The Map View has been located in the Object library

20. As you drag the Map View onto the canvas, it instantiates itself into a blank full-screen blue image as shown in Figure 9-23. Keep dragging it until it's roughly centered over the canvas and drop it.

Figure 9-23. Dragging an MKMapView onto the View Controller

21. Now that you have the Map View correctly placed onto the View Controller, you need a way to programmatically access it. To do that, you'll add an outlet for the MKMapView. First, open the Assistant editor by clicking the appropriate toolbar button. You'll see a new window with the code in the ViewController.h file visible. This is where you need to add your outlet as well as a few other modifications. See Figure 9-24.

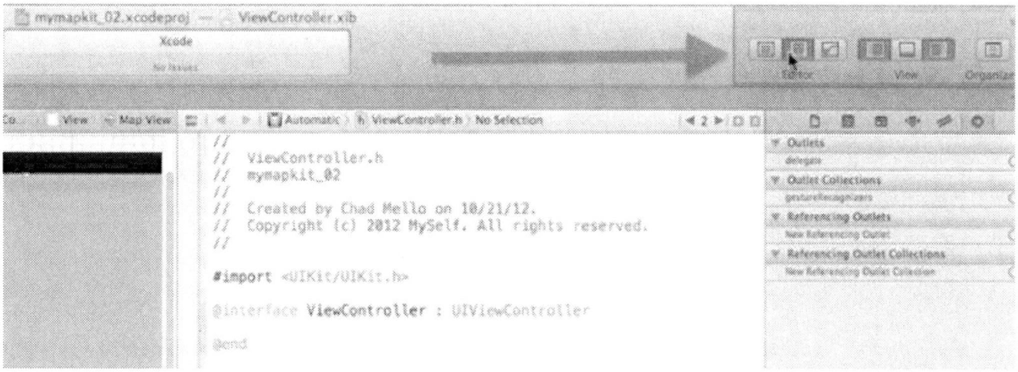

Figure 9-24. Open the Assistant editor

22. To insert an outlet, move your mouse pointer over the View Controller canvas where you just placed a new Map View. With the pointer over the Map View, hold down the Control key and start dragging it over to the header file to the right of it. At this point you will see a "fishing line" (sometimes called a line) connecting it to the MapKit, just as with buttons in earlier chapters.

23. Drag that line over to the code window where you see the source for ViewController.h. Direct the line for the outlet just below the line that reads @interface ViewController: UIViewController. Drop the outlet in place. See Figure 9-25.

Figure 9-25. Inserting a new outlet by dragging it into the Assistant editor window

24. Name the outlet `mapView` while leaving the rest of the default options as they are in the dialog. Press Enter or click Connect to create the outlet. See Figure 9-26 for details.

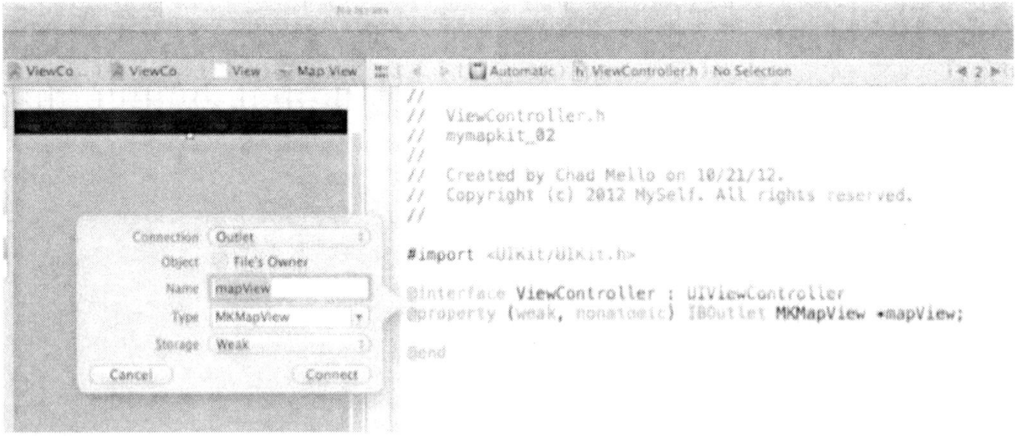

Figure 9-26. Dropping and labeling the new outlet for your Map View. Notice the new @property line added to ViewController.h

25. Close the Assistant editor by clicking the Standard editor button to the left of the Assistant editor in the toolbar. This hides the Assistant editor from view once again. You're finished with the Interface Builder.

Coding the View Controller

Now it's time to get serious. I've included some boilerplate code in DemoMonkey that you can drop into place. I'll explain how this works for `ViewController.h` so you'll know how to do it for the rest of the code. However, I'll go over each line of code separately so you can also follow along by typing the code (which appears after step 28).

26. You'll start, as always, with the header file. Open your header file by clicking `ViewController.h` inside the root project folder. It will look similar to Figure 9-27. Select all the code in the `ViewController.h` window and delete it. See Figure 9-27.

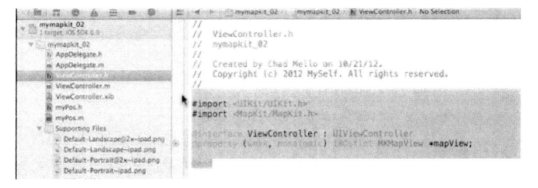

Figure 9-27. Select the code in ViewController.h and delete it. It will be replaced with code from DemoMonkey

27. Here's where you can use DemoMonkey to speed up your coding efforts. Drag in the DemoMonkey code: select line 03 `ViewController.h` from the DemoMonkey window as shown in Figure 9-28. If you prefer to type the code, keep reading.

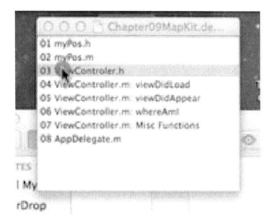

Figure 9-28. Drag 03 ViewController.h from the DemoMonkey window. This item contains the new code for your ViewController.h file

28. Then drag and drop it into the Code editor window. See Figure 9-29.

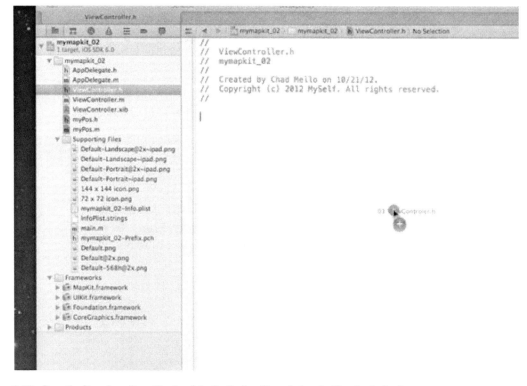

Figure 9-29. Drop the item from DemoMonkey into the Code editor window for ViewController.h

Let's examine the source code for `ViewController.h`. Whether you typed it or dragged it from DemoMonkey, it should look like the code in Figure 9-30 and as listed here:

```
#import <UIKit/UIKit.h>
#import <MapKit/MapKit.h>
#import "myPos.H"
@interface ViewController : UIViewController<MKMapViewDelegate>
@property (weak, nonatomic) IBOutlet MKMapView *mapView;
@end
MKCoordinateRegion uccsRegion;
// buttons that will be on our navigation toolbar
UIBarButtonItem *mapLayer1Button;
UIBarButtonItem *mapLayer2Button;
UIBarButtonItem *mapLayer3Button;
UIBarButtonItem *userLocationButton;
UIBarButtonItem *uccsLocationButton;
```

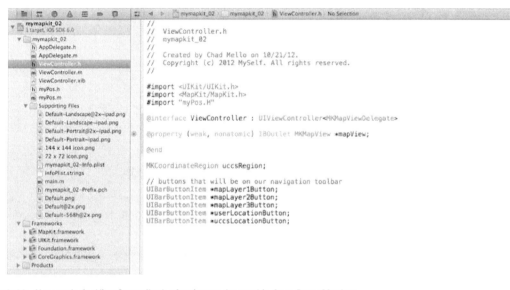

Figure 9-30. New code for ViewController.h after it was dragged in from DemoMonkey

I'm going to talk a little about what you did so you have a good understanding.

- The first thing is you told your app that you've imported all necessary code from the MapKit framework; you did this with

  `#import <MapKit/MapKit.h>` under the line `#import <UIKit/UIKit.h>`

- You told the header file that you'll be using the `MKMapViewDelegate` protocol. As you move around with your app, you need to update your records of where you were and where you are now. The `MKMapViewDelegate` protocol defines a set of optional methods that does exactly what you need to update your records. You did this by adding the `<MKMapViewDelegate>` protocol for the controller class:

```
@interface ViewController : UIViewController<MKMapViewDelegate>
```

■ Next, you defined the outlet and the property at the same time with this:

```
@property (weak, nonatomic) IBOutlet MKMapView *mapView
```

■ You also needed to define a region on the map that's focused on where you are. In your case it's the area around UCCS. You used a special data structure, designed for this very purpose, called `MKCoordinateRegion`:

```
MKCoordinateRegion uccsRegion
```

■ Lastly, you defined a few toolbar-like buttons that you want the user to see in the UI. These `UIBarButtonItem` classes let the user interact with your app. Each line of code defined a different button (I explain them in the next section):

```
// buttons that will be on our navigation toolbar
UIBarButtonItem *mapLayer1Button;
UIBarButtonItem *mapLayer2Button;
UIBarButtonItem *mapLayer3Button;
UIBarButtonItem *userLocationButton;
UIBarButtonItem *uccsLocationButton;
```

29. Once you're done, save it. Your code should look like the code in Figure 9-30. You're finished with your View Controller's header file.

Dealing with the View Controller's Implementation

As mentioned in the introduction to this chapter, controlling and working with the MapKit framework is not a trivial matter. Daunting as this area can be, I couldn't leave this chapter out of the book. I feel that you'll agree after you've finished this chapter.

After doing the necessary importing of your myPos header file and the synthesis of the View Controller that you just set up in the header file, you need to do a few other things:

■ Set up the coordinates of the UCCS Engineering and Applied Science building in the `viewDidLoad` method.

■ Set up your toolbar buttons and add them to your main Navigation Bar at the top of the app in the `viewDidAppear` method.

■ Make a pin drop down onto the exact latitude and longitude set forth in the `viewDidAppear` and put an annotation on it that states this is the office of Dr. Lewis.

■ Tell the Map View to display the user's current location on the map in the `viewDidAppear` method.

■ Respond accordingly when a user taps one of your buttons in the Navigation Bar.

The Map View can show the map in one of three ways:

- *Standard*: Displays a typical map view with street names and other details.

- *Satellite*: Displays an overhead view as seen from satellites orbiting above the Earth.

- *Hybrid*: Displays a combined view of both the Standard and the Satellite views.

You'll set the map type to a Hybrid map by default, but the user will be able to change that by tapping one of three buttons. Also, if you'd like, you'll be able to swap out the UCCS latitude/longitude for a different location of your choice. You just need to have those coordinates handy. You can obtain them from the web site mentioned early in this chapter or from Google Earth or Google Maps.

30. You'll now code the viewController.m file. Open it up and you'll see the default code, as shown in Figure 9-31; go ahead and delete that. To speed things up, you can now drag the boilerplate code from DemoMonkey using Chapter09MapKit.demoMonkey and drop it into the file. The finalized code in ViewController.m will look a quite a bit different from the original code supplied by Xcode in Figure 9-31. In case you want to type the code yourself, it is provided in its entirety at the end of this chapter. The rest of the section looks at the important parts.

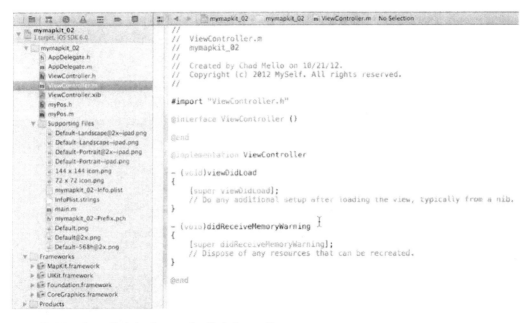

Figure 9-31. The View Controller's implementation file before coding

viewDidLoad

Let's go through each method, starting with viewDidLoad:

- First, set the Map View to enable zoom and scroll and set the map type to Hybrid (displays both map and satellite views):

```
// Setup map features
[_mapView setZoomEnabled:YES];
[_mapView setScrollEnabled:YES];
[_mapView setMapType: MKMapTypeHybrid]
```

- Then, set up your UCCS coordinates. The positive latitude value denotes north of the equator, and the negative longitude value denotes west of the prime meridian (this is where you can place your own coordinates, if you want to):

```
/*
    Create region of UCCS campus centered on
    Engineering & Applied Science building.
*/
    uccsRegion.center.latitude= 38.89350;
    uccsRegion.center.longitude = -104.800500;
    uccsRegion.span.longitudeDelta = 0.01f;
    uccsRegion.span.latitudeDelta = 0.01f;
```

viewDidAppear

Now let's look at viewDidAppear:

- First, create a new instance of your annotation class that you defined inside the myPos files:

```
// Create pin (annotation) to display at our UCCS coordinate
myPos *ann = [[myPos alloc] init];
```

- Next, define your buttons that will be displayed on the Navigation Bar. There are five buttons in all: two location buttons and three buttons related to the type of map the user wants to see. When you create these buttons, you pass in the method that will handle the button presses:

  - barButtonMapLayer1Pressed, barButtonMapLayer2Pressed, and barButtonMapLayer3Pressed methods handle the button taps that change the map type.

  - whereAmI, and whereIsUCCS handle the location buttons when the user taps them.

```
// Initialize bar buttons for selecting map overlays
mapLayer1Button =[[UIBarButtonItem alloc] initWithTitle:
                @"Map" style:UIBarButtonItemStyleBordered target:self
action:@selector(barButtonMapLayer1Pressed:)];
```

```
mapLayer2Button =[[UIBarButtonItem alloc] initWithTitle:
                        @"Satellite" style:UIBarButtonItemStyleBordered target:self
action:@selector(barButtonMapLayer2Pressed:)];

mapLayer3Button =[[UIBarButtonItem alloc] initWithTitle:
                        @"Hybrid" style:UIBarButtonItemStyleBordered target:self
action:@selector(barButtonMapLayer3Pressed:)];

userLocationButton =[[UIBarButtonItem alloc] initWithTitle:
                        @"Where Am I?" style:UIBarButtonItemStyleBordered target:self
action:@selector(whereAmI:)];

uccsLocationButton =[[UIBarButtonItem alloc] initWithTitle:
                        @"Where is UCCS?" style:UIBarButtonItemStyleBordered
target:self action:@selector(whereIsUCCS:)];
n:region animated:YES];
```

▨ Now add your new buttons to the Navigation Bar. Do that by adding the buttons
  into arrays and passing one array to the setLeftBarButtonItems method and
  the other array to the setRightBarButtonItems method of your navigationItem
  class.

```
//array that holds our right-group toolbar buttons
NSMutableArray *arr = [NSMutableArray arrayWithObjects:mapLayer3Button, mapLayer2Button,
mapLayer1Button,nil];

//add our right-group toolbar buttons
[self.navigationItem setRightBarButtonItems: arr animated:YES];

//array that holds our left-group toolbar buttons
arr = [NSMutableArray arrayWithObjects:userLocationButton, uccsLocationButton,nil];

//add our left-group toolbar buttons
[self.navigationItem setLeftBarButtonItems: arr animated:YES];
```

▨ Next, set the title of your application into the top Navigation Bar so that it's
  clearly visible.

```
//set app title on the navigation bar
self.navigationItem.title=@"My Advanced MapKit App";
```

▨ Next, set the title, subtitle, and the coordinate of your annotation object. Note
  that you set the coordinate to be that of the UCCS region you initialized in the
  viewDidLoad.

```
//setup our annotation
ann.title = @"Chad Mello";
ann.subtitle=@"UCCS Engineering & Applied Science";
ann.coordinate = uccsRegion.center;
```

▨ The next line seems innocuous, but it's a rather subtle trick. This code isn't even required; but if you want to provide some of your own fancy modifications to the way annotations behave and look, you'll need to supply your own implementation for doing that. Invoking the setDelegate method of the Map View will cause it to call your own delegate for getting an Annotation View for display. I don't elaborate too much on this here, but be aware that to do highly customizable things with MapKit (custom shapes and overlays, custom annotations, and so on), this is the technique you'll find yourself using. I briefly cover the viewForAnnotation delegate associated with this code, but I don't get very detailed.

```
/*
   inform the mapview that we will supply
   the view for displaying our pin (annoation).
*/
[_mapView setDelegate:self];
```

▨ Now you need to drop your annotation/pin onto the map at the center of the location you previously specified when you set ann.coordinate = uccsRegion.center.

```
//drop pin in front of UCCS Engineering building.
[_mapView addAnnotation:ann];
```

▨ Lastly, for this method, tell your Map View to display an animated point on the map that shows where the user is currently standing.

```
//tell mapview to show where user currently is on the map
_mapView.showsUserLocation = YES;
```

whereAmI

Now it's time to look at the whereAmI method:

▨ Begin by defining a region that stores the coordinates of where the user is currently standing. You need to set the region's center to be the user's location. These coordinates are retrieved from the Map View itself. Having this function built into the Map View spares you from having to do any more coding to get this information:

```
//zoom mapview in to where user is located
MKCoordinateRegion region;
region.center = self.mapView.userLocation.coordinate;
```

▨ Set up your span area and define the span size:

```
MKCoordinateSpan span;
span.latitudeDelta  = 1;
span.longitudeDelta = 1;
```

- Set the region span using the span you just created. To do that, you need to invoke the setRegion method of the Map View, which forces the Map View to locate that region on the map, move to it, and zoom it into view. Note that whereIsUCCS works the same way, but it only needs to call the setRegion method; the rest of the work was done in the viewDidLoad method:

```
region.span = span;
[self.mapView setRegion:region animated:YES];
```

- Finally, you handle the user's touches to change the map view type. Note: the user may choose any map type at any time by touching the button of that desired type:

```
-(void)barButtonMapLayer1Pressed:(id)sender{

    // Switch map layer to standard map view
    [_mapView setMapType: MKMapTypeStandard];
}

-(void)barButtonMapLayer2Pressed:(id)sender{

    // Switch map layer to satellite view
    [_mapView setMapType: MKMapTypeSatellite];
}

-(void)barButtonMapLayer3Pressed:(id)sender{

    // Switch map layer to hybrid (both map and satellite) view
    [_mapView setMapType: MKMapTypeHybrid];
}
```

viewForAnnotation

To wrap things up, as promised, there are a couple things you need to know to understand the viewForAnnotation code (which is in DemoMonkey under "07 ViewController.m: Misc Functions" and is also listed at the end of the chapter).

- viewForAnnotation creates a *delegate method* that manages your annotation during zooming and scrolling. In other words, it keeps track of where the user is—even when the user scrolls, zooms in, or zooms out of your map.

- viewForAnnotation creates a *static identifier*, which controls your *queue*. If it can't *dequeue* your annotation, it will allocate one that you choose. I've also included code that changes the pin color to red, and I've allowed *callout views*.

```
-(MKAnnotationView*)mapView:(MKMapView*)mV viewForAnnotation
```

Modifying the AppDelegate.m Implementation file

Usually, you wouldn't have to do anything in this part of the code, but this is a quick, Single View Application yet you're placing buttons on the Navigation Bar at the top. A simple UIViewController doesn't inherently possess the ability to display its own toolbar-like Navigation Bar. In order to get this Navigation Bar, you've to rely on another type of View Controller called UINavigationController. In AppDelegate.m, you set a UINavigationController to be the Root Controller (the starting controller) instead of your own ViewController class.

The didFinishLaunchingWithOptions method listed next sets your ViewController inside the UINavigationController. Now, the UINavigationController can draw a Navigation Bar at the top of the view that can hold your tool buttons. You can replace all the code in AppDelegate.m from DemoMonkey, line "08 AppDelegate.m":

```
- (BOOL)application:(UIApplication *)application
didFinishLaunchingWithOptions:(NSDictionary *)launchOptions
{
    // Here, we inject a standard navigation controller so that we can utilize the navigation
toolbar.
    // A stand-alone single view UI controller cannot display a navigation toolbar on its own.
    UINavigationController *navcon = [[UINavigationController alloc] init];
    // create our app window
    self.window = [[UIWindow alloc] initWithFrame:[[UIScreen mainScreen] bounds]];
    // load our main map view controller.
    self.viewController = [[ViewController alloc] initWithNibName:@"ViewController" bundle:nil];
    // push our main map view controller onto the navigation controller's stack
    [navcon pushViewController:self.viewController animated:NO];
    //set the root controller to our navigation controller
    self.window.rootViewController = navcon;
    [self.window makeKeyAndVisible];
    return YES;
}
```

The End Result: Running Your iPad MapKit App

If everything was entered correctly, you should be able to compile this code and run it in the iPad Simulator. If you get errors or other messages while trying to run your app, look over each file very carefully and correct any bugs you see.

Before attempting to do anything else, though, save your code. You need to get yourself in the habit of saving your code often. As we were walking through this exercise, you should've been saving your code after each major step, and maybe every so often in between as well. As shown in Figure 9-32, click the Run button to see the results of your hard work.

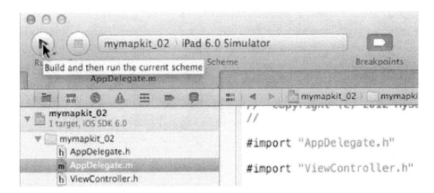

Figure 9-32. Click the Run button to compile and run your program in the iPad Simulator

After a few moments, you should see your app's splash screen in the Simulator. See Figures 9-33, 9-34, and 9-35.

Figure 9-33. *Your app's splash screen is shown while it loads into memory*

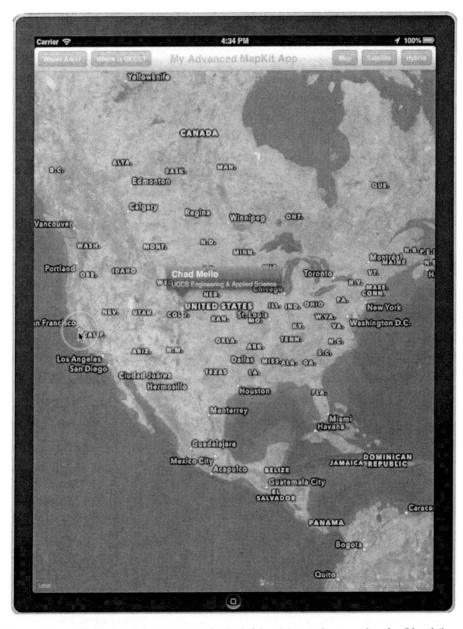

Figure 9-34. Your app's user interface showing the annotation (red pin) and the user's current location (blue dot)

Figure 9-35. Your app's user interface showing the annotation (red pin) and the UCCS Engineering & Applied Science building, after touching the Where is UCCS? button

Being a programmer is hard work, but it's also rewarding! In this chapter, you created a somewhat robust app—but it's nowhere near the professional quality people have come to expect from modern apps. Creating a fully functioning iPhone or iPad app can take weeks, even months in many cases. Try building this app out on your own. Maybe you can add some more features, buttons, and views to extend it far beyond what we covered here. With enough effort, you could be on your way to creating an app worthy of publishing on Apple's app store for the whole world to see and use.

Source for ViewController Implementation

As mentioned earlier in the chapter, here's the code for the View Controller implementation file so you can type it in yourself:

```
#import "ViewController.h"

@interface ViewController ()

@end

@implementation ViewController

- (void)viewDidLoad
{
    [super viewDidLoad];

    // Setup map features
    [_mapView setZoomEnabled:YES];
    [_mapView setScrollEnabled:YES];
    [_mapView setMapType: MKMapTypeHybrid];

    /*
     Create region of UCCS campus centered on
     Engineering & Applied Science building.
     */
    uccsRegion.center.latitude= 38.89350;
    uccsRegion.center.longitude = -104.800500;
    uccsRegion.span.longitudeDelta = 0.01f;
    uccsRegion.span.latitudeDelta = 0.01f;
}

-(void) viewDidAppear:(BOOL)animated
{
        // Create pin (annotation) to display at our UCCS coordinate
    myPos *ann = [[myPos alloc] init];

    // Initialize bar buttons for selecting map overlays
    mapLayer1Button =[[UIBarButtonItem alloc] initWithTitle:
                    @"Map" style:UIBarButtonItemStyleBordered target:self
action:@selector(barButtonMapLayer1Pressed:)];

    mapLayer2Button =[[UIBarButtonItem alloc] initWithTitle:
                    @"Satellite" style:UIBarButtonItemStyleBordered target:self
action:@selector(barButtonMapLayer2Pressed:)];

    mapLayer3Button =[[UIBarButtonItem alloc] initWithTitle:
                    @"Hybrid" style:UIBarButtonItemStyleBordered target:self
action:@selector(barButtonMapLayer3Pressed:)];
```

```
    userLocationButton =[[UIBarButtonItem alloc] initWithTitle:
                        @"Where Am I?" style:UIBarButtonItemStyleBordered target:self
action:@selector(whereAmI:)];

    uccsLocationButton =[[UIBarButtonItem alloc] initWithTitle:
                        @"Where is UCCS?" style:UIBarButtonItemStyleBordered target:self
action:@selector(whereIsUCCS:)];

    //array that holds our right-group toolbar buttons
    NSMutableArray *arr = [NSMutableArray arrayWithObjects:mapLayer3Button, mapLayer2Button,
mapLayer1Button,nil];

    //add our right-group toolbar buttons
    [self.navigationItem setRightBarButtonItems: arr animated:YES];

    //array that holds our left-group toolbar buttons
    arr = [NSMutableArray arrayWithObjects:userLocationButton, uccsLocationButton,nil];

    //add our left-group toolbar buttons
    [self.navigationItem setLeftBarButtonItems: arr animated:YES];

    //set app title on the navigation bar
    self.navigationItem.title=@"My Advanced MapKit App";

    //setup our annotation
    ann.title = @"Chad Mello";
    ann.subtitle=@"UCCS Engineering & Applied Science";
    ann.coordinate = uccsRegion.center;

    /*
     inform the mapview that we will supply
     the view for displaying our pin (annoation).
    */

    [_mapView setDelegate:self];

    //drop pin in front of UCCS Engineering building.
    [_mapView addAnnotation:ann];


    //let mapview to show where user currently is on the map
    _mapView.showsUserLocation = YES;

    [super viewDidAppear:animated];

}

-(void)whereAmI:(id)sender{

    //zoom mapview in to where user is located

    MKCoordinateRegion region;
    region.center = self.mapView.userLocation.coordinate;
```

```
    MKCoordinateSpan span;
    span.latitudeDelta  = 1;
    span.longitudeDelta = 1;
    region.span = span;

    [self.mapView setRegion:region animated:YES];

}

-(void)whereIsUCCS:(id)sender{

    // zoom mapview in to where UCCS campus is located
    [_mapView setRegion:uccsRegion animated:YES];
}

-(void)barButtonMapLayer1Pressed:(id)sender{

    // Switch map layer to standard map view
    [_mapView setMapType: MKMapTypeStandard];
}

-(void)barButtonMapLayer2Pressed:(id)sender{

    // Switch map layer to satellite view
    [_mapView setMapType: MKMapTypeSatellite];
}

-(void)barButtonMapLayer3Pressed:(id)sender{

    // Switch map layer to hybrid (both map and satellite) view
    [_mapView setMapType: MKMapTypeHybrid];
}

-(MKAnnotationView*)mapView:(MKMapView*)mV viewForAnnotation:(id<MKAnnotation>)annotation
{
    // Return annotation view that will make the
    // annotation visible on the map view.

    MKPinAnnotationView *pinView = nil;
    if (annotation!=_mapView.userLocation)
    {
        static NSString *defaultPinID = @"com.rorylewis";
        pinView=(MKPinAnnotationView*)[_mapView
dequeueReusableAnnotationViewWithIdentifier:defaultPinID];

        if(pinView==nil)
            pinView=[[MKPinAnnotationView alloc] initWithAnnotation:annotation
reuseIdentifier:defaultPinID];

        pinView.pinColor=MKPinAnnotationColorRed;
        pinView.canShowCallout=YES;
        pinView.animatesDrop=YES;
    }
```

```objc
    else
    {

        [_mapView.userLocation setTitle:@"I am here!"];
    }

    return pinView;
}

- (void)didReceiveMemoryWarning
{
    [super didReceiveMemoryWarning];
    // Dispose of any resources that can be recreated.
}

- (NSUInteger)supportedInterfaceOrientations
{
    // We support all orientations, but NOT upside down.
    return UIInterfaceOrientationMaskAllButUpsideDown;
}

- (UIInterfaceOrientation)preferredInterfaceOrientationForPresentation
{
    // We "suggest" or "prefer" rotating to the left for best view.
    return UIInterfaceOrientationLandscapeLeft;
}

@end
```

Chapter 10

Storyboarding to Multimedia Platforms

This is the last chapter of the book, and I have been looking forward to writing this chapter for a long time. This is the capstone app, if you will, the app that teaches you how to market your restaurant, business, or whatever you like to various multimedia platforms. I chose to promote a band for this app because it involves iTunes, and many of my students struggle with iTunes. In the lecture hall, I first walk through the app with the students as they imagine they've discovered a band called The Beatles. They then market that band on the Web, YouTube, and iTunes. In the second half of this project, the students create their own business that they market in a similar but much more creative manner.

Unfortunately, due to copyright issues, it is not permissible to show pictures of The Beatles in a book that's not authorized by The Beatles. For the purposes of this book, I've created some dummy sites on the web, with pictures of myself playing guitar, and iTunes sites where I have songs from many years ago (1997). I will show you where to get Beatles URLs (public domain) and how to make the site — first for The Beatles, as I do in class, and then to promote other bands and types of media. Hopefully, you'll have your own business — such as a restaurant, bead shop, consulting service, or whatever — that you can make a promotional app for and put on the iTunes Store so that people can download it for free.

How does this work? Back in Chapter 1, I explain the exact process of how you can make money from your app on the Internet. Here I teach you how to market your business and set up your app, possibly for free to begin with. Let's say you have a babysitting business. After you learn how to manage The Beatles web site, you can make an app for the babysitting business and upload it to the App Store for free downloads. In the old days, we used to hand out cards. Now we hand out apps. You let parents and potential parents, customers of your babysitting service, know that they can download your babysitting business's app for free and, with a password that only works for a limited time (and only if they are potential parents), view their babies on a live webcam any time of day. They can also see other children being taken care of by your staff. They can get updates on snow days and birthdays and pay their bill, all through your app. By word of mouth, those parents will tell other parents how great your business is based solely on how convenient and cool your app was.

This approach can work for other types of businesses; you just need to be creative. Innovation is your department. But hey, you had to have a huge innovative streak to buy this book — and if you're still reading this, you're well into the realm of Geekdom. So, I have full faith that you have everything you need to make a wonderful app for your business, another person's business, or yourself. All you need is the technical know-how, and I'll teach you that right here, right now, so let's go!

myiTunes: A Master-Detail Application (iPad)

myiTunes is based on one of the more daunting methods of creating a Storyboarding app: the Master-Detail Application. I say this because my new students often experience challenges with multiple Master Views and multiple Detail Views. For my more experienced students who've worked with earlier versions of Xcode, there are no more Root View Controller or `MainWindow.xib` files. However, Master-Detail Applications empower the iPad's Split View and Popover View, together with incredible Storyboarding technology. As if this weren't enough, I also throw into the mix the ability to access iTunes, Facebook, Google+, pages that have videos, and, of course, the two iPad splash screens with cool icons that all add up to a beautiful, marketable app just waiting to boost you, your business, or someone else's business into the stratosphere—loudly!

iTunes requires some controversial, quirky, and not-so-user-friendly means of accessing its store. I go through that process step by step, including the ability to look up bands, videos, and podcasts. I don't cover other multimedia platforms in the example because that would be overload, but I do explain how to convert your media from images to videos and so forth. I also include code to access these other forms of multimedia and offer boilerplate code you can download. So, even though you don't use all these types of media in this project, they are there for you.

One thing about terminology before we proceed: we will be talking about Split Views and Popover Views in this app. These are the supercool tables and drop-down menus that, depending how you hold your iPad, invoke a table for the user to use. The Split View shows two panels side by side. In Landscape orientation, the Master View is embedded on the side. However, in Portrait orientation the Split View appears as a Popover that looks like it's lying on top of the existing view — like a drop-down menu sitting on top of what was underneath it (see Figure 10-25). But it can't be that it works like a dialog box or drop-down menu. One student recently asked me, "Dr. Lewis, can we pimp out the Popover!?" Hmmm … nope! You can't tweak, pimp out, or change much. But the issue is whether you want to or not, and the answer is *probably not*. Popovers are sophisticated and elegant and show the user that you, the developer who programmed them, are awesome!

So let's get on with the preliminaries so you can start on your app.

Preliminaries

This chapter's download files are a DemoMonkey file and images. You'll find these files at `http://bit.ly/ULpM9P`. You can download the sample code that I programmed on the video here: `http://bit.ly/ULp01m`. To view the screencast of this chapter's exercise, go to `http://bit.ly/UnfI37`. If you need more help, go to the forum at `http://bit.ly/oLVwpY`.

First, I show you the code from 30,000 feet, for a very broad overall view of the landscape. Then, as you drill down, keep the big picture in mind. But first, take a sneak peak at the Storyboard Popover in Figure 10-26 at the end of this chapter, which illustrates how after tapping the app's icon, the first screen shows the iPad's Popover as it lies "on top" of the screen "below" it. It's really cool and certainly something that every Xcode programmer should learn. What you'll be programming here, from a broad perspective, goes like this:

1. Set up the Popover in the Storyboard.

2. Code the interaction to the multimedia platforms.

3. Tweak the Popover to grab the platforms correctly.

A New Master-Detail Template

Let's get started with the app.

1. You will use a Master-Detail Application. So, open Xcode and ⌘+⇧+N, as shown in Figure 10-1. After selecting the Master-Detail Application, Press Enter/Return.

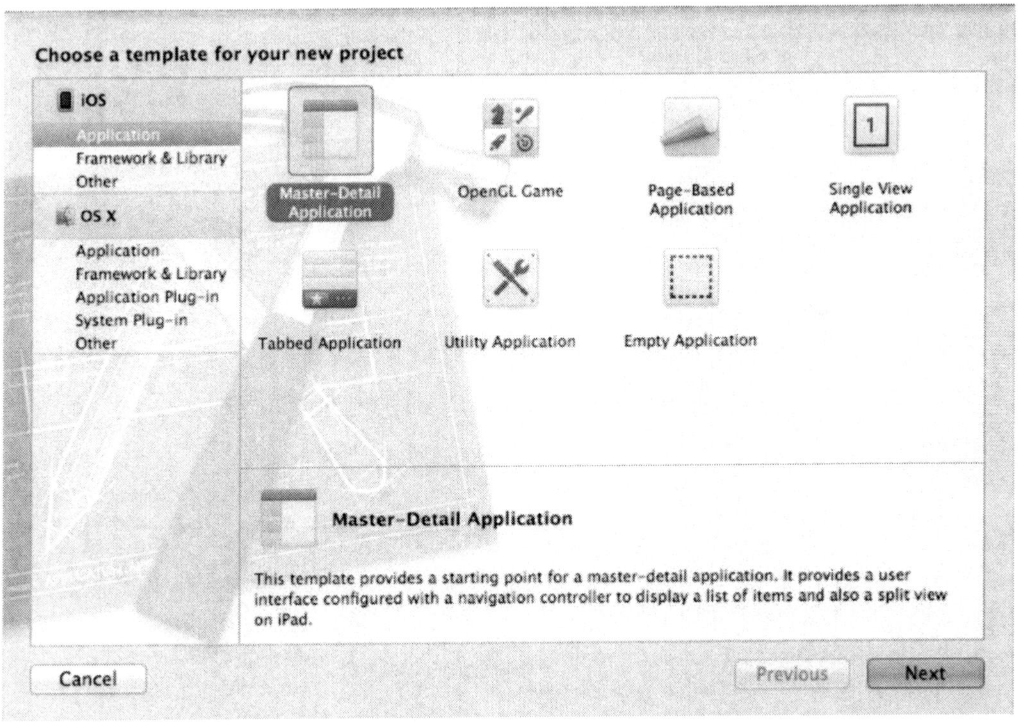

Figure 10-1. Select the Master-Detail Application icon and press Return or click Next

2. In order to follow along with me as closely as you can, name it myiTunes, select iPad in the Devices drop-down, and check Use Storyboards and Use Automatic Reference Counting, as shown in Figure 10-2.

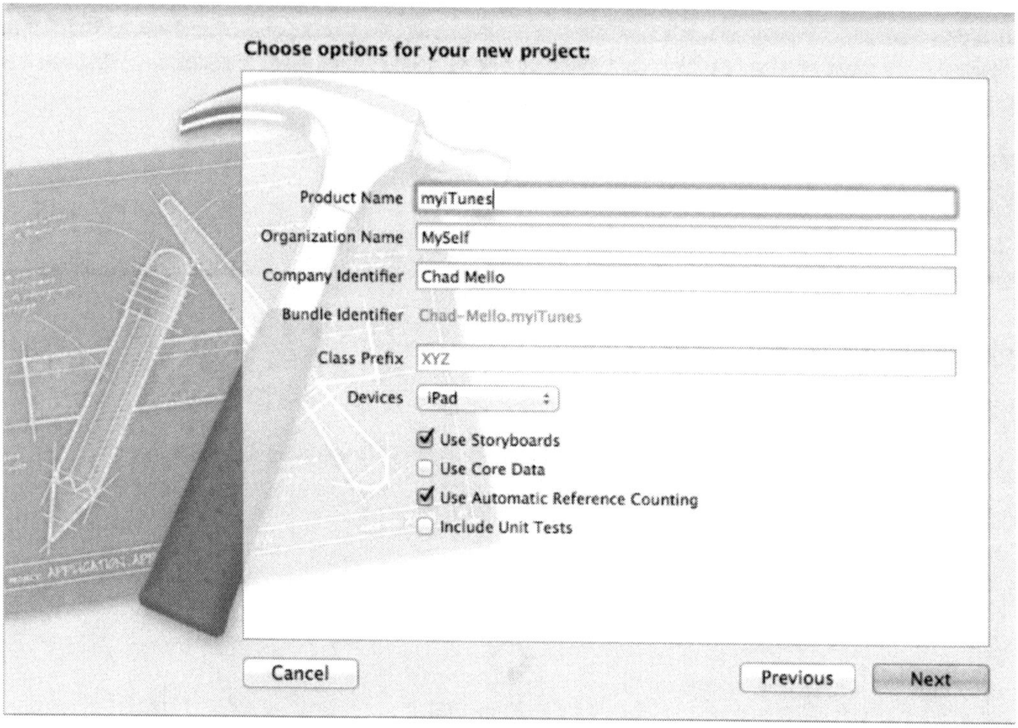

Figure 10-2. Name your app myiTunes, making sure Use Storyboards and Use Automatic Reference Counting are checked

Bring in the Images!

Make sure you've downloaded the images and boilerplate code onto your desktop from http://bit.ly/ULpM9P.

3. Drag in the 72 × 72 px iPad icon and the 144 × 144 iPad icon into the App Icons box. Drag the iPadSplash 769 × 1004 and iPadSplash 1536 × 2008 splash screens into the Launch Images Landscape box. And drag the iPadSplash 1024 × 748 and iPadSplash 2048 × 1496 splash screens into the Launch Images Portrait boxes, as shown in Figure 10-3.

Figure 10-3. Drag in your graphics

4. You always want to keep things nice, orderly, and in their proper place, and note that the files holding the images you just dragged into Xcode are in the root directory. Drag them into their proper location: the Supporting Files folder, as shown in Figure 10-4.

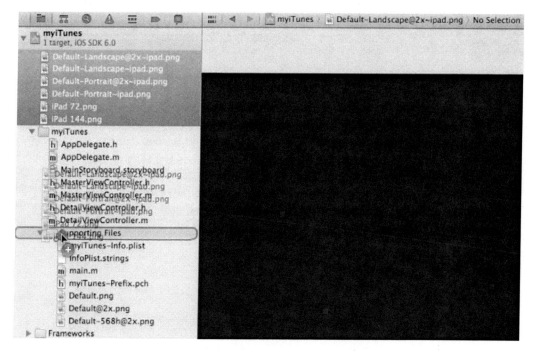

Figure 10-4. Drag the images into the Supporting Files folder

Organize the Popover in Storyboard

The first thing you'll do is set up the Popover in the Storyboard. I'm going to be fairly inventive and artful but won't overboard with beautiful Popover bells and whistles so that I don't take away from my two goals: teaching you to set up the Storyboard and teaching you to write the code behind the Storyboard. However, once you complete this project, you'll have opened the doors to rooms where you can tinker around later. For right now, let's keep it simple.

5. Select `MainStoryboard.storyboard`, as shown in Figure 10-5.

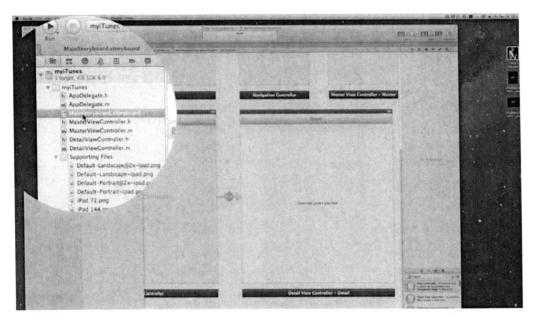

Figure 10-5. Select the Storyboard

6. Before we get too far, let's first absorb what Xcode has instantiated in the initial Master-Detail Application screen. In the bottom right-hand corner in white is Detail View Controller – Detail. To its left and partially hidden is the Navigation Controller. In the upper right-hand side is the Master View Controller – Master, Navigation Controller, and (partially hidden) the Split View Controller Scene. You'll probably spend most of your time programming the Popover, which is the Master View Controller – Master, and after that the Detail View Controller – Detail (the meat and potatoes of your app).

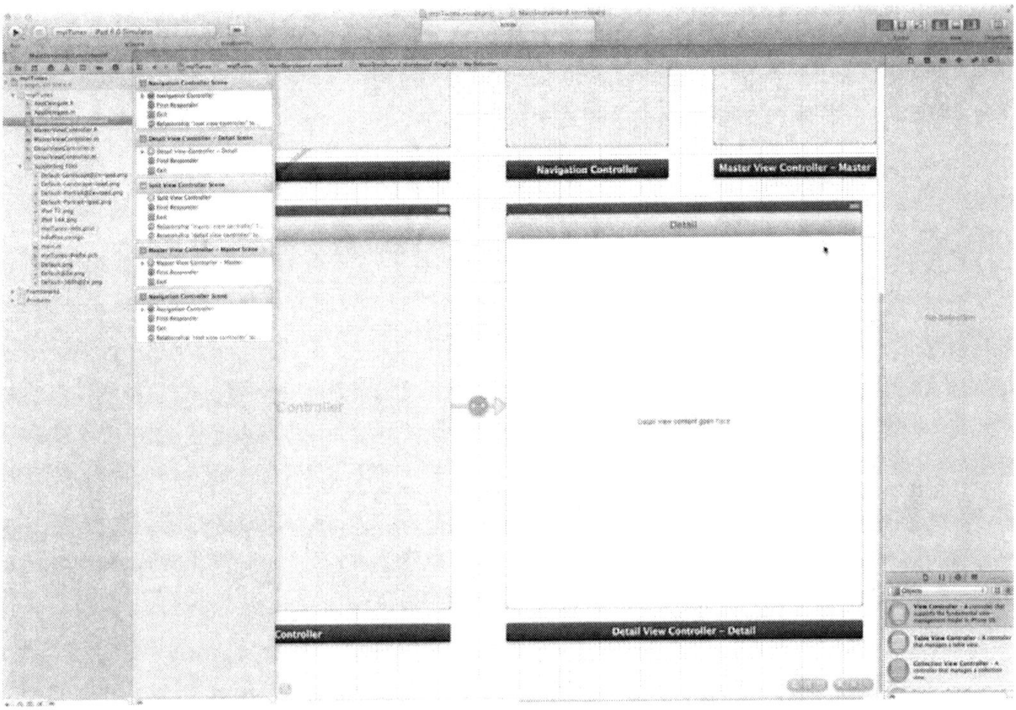

Figure 10-6. The initial Master-Detail Application screen

7.   Figure 10-15 shows all the Table Views and their levels in the left-hand
     sidebar called the Document Outline, inside the box called Master View
     Controller – Master Scene. That's what you'll be working toward in the next
     few steps. There are two ways to populate these Table Views with what you
     want: the long, boring way and the organized and very efficient way. Stick to
     this simple rule:

*Create one Table View with all its sub-attributes. Then, once you have one done
exactly the way you want it, duplicate the entire set.*

Go ahead and select Table View in the Master View Controller – Master scene, as shown in
Figure 10-7.

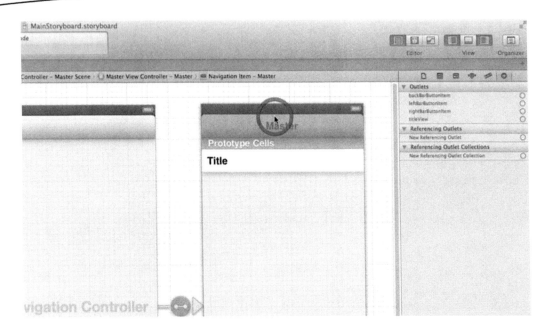

Figure 10-7. Select the Master View Controller – Master

THE BIG PICTURE

1. Set up the Popover in the Storyboard.

    1.1   **Create a group.**

        1.1.1.   Set up the attributes of each Table View Cell – Cell in the group.

    1.2.   Duplicate the group as required.

    1.3.   Label all the cells.

2. Code the interaction to the multimedia platforms.

3. Tweak the Popover to grab the platforms correctly.

---

8. Open the Attributes Inspector in the Utilities pane and ensure Static Cells is selected from the Content drop-down menu, as shown in left-hand image in Figure 10-8. Remember that I advised you to make one cell perfect and duplicate it in order to be efficient? This is where you start that process. Also make sure that the number of cells is only 1, as shown in the right-hand image in Figure 10- 8.

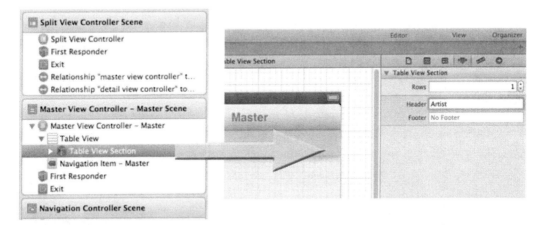

Figure 10-8. *Select Static Cells and change Sections to 1*

9.   This can get tricky, so pay attention to this very simple step: go back to the Documents Outline and, inside your Master View Controller – Master Scene, select Table View Section, as shown in the left-hand image in Figure 10-9. Name this cell Artist. Later, you'll change these names when you copy and paste them. For now, simply go over to the Attributes Inspector and first change the number of rows from 3 to 1 and then name it Artist, as shown in the right-hand image in Figure 10-9.

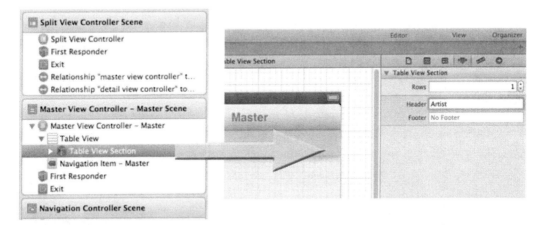

Figure 10-9. *Name the Table View Cell – Cell Artist*

10.   You want to create subtitles in each Table View Cell – Cell because they tell you and, most importantly, the user what you'll see or where you'll be going if you select this option. So, go back to the Documents Outline. If the Table View Section isn't expanded, expand it. Once your Table View Section is expanded, select Table View Cell – Cell, as shown in the left-hand image in Figure 10-10. In the Attributes Inspector, change the Style from Basic to Subtitle, as shown in the right-hand image in Figure 10-10.

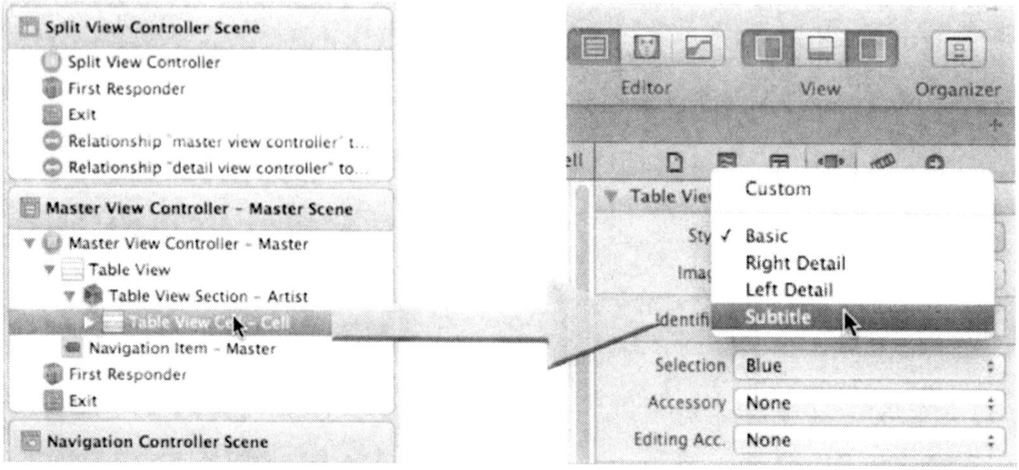

Figure 10-10. Create subtitle in the Table View Cell – Cell

11.   In Figure 10-11, you can see Subtitle under Title in your cell. That's exactly
      what you want. While you're here, add disclosure indicators (>) to give the
      user a sense of the direction that they will be travelling in when they select a
      particular cell. In the Accessory field, just under the Style section you were in,
      select Disclosure Indicator, as shown in Figure 10-11.

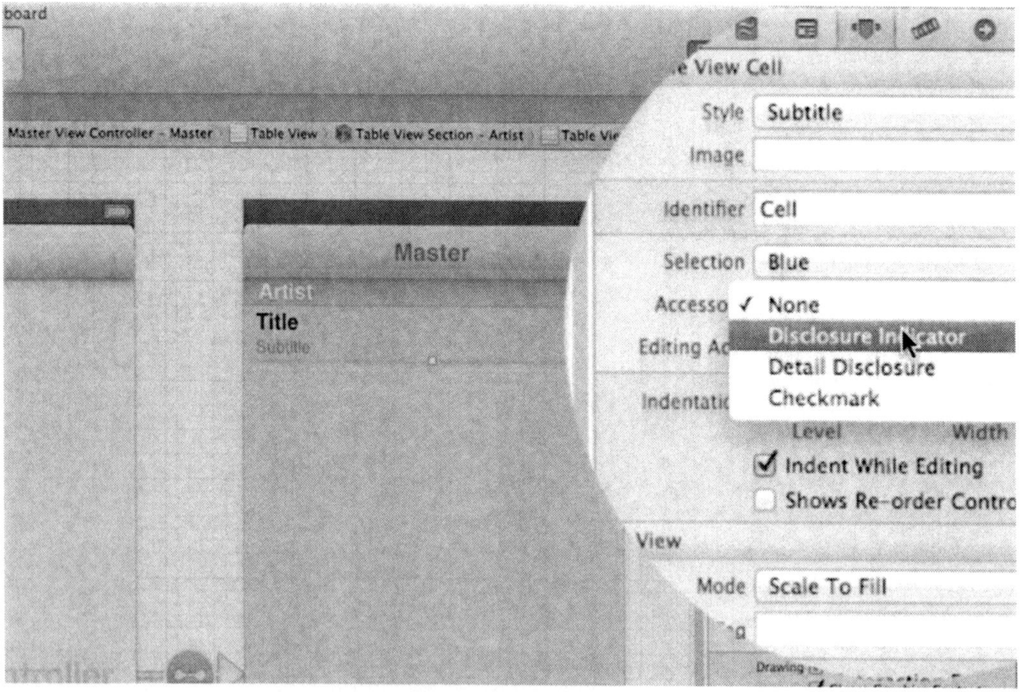

Figure 10-11. Create disclosure indicators for each Table View Cell – Cell

12.   Ahh … look at that beautiful disclosure indicator and subtitle you've just created in Figure 10-12. Beautiful! The next "Big Picture" section shows that you're about to embark on setting up the Table View Section (1.1.2.). Go back to the Documents Outline and select the Table View Section, as shown in Figure 10-12.

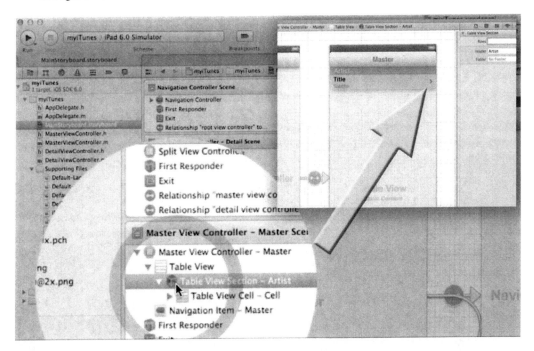

Figure 10-12. Go back up one level to the Table View Section

THE BIG PICTURE

---

1.   Set up the Popover in the Storyboard.

   1.1.   Create a group.

      1.1.1.   Set up the attributes of each Table View Cell – Cell in the group.

         1.1.1.1.   Static cells, grouped style, subtitles, and disclosure indicators.

      1.1.2.   Set up the Table View Section.

         1.1.2.1.   Create a header and create two rows.

   1.2.   Duplicate the group as required.

      1.2.1.   Go to the Master Scene and make four sections.

   1.3.   Label all the cells.

2.   Code the interaction to the multimedia platforms.

3.   Tweak the Popover to grab the platforms correctly.

13. You haven't labeled any Table View Cell – Cells yet. You only do this in step
     1.3 in "The Big Picture," which is the last step for two reasons. First, it takes
     time and second, you'll change them. However, in this instance, you need to
     select the Table View Section and go to the Header in the Attributes Inspector
     and give it a "dummy" label to give you something (anything) to edit when
     you duplicate these cells. Label this group with the name of your first group:
     Artists. Then, create two rows, as shown in Figure 10-13, because you'll only
     have two rows of cells in each group. (You may want more. Always err on the
     side of creating more cells, because you can delete them easily, but if you
     have to recreate them, you often will have to spend time formatting them.)

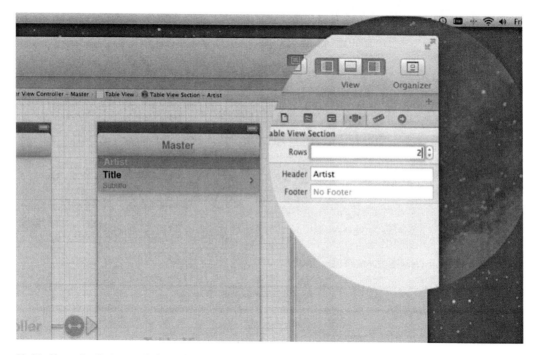

Figure 10-13. Name the first group Artist and create two rows

14. You've now created one group exactly as you want it. Go back to the original
     Table View where you began and make four sections, as shown in Figure 10-14.

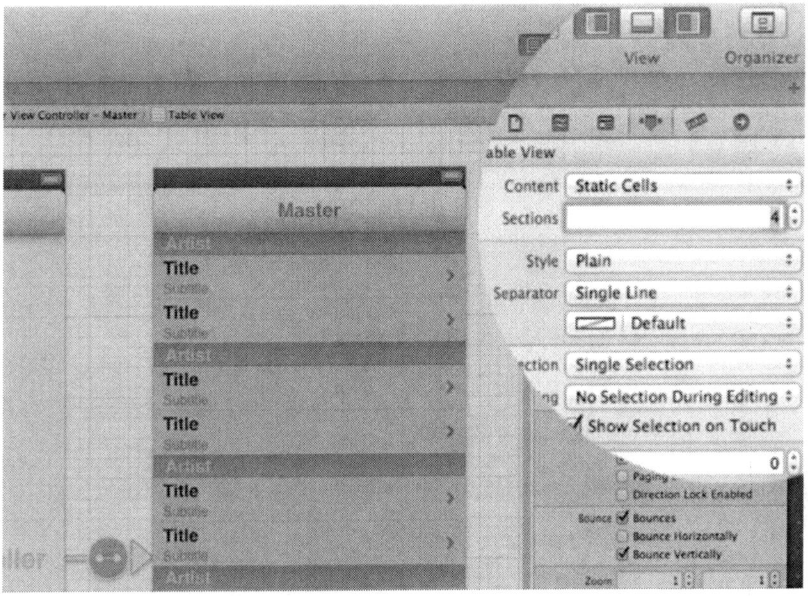

Figure 10-14. Only now do you create all your sections

15. Of course, you'll do things differently when you create your own, but for now name your four groups: Artists, Albums on iTunes, Songs, and Pictures. These four groups will facilitate the band's (I give you the Beatles links when I get to the code) presence on the Web and iTunes, under Artists, then Albums. For the Beatles, there will be many albums. For this example, you're only using two, and likewise for Songs and Pictures. Note some subtitles tell the user that they'll go to iTunes and some tell the user they'll go to the Internet. Name all the cells, as shown in Figure 10-15. Remember, you can simply double-click the cell to create a name.

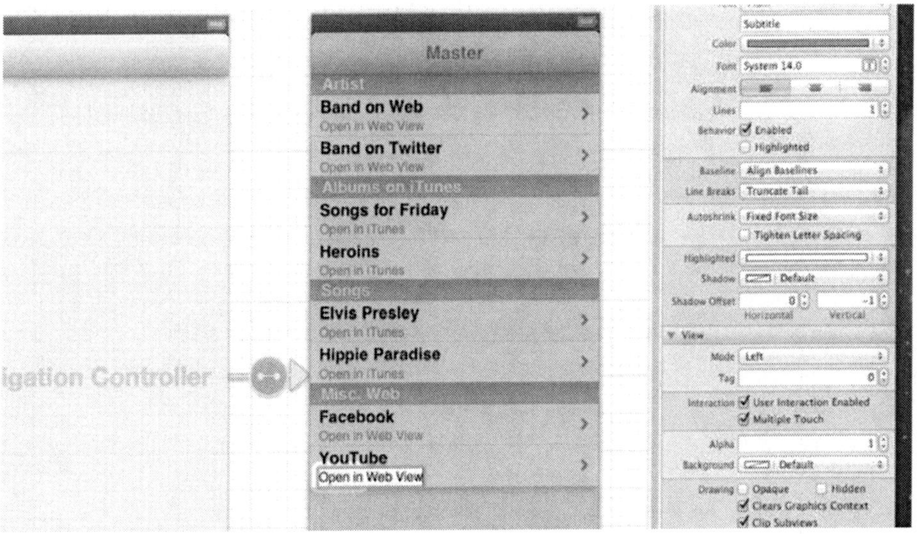

Figure 10-15. Name the cells and headers

Coding the myiTunes App

I really want to keep this really, really, really simple. You'll do two broad things when you code: first you create code that hooks up to what you want to happen when each cell is tapped and then you make sure your views connect correctly with the WebViews.

THE BIG PICTURE

1. Set up the Popover in the Storyboard.

    1.1. **Set up the header for the Master View Controller.**

    1.2. **Set up the header for the Detail View Controller.**

2. Code the interaction to the multimedia platforms.

    2.1. Master View Controller.

        2.1.1. Code for each cell that is selected.

    2.2. Detail View Controller.

        2.2.1. Connecting the views to the WebViews

3. Tweak the Popover to grab the platforms correctly.

---

16. Start by looking at the Master View Controller. First make sure your header allows you to do all the things you need to do in your implementation file. Save everything, close the utilities, open the Navigator, and open up MasterViewController.h. You need to delete the existing @interface so you can replace it with your own. Select it as shown in Figure 10-16 and delete it.

Figure 10-16. Start to create an NSURL to hook up to iTunes

17. You're now going to begin to make sure that you can embed web content into your app using the UIWebView. Simply create a UIWebView object, attach it to a window, and then send it a request to load web content. You can either code this yourself, as I show in a moment, or use DemoMonkey. If you're using DemoMonkey, open up the DemoMonkey file "MasterViewController.h: interface" and drag it over to where you just deleted the @interface one step ago. This is indicated by arrow 1 in Figure 10-17. What you did here is the MasterViewController declaration to accommodate both your table and WebView components.

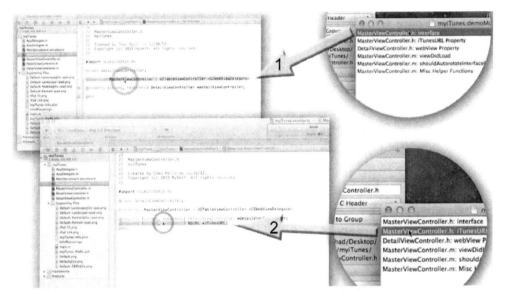

Figure 10-17. Paste the first two DemoMonkey files into the MasterViewController header file

Next, create an @property so you can later use an NSURL object to manipulate a URL to point to the iTunes Store. Either type in the NSURL @property as shown after this step or, if you're using DemoMonkey, select the second DemoMonkey file "MasterViewController.h: iTunes URL" and drag it immediately beneath the @property for the Detail View, as indicated by arrow 2 in Figure 10-17. The NSURL @property code you've just dragged in is what you'll need every time you want to incorporate URLs that connect to iTunes.

These two steps will soon become as common as getting in your car and turning the ignition key. When you want an @interface for a Split View Controller to accommodate a table for web viewing that includes iTunes URLs, you enter the following code:

```
#import <UIKit/UIKit.h>

@class DetailViewController;

@interface MasterViewController : UITableViewController <UIWebViewDelegate>
@property (strong, nonatomic) DetailViewController *detailViewController;
@property (strong, nonatomic) NSURL *iTunesURL;
@end
```

18. Save your MasterViewController.h and open the DetailViewController.h file. You now want to make sure DetailViewController can also accommodate the UIWebView outlets. Either type in the code as shown after this step or drag the DemoMonkey file "DetailViewController.h: webView Property" over between the @property detailItem and @property detailDescriptionLabel, as shown in Figure 10-18. Note that when you go back to tweak the Storyboard to be able to have the DetailViewController access the Internet, you'll connect this to your UIWebView.

```
#import <UIKit/UIKit.h>

@interface DetailViewController : UIViewController <UISplitViewControllerDelegate>

@property (strong, nonatomic) id detailItem;
@property (strong, nonatomic) IBOutlet UIWebView *webView;
@property (weak, nonatomic) IBOutlet UILabel *detailDescriptionLabel;
@end
```

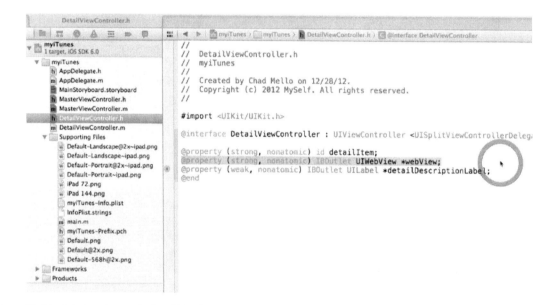

Figure 10-18. Select and open the DetailViewController header file

Coding MasterViewController

In DetailViewController, you need to set up LocateArtistPageInSafari, LocateArtistPageInItunes, LocateMoviePageInItunes (you don't use this one here, but I thought you may like to have it at your disposal), and StartExternalAppWithURL. The "Big Picture" section shows where you are, in bold.

THE BIG PICTURE

1. Set up the Popover in the Storyboard.

   1.3. Set up the header for the Master View Controller.

   1.4. Set up the header for the Detail View Controller.

2. **Code the interaction to the multimedia platforms.**

   2.1. Master View Controller.

      2.1.1. Code for each cell that is selected.

   2.2. Detail View Controller.

      2.2.1. Connect the views to the WebViews.

3. Tweak the Popover to grab the platforms correctly.

---

19. You need to make sure your app still runs regardless of the orientation of the iPad (Split View, in Landscape, and Popover in Portrait) and have a set of cases of events that you'll trigger if a cell is selected. Drag the DemoMonkey file "MasterViewController.m: shouldAutorotateToInterfaceOrientation" over between the `viewDidLoad` and `DidReceiveMemoryWarning` methods, as shown in Figure 10-19. Let's step back for a minute now and have a look at the Big Picture.

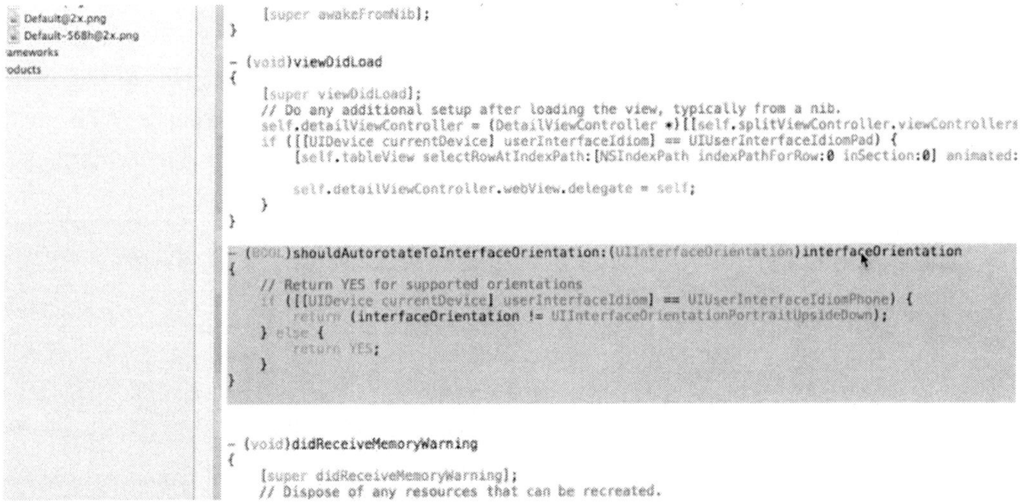

Figure 10-19. Drag in the shouldAutorotateToInterfaceOrientation method

---

THE BIG PICTURE

1.   Set up the Popover in the Storyboard.

2.   Code the interaction to the multimedia platforms.

    2.1.   Master View Controller.

        2.1.1.   Code for each cell that is selected.

            2.1.1.1.   Header material.

        2.1.1.2.   viewDidLoad.

            2.1.1.3.   Set orientations (just done in Figure 10-19).

            2.1.1.4.   Case statements.

            2.1.1.5.   Private methods.

    2.2.   Detail View Controller.

        2.2.1.   Connecting the views to the WebViews.

3.   Tweak the Popover to grab the platforms correctly.

---

20.   You need to select everything from the `insertNewObject` method until the `@end` statement to add your miscellaneous code that includes your `case` statements and private methods. Select it, as shown in Figure 10-20, and delete it.

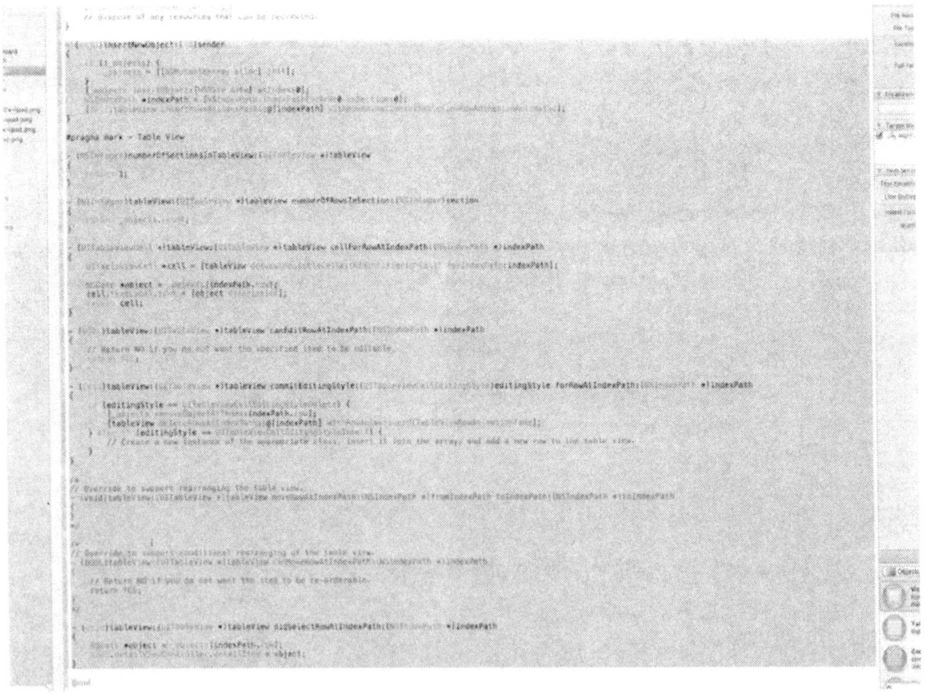

Figure 10-20. Delete from the insertNewObject method to the @end

21. You need to first convert your section and row numbers from a linear index to rows when counting from top to bottom and then add your private methods. Drag in the DemoMonkey file "MasterViewController.m: Misc Helper Functions" and place it where you've just deleted all the code in the last step (you can see the case statements have been added in Figure 10-21; I cover them in detail in a moment). I've purposely left some of the code that you deleted and put in Override comments to let you know what it is you're overriding (telling our code to ignore) and what it is you've replaced. The four overrides are as follows:

```
// Override to support conditional editing of the table view.
// Override to support editing the table view.
// Override to support rearranging the table view.
// Override to support conditional rearranging of the table view.
```

Figure 10-21. *Your case statements*

Note that these four overrides make the compiler ignore code that was already not needed for this application. When you uncomment the code, it provides more control over the default behavior of the Table View. This is what's known as overriding.

Before you start working on the case statements, which will look at what type of link is invoked, depending on the button tapped by the user, you need to do a little housekeeping. As noted earlier, you need to convert your section and row numbers into a linear index of rows when counting from top to bottom. As shown in the override comments, you assume that the first section is two rows and all others are one row. You can, of course, choose your own iTunes links to The Beatles, as mentioned earlier — or to any band, lecture, movie, or podcast you choose. They are obtained from iTunes Link Maker (http://itunes.apple.com/linkmaker/) as recommended in the iTunes Link Maker FAQ (www.apple.com/itunes/linkmaker/faq/).

For those who need to dig a little deeper, the following code is the function that contains the switch block. The first line is the function's definition, and in the second line it fetches the actual row index that was selected by the user. It's this line (indexPath.section*2 + indexPath.row) that makes sure that the first section is two rows and all others are one row.

```
- (void)tableView:(UITableView *)tableView didSelectRowAtIndexPath:(NSIndexPath *)indexPath
{
NSInteger nSelectedRowIdx = indexPath.section *2 + indexPath.row;
    switch (nSelectedRowIdx) {
```

Now you need to make the case statements that will keep tabs on what selection the user taps in your list that you've ordered sequentially. You have four sections: ARTIST, ALBUMS IN ITUNES, SONGS, and PICTURES. Remember that you gave two options for each selection, which means you need to have two cases within each of them. I lay it out in the "Big Picture" section.

THE BIG PICTURE

1. Set up the Popover in the Storyboard.

2. Code the interaction to the multimedia platforms.

    2.1.   Master View Controller.

        2.1.1.   Code for each cell that is selected.

            2.1.1.1.   Header material.

            2.1.1.2.   viewDidLoad.

            2.1.1.3.   Set orientations.

            2.1.1.4.   Case statements.

                2.1.1.4.1.   ARTISTS.

                    2.1.1.4.1.1.   Case 0.

                    2.1.1.4.1.2.   Case 1.

                2.1.1.4.2.   ALBUMS.

                    2.1.1.4.2.1.   Case 2.

                    2.1.1.4.2.2.   Case 3.

                2.1.1.4.3.   SONGS.

                    2.1.1.4.3.1.   Case 4.

                    2.1.1.4.3.2.   Case 5.

Accordingly, the code is as follows:

```
/////////>>>>>>>>>>        ARTIST      <<<<<<<<<<<<<<<<<

case 0: // in Safari (Artist) RLB on WEB
{
    NSURL *urlInSafari = [NSURL URLWithString:@"http://bit.ly/VAggDR"];
    [self LocatePageInSafari: urlInSafari];
}
    break;

case 1: // in Twitter
{
    NSURL *urlInItunes = [NSURL URLWithString:@"https://twitter.com/RoryLewisBand"];
    [self LocatePageInSafari:urlInItunes];
}
    break;

/////////>>>>>>>>>>   ALBUMS IN ITUNES  <<<<<<<<<<<<<<<<<

case 2: // in iTunes (Songs) SONGS FOR FRIDAY
    //[self LocateArtistPageInItunes];
{
    NSURL *urlInItunes = [NSURL URLWithString:@"itms://itunes.apple.com/us/album/songs-for-
friday/id408548641?uo=4"];
    [self StartExternalAppWithURL:urlInItunes];
}
    break;

case 3: // in iTunes (Songs) HEROINES
    //[self LocateArtistPageInItunes];
{
    NSURL *urlInItunes = [NSURL URLWithString:@"itms://itunes.apple.com/us/album/heroines/
id461113548?uo=4"];
    [self StartExternalAppWithURL:urlInItunes];
}
    break;
```

```
        ///////// >>>>>>>>>>        SONGS      <<<<<<<<<<<<<<<<<

        case 4: // in iTunes (Songs) Elvis Presley
            //[self LocateArtistPageInItunes];
        {
            NSURL *urlInItunes = [NSURL
URLWithString:@"itms://itunes.apple.com/us/album/elvis-presley/id461113548?i=461113566&uo=4"];
            [self StartExternalAppWithURL:urlInItunes];
        }
            break;

        case 5: // in iTunes (Songs)
            //[self LocateArtistPageInItunes];
        {
            NSURL *urlInItunes = [NSURL
URLWithString:@"itms://itunes.apple.com/us/album/hippie-paradise/id408548641?i=408549591&uo=4"];
            [self StartExternalAppWithURL:urlInItunes];
        }
            break;

        ///////// >>>>>>>>>>        PICTURES    <<<<<<<<<<<<<<<<<

        case 6: // in Safari (Artist) RLB on WEB
        {

            NSURL *urlInSafari = [NSURL URLWithString:@"http://on.fb.me/nFwQj6"];
            [self LocatePageInSafari:urlInSafari];
        }
            break;

        case 7: // in Safari (Artist) RLB on WEB
        {
            NSURL *urlInSafari = [NSURL
URLWithString:@"http://www.youtube.com/watch?v=ANpjUmyaE94"];
            [self LocatePageInSafari:urlInSafari];
        }
            break;

    }

    //[self DeselectRow];
}
```

Now you need to create your helper routines to process redirects prior to handing off to iTunes Store. Specifically, you need to process a LinkShare/TradeDoubler/DGM URL into something the iPhone can handle, if you choose to use a universal app on your own that does include the iPhone. For more information, check out http://developer.apple.com/library/ios/#qa/qa1629/_index.html.

```
- (void)openReferralURL:(NSURL *)referralURL {
    //NSURLConnection *conn =
    (void)[[NSURLConnection alloc] initWithRequest:[NSURLRequest requestWithURL:referralURL]
delegate:self startImmediately:YES];
}
```

Save the most recent URL as a safety measure (just in case multiple redirects occur). Note that
iTunesURL is an NSURL property in this class declaration:

```
- (NSURLRequest *)connection:(NSURLConnection *)connection willSendRequest:(NSURLRequest *)request
redirectResponse:(NSURLResponse *)response {
    self.iTunesURL = [response URL];
    NSLog(@"RxURL [%@]",[self.iTunesURL absoluteString]);
    return request;
}
```

Okay, no more redirects. Use the last URL that you saved:

```
- (void)connectionDidFinishLoading:(NSURLConnection *)connection {
    [self StartExternalAppWithURL:self.iTunesURL];
}
```

This is a little technical, but you need to have an iTMS link (a special kind of URL/link protocol
used for iTunes' links and URLs) to get out there into the ether. The little method called
StartExternalAppWithURL allows your iTMS links:

```
-(void)StartExternalAppWithURL:(NSURL *)theURL
{
    NSLog(@"UsingURL [%@]",[theURL absoluteString]);
    [[UIApplication sharedApplication] openURL:theURL];

    [self DeselectRow];
}
```

Almost done. You just need to deselect your last selected table cell so that when the view reappears,
it's not still selected. You do this after your external app start has been requested because this
object is *not* informed of view leaving *or* the app restarting from the background when it's resumed
without adding additional plumbing.

```
-(void)DeselectRow
{
    // Unselect the selected row if any
    NSIndexPath* selection = [self.tableView indexPathForSelectedRow];
    if (selection) {
        [self.tableView deselectRowAtIndexPath:selection animated:YES];
    }
    [self.tableView reloadData];
}
```

Last bit: three Artist pages in Safari (case 0) and the cases for 6 and 7.

```
-(void)LocatePageInSafari: (NSURL *)theURL{

    // if we have an iPAD...
    if ([[UIDevice currentDevice] userInterfaceIdiom] == UIUserInterfaceIdiomPad) {
        // then open page in detail view (UIWebView)
        NSURLRequest *urlRequest = [NSURLRequest requestWithURL:theURL];
        [self.detailViewController.webView loadRequest:urlRequest];
    } else {
        // else we have an iPhone/iPod Touch so open in external safari
        [self StartExternalAppWithURL:theURL];
    }
}

@end
}
```

Coding DetailViewController

That was something else, wasn't it!? Just as an aside, when I first began wrapping my head around Storyboarding for my class, the beta version kept changing every week. Not only had I never seen a Storyboard before, but the code was changing constantly, yet I had to teach it in the lecture hall. I had many sleepless nights. But here's the deal. If you master this app and Storyboarding, you're well on your way to huge success in programming. You don't have to know everything I've talked about—you can simply learn when to use it. In DetailViewController, you need to set up your UIWebview—but first let's have a look at The Big Picture. (The good news here is that you don't actually code the DetailViewController—you do it via Storyboarding.

THE BIG PICTURE

1. Set up the Popover in the Storyboard.

2. Code the interaction to the multimedia platforms.

    2.1.   Master View Controller.

    2.2.   Detail View Controller.

        2.2.1.   Connecting the views to the WebViews.

3. Tweak the Popover to grab the platforms correctly.

---

22. Save everything. Go back into Storyboard, close the Navigator, open up the Utilities, and open up the Library. Your Table View Cell is where your WebViews are shown, so you need a WebView located there. Go back to Storyboard and either delete the label or not at this point. It makes no difference, because as you'll see in the next step, when you move the WebView up the hierarchy table, the label disappears. Regardless of whether you delete the label or not, select Table View Cell – Cell and drag a Web View onto the Detail View Controller - Detail, as shown in Figure 10-22.

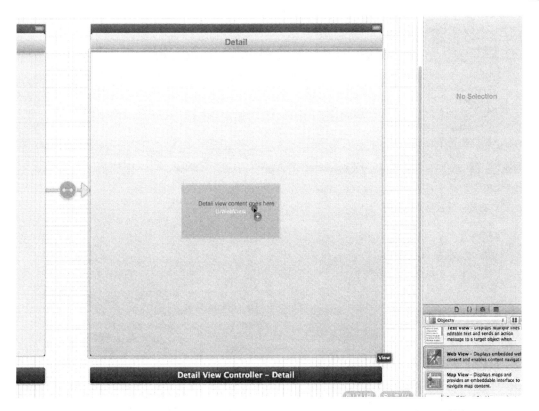

Figure 10-22. Go back to Storyboard, select the Table View Cell – Cell, and drag a WebView onto the Detail View

Finalizing the Storyboard

The only thing you still need to do is connect something that wasn't there when you began: the `webView` – `UIWebView` connection in the code. Now that it's there, you need to go back into Storyboard and connect them.

23.   Before you connect the WebView up, here's a cool little trick: remember when you moved the WebView in you just left it that size? Well, here's way to guarantee perfect size control no matter what elements you add into your code at different layers. Open Storyboard again, go to the Documents Outline, go to the Detail View Controller – Detail Scene, and select the WebView. Drag it upward above the view and drop it there. The old view disappears, as shown in Figure 10-23, and the WebView is now in control and fills up the entire area. Okay, now let's make those connections.

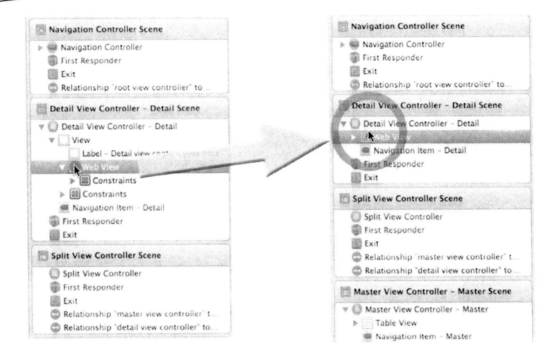

Figure 10-23. *Move WebView up to fill the iPad screen*

24. Keeping the Detail View Controller - Detail selected, as shown, go back to the Connection Inspector and drag from the `webView` to the `UIWebView`, as shown in Figure 10-24. Save it.

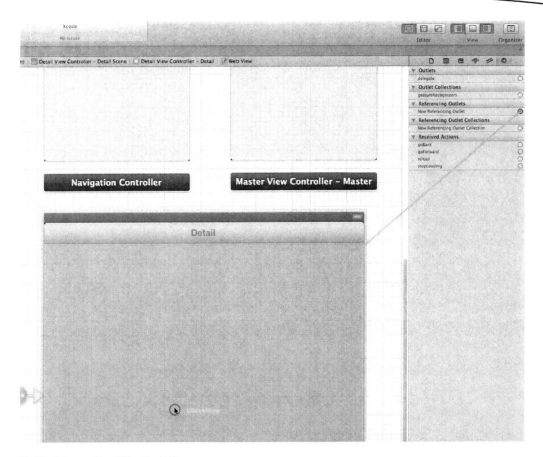

Figure 10-24. Select myDetailViewController

Note   Now connect your iPad to your Mac and, rather than selecting iPad Simulator, select iOS Device. You can run it on the Simulator if you like, *but iTunes cannot run inside the Simulator*, so all the iTunes links won't work. Once you've connected your iPad to your Mac, Click Run.

25.   Once your app has completed building, which may take a few seconds, you'll see the icon appear, as shown in Figure 10-25. Once you click the icon, you will immediately see the Popover screen. The first time you select it, it won't show anything underneath. However, once you select a page and then select the Popover again, it keeps the underlying image below the Popover; mine was the YouTube site, as shown in Figure 10-25.

Figure 10-25. *From the icon through to the Popover*

26. Figure 10-26 shows the flipping while using the web site case.

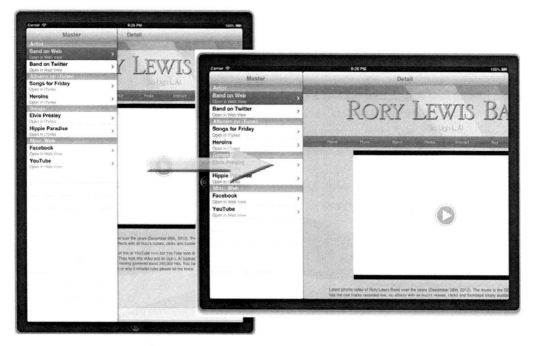

Figure 10-26. *Orientation working with the Web*

In Ending

This has been a wonderful journey, but it's really only the start. As I've gone through this third edition, I can't help but think of all the fresh minds that will read these exercises and struggle through them—and then break through to create awesome apps and make money! How many more of my students and readers of this book will work at Apple!? Wow! It's been a great motivation for me to think about this.

I hope to see you all on the forum. I do not answer emailed questions, but I will answer those exact same questions if you post them on the forum (`http://bit.ly/oLVwpY`) because then everybody can share my answers. I encourage you to help. No matter how much of a beginner you are, get into the forum and help others. Helping others speeds up your journey.

Peace.

Dr. Lewis

Index

T

U, V, W